150 Uplifting Short Stories for Seniors

A Treasury of Nostalgic, Humorous, and Easy-to-Read Stories to Warm the Hearts, Laughter, and Bring Joy to Their Days

Victoria Bennet

© Copyright VICTORIA BENNET. All Right Reserved.
Copyright Protected with
www.ProtectMyWork.com,
Reference Number: 17730200623S042

The content contained within this book may not be reproduced, duplicated or transmitted without direct written permission from the author or the publisher. Under no circumstances will any blame or legal responsibility be held against the publisher, or author, for any damages, reparation, or monetary loss due to the information contained within this book. Either directly or indirectly.

Legal Notice:
This book is copyright protected. This book is only for personal use. You cannot amend, distribute, sell, use, quote or paraphrase any part, or the content within this book, without the consent of the author or publisher.

Disclaimer Notice:
Please note the information contained within this document is for educational and entertainment purposes only. All effort has been executed to present accurate, up to date, and reliable, complete information. No warranties of any kind are declared or implied. The content within this book has been derived from various sources.
By reading this document, the reader agrees that under no circumstances is the author responsible for any losses, direct or indirect, which are incurred as a result of the use of information contained within this document, including, but not limited to, errors, omissions, or inaccuracies.

"Dedicated to all the seniors who have graced our lives with the sharing of their stories, sparked our days with laughter, and imparted timeless wisdom that guides our paths. You, with your rich tapestry of experiences, make our world richer, fuller, and profoundly more meaningful. In your honor, these stories unfold, mirroring the strength, resilience, and joy that truly define growing older."

TABLE OF CONTENTS

INTRODUCTION   8

1. The Marvelous Memory Café   9
2. The Pronunciation Gap   11
3. The Case of the Missing Dentures   12
4. A Priest, a Nun, and a Frosty Cabin   13
5. Jolly's Pinch: A Robotic Tale of Truth and Laughter   14
6. The Farmer's Wit: A Splash of Humor by the Pond   15
7. The Curious Case of the Crumbling Cupboard   16
8. Whack and Banter: The Story of a Naughty Marriage   17
9. Bare Feet and Warm Hearts: A Lesson in Humanity   18
10. High Seas Humor: Captain Reynolds and the Colors of Courage   19
11. The Invisible Chef   20
12. The Precious Stone and the Gift of Kindness   22
13. The Memory Chronicles: Erik and Milly's Sweet and Savory Adventures   23
14. The Wishful Trio: Genie's Surprise and Manager's Strategy   24
15. The Kissed Mirrors Conundrum: A Janitor's Cunning Solution   25
16. Waves of Laughter: The Shellebration Coast Chronicles   26
17. The Maid's Clever Negotiation   29
18. Whiskers and Serenity: A Tale of Unexpected Companionship   30
19. The Curious Case of Charlie   31
20. Silver Gems and Golden Bonds: A Grandfather's Legacy   32
21. Split Pants and Giggles: The Hilarious Adventures of the Mirthwood Comedian   35
22. Feathered Gossip: A Parrot's Hilarious Antics   37
23. Adventures in Swimwear: Tales of Mishaps and Laughter   38
24. Yoga and Laughter: The Misadventures of Fred   39
25. A Chili Adventure with Unforeseen Consequences   40
26. The Mystery of the Vanishing Slippers   41
27. Serendipity Springs: A Campground of Unexpected Adventures   43
28. The Bacon Caper: A Salad Bar Mishap   44
29. Mildred's Colorful MixUp   46
30. The Whimsical Adventures of the Polka Dot Hat   47
31. A Hilarious Tale of Spicy Wings and Enduring Friendship   48
32. Insomniac Chronicles: A Comedy of Errors   49
33. Bubbles, Bubbles Everywhere   50

#	Title	Page
34.	The Thanksgiving Stranger	52
35.	A Comical Encounter with An Unconventional Genie	53
36.	Oliver the Goat: A Tale of Horned Hijinks	54
37.	The Not-So-Quiet Game Night	55
38.	The Misadventures of Professor Quirky	57
39.	The extravagant Weather Machine	58
40.	The Wacky Wedding Planners	60
41.	The Absurd Antique Auction	61
42.	The Whistleblower's Whimsy	63
43.	The Fantastical Gardening Club	64
44.	The Eccentric Book Club	66
45.	The Great Escape Room Caper	67
46.	The Whimsical Cupcake Quest	69
47.	The Love Potion MixUp	70
48.	A Soldier's Unexpected Humor	72
49.	The Noisy Nighttime Conundrum	73
50.	Melodies and Mirth: The Tuna Can MixUp	74
51.	The Prankster's Harvest: Hilarious Culinary Adventures	75
52.	Feathers and Typo Tangles: A Writer's Tale Adventures	76
53.	The DIY Defender: A Hilarious Tale of Package Protection	77
54.	The Surprise Senior Talent Show	79
55.	The Great Bingo Caper	80
56.	The Unforgettable Road Trip	82
57.	The Hilarious Haunted House	83
58.	The Time-Traveling Mixup	84
59.	The Enchanted Pages: A Whimsical Literary Journey	86
60.	The Wacky Science Fair	89
61.	The Secret Language of Cats	90
62.	The Extraordinary Extraterrestrial Expedition	92
63.	The Neighbor's Help	93
64.	The Zany Zookeepers	94
65.	The Marvelous MindReading Mystery	95
66.	The Mirthful Mystery Cruise	97
67.	The Hilarious History Class	98
68.	The Ridiculous Robot Butler	99
69.	In the Realm of the silly Bugs	100
70.	Adventures of Grandpa and Little Amelia	101
71.	The Hilarious Hair Salon	102
72.	The Cracked Pot's Beauty: Embracing Imperfections	104

#	Title	Page
73.	The Scented Shenanigans: A Prank with a Fragrant Twist	105
74.	The Inner Menagerie: A Tale of Self-Mastery	106
75.	Hilarious Home Improvement Misadventures	107
76.	Checkmate and Chuckles: The Chess Battles of Arthur and Martha	108
77.	The Hilarious Adventures of a Photographer and a Bewildered Pilot	109
78.	The Unstoppable Optimist	111
79.	The Fantastic Food Truck Adventure	112
80.	Winter Whims and Flour Follies	113
81.	Garage Doors and Unforeseen Laughter	114
82.	The Hash Brown Redemption: From Mishaps to Culinary Triumph	115
83.	The Escapades of Granny Giggles	117
84.	The Hilarious Home Makeover	118
85.	The Outrageous Office Shenanigans	119
86.	The Art of Forgery: A Hilarious Report Card Caper	120
87.	The Mysterious Case of the Vanishing Socks	121
88.	The TimeTraveling Troupe	122
89.	The Colorful Wisdom of Grandma	123
90.	The Legendary Pillow Fight	124
91.	From Grandma's Kitchen: The Journey of a Sour Dough Starter	126
92.	A Memorable Christmas Prayer on the Farm	127
93.	The Sneaky Sweethearts	128
94.	An Unforgettable SkyHigh Story	129
95.	A Comical Courtroom Clash	130
96.	Melodies in the Night: An Unconventional Serenade	131
97.	Language and Laughter: Boys vs. Girls	132
98.	Of Fines and Folly: The Farmer and the Government Inspectors	133
99.	Misunderstandings and Mirth: A Tale of Kisses and Slaps	134
100.	Racing, Robbery, and a Witty Ruse	136
101.	The Scales of Justice: The Baker and the Farmer	137
102.	The Mysterious Man and His Majestic Companion	138
103.	The Unforgettable Love: A Tale of Memory and Connection	139
104.	Seasons of Perception: The Tale of the Distant Apple Tree	140
105.	Ingenious Initiatives	141
106.	Lost in Translation: A Hilarious Bus Exchange	142
107.	The Great Race: Speeding, Laughter, and a Clever Excuse	143
108.	An Unexpected Adventure with a Talking Frog	144
109.	The Seductive Serenade: A Tale of Curiosity and Monastic Secrets	145
110.	Unclad Occupations: Hilarity Unveiled on the Sands	147
111.	The Wit of a Cowboy	148

112.	Grandpa's Clever Coup: A Tale of Luxury Cars and Shrewd Tricks	149
113.	Wrinkles and Wonder: Embracing Imperfect Perfection	150
114.	The Love Dress: Rekindling the Flame of Desire	151
115.	The Magical Anniversary	152
116.	The Grand Bargain: The Quirky Life Contracts of Creation	153
117.	From Silence to Unstoppable Banter	154
118.	The Hilarious Trials of the Clever Doctor and the Prankster Lawyer	155
119.	The Wisdom in the Coffee Cup: A Lesson on Life's True Essence	156
120.	The Suitor's Witty Quest and the Challenge of the Lake	157
121.	Pushed the Limits: A Hilarious Hunting Mishap	158
122.	The Woodcutter's Wisdom: Finding Balance for Productivity	159
123.	The Cookie Thief: A Divine Twist of Sweet Indulgence	160
124.	From Rags to Riches and Back Again: A Gamble Gone Awry	161
125.	The King's Quest for the Extraordinary Tale	162
126.	The Epic Wheelchair Race	163
127.	The Sunday Ritual: A Story of Making a Difference	164
128.	The Giggling Gnome's Wisdom	165
129.	Embracing Your Unique Worth	167
130.	The Power of Balance in Life's Challenges	168
131.	Challenging Mental Barriers to Personal Growth	169
132.	Etched in Stone: The Power of Forgiveness and Gratitude	170
133.	The Roommate Riddle: A Tale of Assumptions and Missing Documents	171
134.	The Speed Limit MixUp: A Hilarious Encounter on Route 19	172
135.	The Ripple of Generosity: A Tale of Shared Happiness	173
136.	Discovering True Wealth: A Journey of Understanding	174
137.	The Sweetest Pear: The Power of Understanding and Empathy	175
138.	When Superman's Excuses Fall Short	176
139.	Bonds Beyond Words: A Tale of Friendship	177
140.	The Seated Soldier: A Lesson in Discipline	178
141.	The Crafty Daughter and The Pebbles of Fate	179
142.	The Seeds of Wisdom: A Journey of Enlightenment	180
143.	Unexpected Reunion: Laughter and Memories in the Afterlife	181
144.	Interstellar Odysseys: The Astronauts' Unforgettable Journey	182
145.	Laughter and Healing in the Doctor's Office	183
146.	The Battle of Colors: A Tale of Harmony and Unity	183
147.	The Echo of Life: Reflections of Our Words and Actions	185
148.	A Jar Full of Life: Prioritizing What Truly Matters	186
149.	The Horoscope and the Art of Fishing	187
150.	The Sieve of Wisdom: The Transformative Power of Reading	188

CONCLUSION 189

INTRODUCTION

DEAR READER, it is with warmth and anticipation that I welcome you to the pages of my book. My name is Victoria Bennett, and I have the immense privilege of being the author or, perhaps more aptly, the curator of the stories you're about to encounter.

As a woman who has seen six decades of life, with its joys, sorrows, and countless moments of laughter, I've come to appreciate the profound richness and wisdom that come with age. It is this richness, this wellspring of shared human experience, that I've endeavored to capture within the pages of this book.

The characters you will meet in this storybook are diverse, vibrant, and, above all, relatable. They are individuals who have lived, who have stories etched in the lines of their faces, and whose eyes bear witness to the world's evolving tapestry. These are men and women who may remind you of your own journey, your friends, your loved ones, and perhaps, even yourself.

Embedded in these narratives are themes of growth, reflection, and the enduring human spirit. They are reminders that the voyage of self-discovery and understanding doesn't end with youth but evolves and deepens throughout our lives. And within each story, you will find echoes of your own strength, resilience, and the wisdom born from your unique life journey.

Each tale is set against the backdrop of different eras - some you might recall with vivid clarity, others before your time yet a part of our shared heritage. Whether reflecting on the post-war boom or the digital revolution that changed everything, you'll be invited to reminisce about the past and consider how these times have shaped our present.

In the tradition of those humor-filled magazines and classic books we all remember fondly, these stories are designed to bring a smile to your face. They are tales of joy, surprise, and hearty laughter, reflecting my belief that no matter our age, we all need a good chuckle.

So, I invite you, dear reader, to join me on this journey. To revisit the past, to laugh and reflect, and to see a bit of yourself in the lives and stories of these characters. As you turn the pages of my collection of tales, may you find enjoyment, insight, and perhaps even a new perspective on this grand adventure we call life.

*As an experienced curator of stories and a lover of shared wisdom, I'm delighted to share this collection with you. While I'm not a professional author in the traditional sense, I'm someone who deeply enjoys weaving tales that entertain, educate, and evoke emotions. Despite the substantial effort put into ensuring the quality and richness of these stories, there might still be areas for improvement. If you spot any errors or have suggestions for future stories, please don't hesitate to contact me at **victoriabennet.stories@gmail.com**. As a token of my appreciation, you will receive a special gift. (Remember to check your email spam folder).*

Thank you for your support and trust. I hope this book brings you joy, laughter, and meaningful reflection.

1. THE MARVELOUS MEMORY CAFÉ

IN THE BUSTLING CITY OF RIVERSIDE, nestled between quaint cobblestone streets, stood a small, unassuming building with a sign that read, "The Marvelous Memory Café." It was a place like no other, where the enchantment of stories and the warmth of human connection permeated the air.

The café was the brainchild of Abigail Williams, a spirited woman with a passion for preserving memories and fostering meaningful connections. Having witnessed the transformative power of storytelling in her own life, Abigail dreamt of creating a space where people of all ages could come together to share their tales and create lasting memories.

As news of the café spread throughout the city, curious souls from all walks of life flocked to its welcoming doors. The interior exuded an air of nostalgia, adorned with vintage photographs, cozy armchairs, and shelves filled with well-worn books. The aroma of freshly brewed coffee mingled with the scent of homemade pastries, creating an irresistible allure.

Each day, the café bustled with activity. Children sat cross-legged on the floor, their wide eyes fixed on the animated gestures of elderly storytellers. Laughter filled the room as young and old shared anecdotes, adventures, and life lessons.

On one particular afternoon, the café was abuzz with anticipation as a group of high school students gathered for a storytelling session. Abigail, the café's vivacious host, welcomed them with a warm smile, her eyes twinkling with excitement. She believed that intergenerational connections held the key to a rich tapestry of memories.

Seated in a circle, the students listened intently as an elderly gentleman named Mr. Johnson began to share his story. His voice trembled with a mix of nostalgia and wisdom as he recounted tales of his youth, painting vivid pictures with his words. The students leaned in, captivated by his every word.

As Mr. Johnson began to recount his memories, the students could almost see the scenes he described come to life before their eyes. His voice carried them back to a time when he was a young boy, playing in the sun-drenched fields of his family's farm.

He reminisced about the summers spent helping his father tend to the crops, the smell of freshly turned earth filling the air. He recalled the joyous laughter and camaraderie shared with his siblings as they chased each other through the fields, their bare feet leaving imprints in the soft soil.

Mr. Johnson spoke of long, lazy afternoons spent fishing by the nearby creek, the water sparkling in the sunlight. He described the thrill of catching his first fish and the simple pleasure of cooking it over an open fire, the smoky aroma filling the air as they savored the meal together.

He painted a picture of winter nights huddled around the crackling fireplace, the warmth of the flames dancing on their faces. He spoke of the games they played, the stories they told, and the sense of togetherness that permeated their cozy home.

Mr. Johnson's memories carried the students to a bygone era, where time seemed to move slower, and connections were cherished. They felt the nostalgia in his words, yearning for a glimpse of a world they had never experienced.

Inspired by Mr. Johnson's narrative, one of the students, Mia, bravely shared her own story of overcoming adversity. She spoke of her grandmother's unwavering support and the strength she found within herself.

As Mia began to share her story, the room hushed in anticipation. She spoke of her beloved grandmother, a remarkable woman who had faced countless challenges in her life. Mia described the struggles her grandmother had endured as a young immigrant, leaving behind her home and family to build a new life in a foreign land.

She recounted how her grandmother had faced discrimination and adversity, battling against prejudice and the limitations imposed upon her. Mia spoke of the long hours her grandmother worked to provide for her family, the sacrifices she made, and the resilience she displayed in the face of hardship.

But Mia's story wasn't just about her grandmother's trials. She emphasized the strength she had witnessed within her grandmother, the unwavering determination that had guided her through every obstacle. She spoke of the love and support her grandmother had shown her, the belief she instilled in Mia that she could overcome any challenge that came her way.

Mia's voice trembled with emotion as she shared her gratitude for her grandmother's unwavering presence in her life. The room was filled with a profound sense of admiration and respect for both Mia and her grandmother as they reminded everyone of the power of resilience and the indomitable spirit that can emerge from even the most difficult circumstances.

As the day turned into evening, friendships blossomed, and the café became a sanctuary for human connection. People from all walks of life found solace in sharing their joys, sorrows, and everything in between. It became a place where memories were cherished, and laughter became the universal language.

The Marvelous Memory Café became a beacon of hope in the community, a place where the threads of human stories intertwined, creating a tapestry of resilience, love, and shared experiences. Its doors remained open, inviting new voices and embracing old friends, ensuring that no memory would be forgotten and no story left untold.

2. THE PRONUNCIATION GAP

IN THE PICTURESQUE STATE OF LOUISIANA, a middle-aged couple named Chase and Maya embarked on a road trip through the charming city of Natchitoches. Little did they know that this journey would lead them not only to new experiences but also to a comical dispute about the pronunciation of the city's name.

As Chase and Maya drove through the unfamiliar streets of Natchitoches, their curiosity was piqued by the captivating sights and sounds around them. However, their sense of wonder quickly turned into a lighthearted argument as they stumbled upon the perplexing name of the city.

"I'm telling you, Maya, it's pronounced 'Natch-ee-toches'!" Chase declared confidently, his voice filled with conviction.

Maya, equally convinced, shot back, "No, no, Chase! It's 'Natch-i-tow-chez'! I'm sure of it!"

Their friendly debate intensified as they continued down the road, neither willing to back down from their viewpoint. The spirited exchange echoed through the car, with each insisting they knew the correct pronunciation.

As hunger began to gnaw at their stomachs, Chase and Maya decided to put their linguistic dispute aside momentarily and seek refuge in a local eatery. With an air of amusement lingering between them, they entered the restaurant and took a seat at the counter.

A pretty, young waitress approached them with a warm smile, ready to take their order. Sensing an opportunity, Chase flashed his own smile and addressed her with a request that held the key to settling their ongoing argument.

"Excuse me, ma'am," Chase said, his tone friendly yet eager. "Before we place our order, we have a little disagreement. Could you please help us settle it once and for all?"

The young waitress, ever accommodating, replied with a cheerful demeanor, "Of course, honey! I'm here to help. What's the issue?" Chase leaned closer and made his request, "Could you please pronounce the name where we are right now, slowly and clearly?"

The waitress's smile widened, sensing the opportunity for a playful twist. She leaned over the counter, looking directly into Chase's eyes, and with an exaggerated drawl, she declared, "Oh, sure thing, sir! You're in 'Burrr-gerrr Kiiing'!"

Chase and Maya exchanged stunned glances, their jaws dropping in unison. A moment of silence hung in the air before erupting into hearty laughter. The realization washed over them that their argument about the city's pronunciation had taken a hilariously unexpected turn.

In that laughter-filled moment, Chase and Maya grasped the moral hidden within their playful squabble. They understood that sometimes, the pursuit of being right can lead to unnecessary tension and misunderstandings. The ability to find humor in our differences and embrace the joy of shared laughter can bridge any divide and bring us closer together.

3. THE CASE OF THE MISSING DENTURES

IN A HEARTWARMING TURN OF EVENTS, the residents of Paradise Nest nursing home found themselves immersed in an unexpected mystery—one that would ignite laughter and camaraderie among the elderly community. The incident, known as "The Case of the Missing Dentures," became a tale of resilience, determination, and the power of unity.

The story unfolded in 1957 within the cozy halls of Paradise Nest, where laughter resonated like a symphony, bringing brightness to the residents' days. Amidst their shared moments of joy, a peculiar occurrence took place—the disappearance of Mr. Jenkins' prized dentures. Mr. Jenkins, known for his forgetfulness, found himself in a state of distress as his infectious toothless grin was suddenly robbed of its charm. Faced with the absence of Mr. Jenkins' cheerful presence, the community rallied together in a flurry of concern and curiosity.

Enter Emily, a quick-witted granddaughter with an adventurous spirit. Driven by a desire to restore the laughter that had temporarily vanished from the nursing home, Emily took on the role of a detective-in-training. With a twinkle in her eye and a determination in her heart, she embarked on a quest to unravel the enigma that had befallen their community.

Equipped with a magnifying glass and fueled by her unwavering resolve, Emily ventured into the vibrant tapestry of Paradise Nest. She sought to engage with the colorful cast of characters that called the nursing home their home, hoping to uncover clues and restore Mr. Jenkins' cherished dentures.

Her journey began in the bustling dining hall, where the tantalizing aroma of freshly cooked meals mingled with animated conversations. There, she approached Mr. Thompson, a notorious joker known for his funny jokes. With a raised eyebrow, Emily inquired, "Mr. Thompson, any funny business with Mr. Jenkins' dentures?" Mr. Thompson, wearing a sly grin, playfully responded, "Oh, my dear, I've pulled many tricks, but I can assure you, I'm innocent this time. Denture-related jokes are not my forte. Besides, I prefer to keep my pranks toothless, just like Mr. Jenkins!"

Undeterred by her initial encounter, Emily continued her investigation, seeking insights from Mrs. Henderson, a gentle soul with a fondness for feathered friends.

In the cozy embrace of Mrs. Henderson's room, adorned with cherished mementos, they shared cups of tea and stories of days gone by. Amidst their conversation, Emily inquired, "Mrs. Henderson, have you seen anything peculiar? Perhaps a bird with a penchant for shiny objects?" Mrs. Henderson chuckled and replied, "Darling, my feathered friends have good taste, but dentures aren't their idea of a delectable snack. I believe they prefer a meal that won't require a trip to the dentist!"

Emily's search led her to the communal game room, where Mr. Ramirez, a retired magician, captivated residents with his whimsical tricks. Enchanted by his sleight of hand, Emily couldn't help but wonder if the magician had played a role in the mysterious vanishing act. With a mischievous glimmer in her eye, she questioned, "Mr. Ramirez, did you make Mr. Jenkins' dentures disappear with one of your magic tricks?" Mr. Ramirez, letting out a hearty laugh, responded, "Ah, my young detective, I assure you, my magic is limited to rabbits and card tricks, not dental appliances! But hey, if you ever need a disappearing act for leftovers, I'm your guy!"

Undeterred by dead-ends, Emily's next encounter brought her to Miss O'Connor, a spirited reader with an imaginative mind. Amidst stacks of books that formed towers of knowledge, Emily and Miss O'Connor delved into tales of daring adventures and far-off lands. As their conversation unfolded, Emily's keen eyes caught a glimmer of metal. With excitement in her voice, she exclaimed, "Miss O'Connor, look what I found! The missing dentures!" Miss O'Connor chuckled and quipped, "Ah, the wonders of literature. It seems those dentures wanted to embark on their own adventure. They must have yearned to join the ranks of legendary characters like Moby Dick and Huckleberry Finn!"

Excitement washed over Emily as she triumphantly reunited Mr. Jenkins with his cherished smile. Laughter cascaded through the nursing home, reigniting the joy that had momentarily slipped away. The residents gathered together, sharing funny stories and lighthearted banter, savoring the return of mirth to their lives.

As the story of the missing dentures faded into memory, the nursing home embraced a renewed sense of community. Laughter resounded through the halls, weaving its way into the tapestry of their days. The missing dentures had become a catalyst for connection, reminding the residents of the strength found in unity and the power of humor.

4. A PRIEST, A NUN, AND A FROSTY CABIN

ON A SNOWY WINTER NIGHT, a priest and a nun found themselves caught in the midst of a treacherous snowstorm. As the blizzard raged on, they trudged through the deep snow, desperately seeking shelter. After what felt like an eternity, they stumbled upon a small cabin, a beacon of hope in the midst of the white wilderness.

Exhausted from their arduous journey, they entered the cabin, grateful for the refuge it offered. Inside, they discovered a modest living space with a single bed, a stack of blankets in the corner, and a sleeping bag laid out on the floor.

Being a gentleman at heart, the priest gallantly turned to the nun and said, "Sister, you must be tired. Please, you take the bed, and I'll sleep on the floor in the sleeping bag."

With a grateful smile, the nun accepted the offer and nestled into the cozy comfort of the bed. The priest, true to his word, zipped himself up in the sleeping bag and prepared to rest.

However, just as the priest was about to drift off into a peaceful slumber, he heard a voice—soft and trembling, yet filled with a hint of discomfort. It was the nun.

"Father," she said, her voice barely above a whisper, "I'm cold."

Without hesitation, the priest unzipped the sleeping bag, braving the cold air as he rose from the floor. He retrieved a blanket and gently placed it over the shivering nun, ensuring her warmth and comfort.

Once again, the priest settled back into the sleeping bag, feeling the fatigue wash over him. But as the seconds ticked by, he heard the nun's voice once more—plaintive and filled with a lingering chill.

"Father, I'm still very cold," she murmured.

Slightly exasperated but driven by compassion, the priest unzipped the sleeping bag for the second time, rising to his feet. With patience, he fetched another blanket and draped it over the nun, hoping to alleviate her discomfort.

As the priest wearily settled back into his sleeping bag, his eyelids heavy with sleep, he heard the nun's voice again—this time, more persistent and tinged with a longing for warmth.

"Father, I'm sooooo cold," she whispered, her plea echoing through the cabin.

At that moment, an idea sparked in the priest's mind. He pondered the situation and came up with a solution, one that would bring some warmth to both of them in this frozen wilderness.

"Sister," the priest declared, his voice filled with playful authority, "I have an idea. Since we're out here in the middle of nowhere, where no one will ever know what happened, let's pretend we're married."

A delighted smile curved the nun's lips, and she purred in agreement, "That's fine by me."

With a sly grin, the priest seized the opportunity and quickly responded, "Well then, my dear, get up and get your own stupid blanket!"

5. JOLLY'S PINCH: A ROBOTIC TALE OF TRUTH AND LAUGHTER

A MAN PURCHASED A ROBOTIC COMPANION NAMED JOLLY and brought it home to his wife and kids. The family was thrilled with their new technological addition. However, what the father didn't disclose was that Jolly had a unique feature: it would give a playful pinch on the butt to anyone who told a lie.

Eager to test out Jolly's truth-detecting ability, the father turned to one of his kids. "Tell me, did you and your brother go to school today?" he asked. The child replied with a resounding "yes," but to everyone's surprise, Jolly playfully pinched the child behind. The father was impressed by Jolly's honesty and enforcement.

Turning his attention to the younger brother, the father inquired, "Where did you go today?" The younger child confidently responded, "To a friend's house," and Jolly refrained from pinching. Satisfied with his conclusion, the father then directed his attention to the older sibling.

"When I asked what you were doing, you said you were watching cartoons. Is that true?" questioned the father. But once again, Jolly mischievously pinched the older child behind. Laughing hysterically, the father couldn't contain his amusement and asked, "Alright, spill the beans. What were you really doing?"

With a sheepish smile, the older child confessed, "We were actually watching a slightly inappropriate movie." The father's amusement quickly turned into outrage as he scolded both of his children for their choice of entertainment. He exclaimed, "How dare you! When I was your age, I wouldn't even dare think of watching such films!"

In an unexpected twist, Jolly turned around and playfully pinched the father behind. Witnessing the entire incident, the wife couldn't contain her laughter. She looked at her husband, locked eyes with him, and remarked, "Are you truly surprised? They're just following in your footsteps, after all. They're just like you. I mean, they are your sons, after all".

At that moment, Jolly turned to the mother and gave her a playful pinch on the behind.

6. THE FARMER'S WIT: A SPLASH OF HUMOR BY THE POND

IN THE SUNNY STATE OF FLORIDA, there lived an elderly farmer named Edwin. Edwin had a thriving fruit orchard near a picturesque pond that added charm to his land. One evening, as the golden sun began to set, Edwin decided to head down to the pond to pick some fresh fruits for his dinner.

With a spring in his step, Edwin grabbed a trusty five-gallon bucket and made his way toward the glistening waters. Little did he know that his routine fruit-picking excursion was about to take an unexpected turn.

As he approached the pond, the sound of joyful laughter and feminine voices reached his ears. Puzzled, Edwin followed the sound and, to his astonishment, discovered a group of young women reveling in the pond's cooling embrace. Their carefree spirits were evident as they splashed and frolicked, completely unaware of Edwin's presence.

As the old farmer drew closer, the women caught sight of him, and their laughter turned to startled gasps. With a mix of embarrassment and urgency, they hurriedly swam to the deeper end of the pond, seeking refuge from the unexpected visitor.

One bold woman spoke up, her voice echoing across the water, "We're not coming out until you leave!"

Edwin, a man of wit and quick thinking, took a moment to ponder the situation. He realized that his unexpected arrival had disrupted the women's private retreat, and he needed to find a way to defuse the tension.

With a playful glimmer in his eye, Edwin raised the bucket high in the air, capturing the attention of the women. He cleared his throat and responded with a lighthearted tone, "Ladies, fear not! I didn't come down here to watch you swim or to disrupt your moment of freedom."

Pausing for dramatic effect, Edwin continued, a subtle gleam in his voice, "You see, I'm actually here to feed the alligator!"

The women's startled expressions quickly transformed into a mix of surprise and amusement. Edwin's unexpected twist had taken them by surprise, catching them off guard. Laughter filled the air as they realized the farmer's clever ruse.

At that moment, the tension dissipated, replaced by a shared moment of lightheartedness.

Edwin had shown them that age was no barrier to wit and quick thinking and never to underestimate the power of a sharp mind.

7. THE CURIOUS CASE OF THE CRUMBLING CUPBOARD

A WOMAN NAMED AMÉLIE PURCHASED A SELF-ASSEMBLY, flat-pack cupboard from her local home goods store. Eager to enhance her bedroom's aesthetic, Amélie carefully read the instructions, counted the pieces, and skillfully assembled the cupboard. She couldn't help but feel a sense of delight as she admired the finished product.

Amélie's quaint home was situated near a bustling railway line and as the trains thundered by, an unexpected occurrence unfolded—the cupboard collapsed. Undeterred by this perplexing misfortune, Amélie meticulously re-read the instructions, disassembled the cupboard, and painstakingly put it back together. However, to her dismay, the same thing happened once more. Each time a train passed, the entire cupboard would crumble, leaving Amélie frustrated and perplexed.

Determined to solve this curious conundrum, Amélie embarked on yet another attempt. She diligently re-re-read the instructions, triple-checking every step, and meticulously re-re-assembled the cupboard. But as fate would have it, the familiar rumble of a passing train led to the cupboard's collapse once again—for the third time.

Growing increasingly exasperated and cross, Amélie decided to contact the customer service department. She explained the perplexing situation, only to be met with disbelief on the other end of the line. The customer service representative insisted that such a scenario was impossible and offered to send a skilled fitter to investigate the matter further.

The appointed fitter arrived at Amélie's home, determined to unravel the mystery behind the collapsing cupboard. With great expertise, he assembled the cupboard, hoping to uncover the root cause of its instability. Yet, as another train passed by, the cupboard crumbled once again, leaving the fitter utterly bewildered.

Driven by a burning desire to solve this enigma, the fitter decided to take an unconventional approach. He resolved to reassemble the cupboard and positioned himself inside it, patiently waiting for the next train to pass. Little did he know that this decision would lead to an unexpected series of events.

Just as the fitter found himself nestled within the cupboard, Amélie's husband, François, returned home. Eager to surprise him with her latest purchase, Amélie directed François to their bedroom, where the splendid cupboard stood. An innocent curiosity took hold of François, and he impulsively opened the cupboard's doors to explore its contents.

To his astonishment, François discovered the fitter concealed inside the cupboard. A tidal wave of misunderstanding washed over him, fueled by the assumption that the fitter was hiding there as Amélie's secret lover.

Shocked and bewildered, François demanded an explanation, unable to fathom the situation unfolding before him.

Caught off guard and desperately searching for an explanation, the fitter blurted out, "You probably won't believe me, but I'm standing here waiting for a train!" His words only served to deepen François' confusion, leaving both men entangled in a web of misunderstandings and humorous misinterpretations.

In the end, it was a tale of extraordinary circumstances and amusing coincidences, reminding everyone involved that sometimes life's quirks can lead to the most unexpected and comical encounters.

8. WHACK AND BANTER: THE STORY OF A NAUGHTY MARRIAGE

IN A QUIET SUBURBAN NEIGHBORHOOD, Mr. Smith sat in his favorite armchair, engrossed in his morning newspaper. The aroma of freshly brewed coffee filled the air as his wife, Mrs. Smith, bustled around the kitchen, preparing breakfast.

Just as Mr. Smith was about to turn the page, he felt a sudden impact on the back of his head. Startled, he looked up to see his wife standing there with a frying pan in hand, a mischievous glint in her eyes.

"Why on earth did you hit me?" Mr. Smith exclaimed, rubbing the spot where the pan had made contact.

Mrs. Smith crossed her arms and replied, "There was a mysterious note in your pocket with the name 'Lucy' written on it."

Mr. Smith chuckled and said, "Oh, dear. 'Lucy' is actually the name of the new coffee blend I've been meaning to try. It's a limited edition!"

Mrs. Smith raised an eyebrow skeptically but remained silent. Little did Mr. Smith know that his witty response had sparked an idea in his wife's mind.

Three days later, as Mr. Smith was engrossed in the sports section of the newspaper, Mrs. Smith stealthily approached him with the frying pan once again.

Whack! Another swift blow to the back of his head.

"Why in the world would you hit me again?" Mr. Smith protested, a mix of surprise and amusement on his face.

With an amused smile, Mrs. Smith retorted, "You better pick up the phone, dear. It's your precious coffee blend calling!"

Mr. Smith looked perplexed for a moment before bursting into laughter. "Oh, I see what you did there! You certainly know how to keep me on my toes, my dear."

Their banter continued as they shared a good laugh, and Mr. Smith marveled at his wife's clever sense of humor. They sat down together, enjoying their breakfast and relishing in the playful dynamic that had always kept their marriage full of laughter and surprises.

From that day forward, the frying pan became a symbol of their shared sense of humor, a playful reminder of the unique bond they shared. It became an inside joke between them, with Mrs. Smith occasionally brandishing it as a lighthearted threat during their playful exchanges.

Their friends and neighbors couldn't help but be entertained by the couple's antics. The Smith's home became a hub of laughter and mirth, where humorous banter and unexpected surprises were always on the menu.

In the end, it wasn't just the clever comebacks or the amusing pranks that made their relationship special. It was the enduring love, laughter, and a shared appreciation for the lighter side of life that made Mr. and Mrs. Smith an inseparable pair.

9. BARE FEET AND WARM HEARTS: A LESSON IN HUMANITY

ON A CHILLY WINTER'S DAY, a little boy stood outside a shoe store, barefooted and shivering. His eyes were fixed on the display window as he longingly peered at the shoes that seemed like treasures to him.

A kind-hearted lady, touched by the sight of the boy, approached him with compassion in her heart. She couldn't help but inquire about his earnest gaze upon the store window.

"My little fellow," she said gently, "why are you looking so intently in that window?"

With innocence and hope in his eyes, the boy replied, "I was asking God to give me a pair of shoes."

The lady's heart melted upon hearing his words. She took the boy's hand, leading him into the store, determined to bring warmth and comfort to his cold, bare feet. She approached the clerk and requested half a dozen pairs of socks for the young boy.

As the clerk hurriedly gathered the socks, the lady asked for a basin of water and a towel. Without hesitation, he fetched the requested items. Together, the lady and the boy moved to the back of the store, away from prying eyes.

There, the lady knelt down, removed her gloves, and gently washed the boy's little feet with care.

She dried them tenderly with the towel, ensuring each tiny toe was warmed and comforted.

In the meantime, the clerk returned, presenting the socks to the lady. She lovingly slid a pair onto the boy's feet, embracing him with warmth and protection. With a generous heart, she purchased a pair of shoes for him, ensuring that his journey would no longer be hindered by the chill of the pavement.

As the lady patted the boy's head, she asked him, "No doubt, my little fellow, you feel more comfortable now?"

Tears welled up in the boy's eyes as he grasped the lady's hand, his voice filled with wonder and gratitude. "Are you God's Wife?" he asked, his voice trembling with emotion.

The lady was taken aback by the boy's question, surprised and touched by his innocent perception. She knelt down, looking into his eyes with a smile.

"My dear child," she replied, her voice warm with affection, "I am not God's Wife, but I am merely someone who saw a need and wished to help. It is through acts of kindness and compassion that we become reflections of the love that God has for each and every one of us."

The boy's eyes sparkled with understanding as he absorbed her words. At that moment, he not only experienced the physical warmth of the socks and shoes but also the warmth of a caring heart that had reached out to him.

From that day forward, the little boy carried with him the lesson of kindness, recognizing that helping others in need is an opportunity to embody the love and compassion that is within all of us.And so, dear reader, let the tale of the lady and the little boy remind us of the power of empathy and the importance of extending a helping hand to those in need. May it inspire us to embrace opportunities for kindness and compassion, for it is in such acts that we touch the lives of others and, in turn, find warmth and fulfillment in our own hearts.

10. HIGH SEAS HUMOR: CAPTAIN REYNOLDS AND THE COLORS OF COURAGE

IN THE VAST EXPANSE OF THE OPEN SEA, a navy captain and his crew sailed their ship with valor and a touch of humor. Captain Reynolds, known for his quick wit and clever strategies, was well-respected by his men.

One sunny day, as the crew went about their duties, the First Mate spotted a pirate ship approaching on the horizon. He hurriedly approached the captain and relayed the urgent news. Without missing a beat, Captain Reynolds calmly turned to a nearby sailor and requested his red shirt.

Confusion filled the sailor's face as he handed over the crimson garment. Unable to contain his curiosity, he asked the captain, "Captain, forgive me for asking, but why do you need a red shirt?"

"A playful gleam danced in Captain Reynolds' eyes as he replied, "Ah, my dear sailor, the reason for the red shirt is to ensure that if I were to bleed during battle, you and the crew wouldn't be disheartened. It helps maintain our morale and keeps us focused on the task at hand!" The crew chuckled at the captain's witty response, appreciating his light-hearted spirit even amidst the imminent threat."

As the pirate ship closed in, a battle ensued. Cannonballs roared through the air, and swords clashed against each other. The crew fought valiantly, with Captain Reynolds at the forefront, his red shirt hidden beneath his commanding presence. Through their collective effort, they repelled the pirates and emerged victorious.

The following day dawned, bringing a surprising turn of events. Word reached the captain that not one but twenty pirate ships were rapidly approaching their vessel. Panic spread among the crew as they prepared for the impending onslaught. Sensing the tension, Captain Reynolds shouted, "Quickly! Fetch me my brown pants!"

Confusion mingled with amusement as the crew hurried to fulfill their captain's request. One brave sailor, unable to suppress his curiosity, asked, "Captain, why brown pants? What do you need them for?"

A sly grin appeared on Captain Reynolds' face as he replied, "Well, my friend, when facing twenty pirate ships, one must always be prepared. These brown pants will come in handy if we encounter any unexpected situations, ensuring our composure remains intact!" Laughter erupted among the crew, momentarily easing their concerns as they enjoyed the captain's quick wit.

11. THE INVISIBLE CHEF

THE SCENT OF FRESHLY BAKED COOKIES wafted through the air halls of Maplewood Manor, where Bennett resided. Bennett was known for his vivid imagination and his knack for storytelling. His tales of wild adventures and fantastical creatures entertained his fellow residents, but sometimes, his imagination would lead him on whimsical escapades of his own.

One sunny morning, as Bennett sat in the communal dining area enjoying his breakfast, he overheard whispers among the staff. "Have you heard about the invisible chef?" one nurse whispered to another. Bennett's ears perked up, his imagination already spinning tales of culinary magic.

Later that day, as Bennett made his way to the dining room for lunch, he couldn't help but notice the tantalizing aroma of a gourmet feast. His taste buds danced with anticipation, but as he entered the room, he couldn't see any chefs bustling about in the kitchen. His eyes widened with wonder. Could it be? Was there truly an invisible chef working their magic in Maplewood Manor?

Determined to uncover the truth, Bennett embarked on his extravagant adventure. Armed with a detective's hat and a magnifying glass, he began his investigation. He questioned the staff, who chuckled at his inquiries but played along with his imaginative quest. They regaled him with tales of a legendary invisible chef who prepared the most exquisite dishes, using secret recipes passed down through generations.

Bennett's adventure took him to every nook and cranny of Maplewood Manor. He followed the scent of freshly baked bread, only to find an empty kitchen. He tiptoed through the herb garden, imagining the invisible chef plucking herbs and spices for their creations. He even snuck into the pantry, convinced he would catch a glimpse of the invisible chef at work.

Throughout his investigation, Bennett encountered a host of witty characters. Martha, the housekeeper, teased him about his invisible companion. "Bennett, dear, are you sure you haven't mistaken the kitchen staff for invisible chefs? I've never seen anyone whip up a soufflé like they do!" Bennett chuckled and replied, "Ah, Martha, the invisible chef is a culinary genius unlike any other. Their magic lies in the secret ingredients only they can see."

Undeterred by Martha's jests, Bennett continued his quest, determined to prove the existence of the invisible chef. One afternoon, he stumbled upon a surprise. In a forgotten corner of the dining hall, hidden behind a curtain, stood a small door. With a mix of curiosity and excitement, Bennett opened it, revealing a hidden passage that led to a clandestine kitchen.

Inside, he found a bustling kitchen filled with pots and pans clanging and ingredients dancing in the air as if by magic. But to Bennett's astonishment, there was no invisible chef to be found. Instead, he discovered a group of dedicated kitchen staff working diligently to prepare meals for the residents. They greeted Bennett with warm smiles and hearty laughter, confessing that the legend of the invisible chef was born out of their creativity and love for their craft.

Bennett's disappointment quickly turned into delight as the staff invited him to join them. Together, they whipped up a delectable feast, sharing stories and laughter as they cooked. Bennett discovered that the true magic of the kitchen wasn't in invisibility but in the camaraderie and joy that went into creating delicious meals.

From that day forward, Bennett became an honorary member of the kitchen crew. He regaled his fellow residents with tales of his adventures, sprinkled with a dash of imagination. The residents reveled in the tales of the invisible chef and eagerly awaited the culinary surprises that awaited them each day.

And so, the legend of "The Invisible Chef" at Maplewood Manor lived on, becoming a beloved part of the nursing home's folklore. Bennett continued to share his imaginative tales, weaving stories of magic and culinary wonders, brightening the spirits of his fellow residents.

Word of the invisible chef and the enchanting meals spread beyond Maplewood Manor. Visitors and guests couldn't resist the allure of the mythical chef, and the nursing home became known for its exceptional cuisine. Families and friends eagerly anticipated their visits, eager to experience the magic of the invisible chef's creations.

But for Bennett and his newfound friends in the kitchen, the true magic lay not in the invisibility but in the joy they found in cooking together and the happiness they brought to others. The invisible chef had become a symbol of the power of imagination, friendship, and the simple pleasures of sharing a delicious meal.

12. THE PRECIOUS STONE AND THE GIFT OF KINDNESS

LONG AGO, IN A PICTURESQUE MOUNTAIN VILLAGE, there lived a wise and good-hearted woman. She had a reputation for her wisdom and selflessness, always ready to lend a helping hand to those in need.

One day, as the wise woman was strolling along a glistening stream, she noticed something sparkling amidst the water. To her surprise, it was a precious stone, glimmering with an otherworldly radiance. Grateful for this unexpected find, she carefully picked it up and placed it in her bag.

The very next day, the wise woman encountered a weary traveler who appeared hungry and downtrodden. Without hesitation, she opened her bag and offered him her humble provisions. The hungry traveler's eyes widened in astonishment as he caught a glimpse of the precious stone nestled among the food.

Unable to contain his greed, the traveler made a bold request. He asked the wise woman to give him the precious stone, envisioning a life of comfort and security. To his surprise, the wise woman agreed without a second thought and handed him the stone. The traveler's heart swelled with joy as he departed, clutching the valuable gem tightly.

Days turned into weeks, and the traveler's excitement began to wane. Though the precious stone held immense value, its weight in his possession felt burdensome. It weighed heavily on his conscience, overshadowing the initial elation. The traveler's heart yearned for something more.

Driven by this newfound awareness, the traveler retraced his steps and returned to the village where he had encountered the wise woman. He sought her out, carrying the precious stone in his trembling hands.

"I've been thinking," he began, his voice filled with sincerity. "The stone you gave me is undeniably valuable, yet it pales in comparison to the kindness and compassion you displayed when you gave it to me. It is not the stone that I seek but rather the essence within you that enabled such selflessness. Please, I implore you to share with me that precious gift."

The wise woman listened intently, a gentle smile forming on her face. She recognized the growth within the traveler and understood the lesson he had learned. She reached out and clasped his hands warmly.

"My dear traveler," she began, her voice filled with warmth, "what you seek lies not in external treasures but within your own heart. The true riches of life are found in acts of kindness, empathy, and selflessness. It is through giving that we receive, and it is in sharing the best parts of ourselves that we create a world of beauty and joy."

The traveler's eyes glistened with understanding as he realized the depth of the wise woman's words. The precious stone, once so coveted, now seemed insignificant compared to the valuable lesson he had learned.

From that day forward, he carried within him the spirit of generosity and kindness, spreading joy wherever he went.

And so, the wise woman's act of selflessness not only touched the traveler's heart but also served as a reminder to all who heard the tale. It taught them that true wealth is not measured by material possessions but by the goodness and love we share with one another.

And so, dear reader, let this story inspire you to embrace the wisdom of the wise woman and recognize the precious gifts that lie within you. May your laughter be abundant, your acts of kindness be plentiful, and your heart forever filled with the truest and most valuable riches life has to offer.

13. THE MEMORY CHRONICLES: ERIK AND MILLY'S SWEET AND SAVORY ADVENTURES

IN A QUAINT LITTLE ABODE, nestled amidst the embrace of time, resided Erik and Milly, an elderly couple who had woven a tapestry of love, laughter, and cherished moments throughout their years together. As the seasons of their lives danced on, they found themselves grappling with an intriguing phenomenon: forgetfulness tiptoeing into the fabric of their everyday existence.

Concerned about their fading memories, Erik and Milly decided it was time to seek advice from their trusted doctor. Perhaps he could shed some light on their situation and offer guidance. With hopeful hearts, they set off to the doctor's office, ready to tackle this new challenge.

Upon sharing their concerns with the doctor, he kindly reassured them that forgetfulness was a common occurrence in old age. To help them cope, he suggested a simple solution: writing things down. By jotting down important details, they could keep track of their thoughts and avoid unnecessary lapses in memory.

With the doctor's advice in mind, Erik and Milly returned home, determined to put this new strategy into action. Excited to give it a try, Milly turned to Erik and made a request.

"Erik, my dear, could you please get me a bowl of ice cream from the kitchen refrigerator?" Milly asked, her eyes sparkling with anticipation.

Erik, confident in his ability to remember such a simple task, replied, "No need to write that down, Milly. I'm sure I'll remember."

Undeterred, Milly added, "Well, Erik, I'd also love some whipped cream with my ice cream. Should I write that down?"

With a dismissive wave of his hand, Erik declared, "No, no need for that. I've got it. You want a bowl of ice cream with whipped cream."

Milly's face lit up with delight as she continued, "Oh, Erik and I'd absolutely adore a cherry on top too. Should I write that down?"

Chuckling at his own impressive memory, Erik assured her, "Don't worry, my love. I've got it all figured out. You want a bowl of ice cream with whipped cream and a cherry on top."

With his confidence soaring, Erik headed into the kitchen to fulfill Milly's sweet desires. However, as time ticked by, Milly grew curious about his prolonged absence. Finally, after what felt like an eternity, Erik returned to the living room with a plate of eggs and bacon.

Milly's eyes widened in surprise as she stared at the unexpected breakfast before her. She turned to Erik, her confusion evident. "Erik, my dear, this is all well and good, but where's the french toast?" she asked, her voice filled with playful exasperation.

Realization dawned on Erik's face as he laughed at his own forgetfulness. It seemed that even with the best intentions, mistakes were bound to happen.

While writing things down can certainly be helpful, it's essential to embrace our human nature and accept that occasional slip-ups and humorous moments are part of life's grand tapestry. Erik and Milly discovered that laughter and love could overcome forgetfulness, turning a simple breakfast mishap into a cherished memory they would share for years to come.

14. THE WISHFUL TRIO: GENIE'S SURPRISE AND MANAGER'S STRATEGY

IN A BUSTLING OFFICE BUILDING, three colleagues embarked on an unexpected adventure during their lunch break. As they strolled along, their eyes fell upon an intriguing object lying on the ground—a dusty old oil lamp. Excitement filled the air as they contemplated the possibility of encountering a mystical genie.

Without wasting a moment, the customer service agent, the administration clerk, and their manager gathered around the lamp and vigorously rubbed it, hoping to unlock the genie's magical powers. To their astonishment, a vibrant puff of smoke erupted from the lamp, revealing the mystical genie.

"I am the genie of the lamp, and I shall grant each of you one wish," declared the genie with a smile.

Eagerly, the customer service agent leaped forward, unable to contain their enthusiasm. "I wish to be whisked away to the Bahamas, where I'll cruise on a speedboat, basking in the sun without a worry in the world!"

In an instant, a dazzling display of lights and smoke enveloped the customer service agent, transporting them to the picturesque shores of the Bahamas.

Next in line, the administration clerk's eyes sparkled with delight. "I desire nothing more than to find myself in Hawaii, lounging on a pristine beach, indulging in endless Pina Coladas alongside the love of my life!"

As if by magic, a whirlwind of smoke swept the administration clerk away, leaving behind only the faint scent of tropical paradise.

Now, it was the manager's turn. With an air of wisdom and authority, the manager pondered their wish carefully. A smirk curled across their face as they made their decision.

"I wish for both of my colleagues to return to the office promptly in 30 minutes," announced the manager, a mischievous glint in their eyes.

In an instant, the genie snapped their fingers, and the enchanting spell was cast. The customer service agent and the administration clerk reappeared, slightly disoriented but back in their familiar office surroundings.

Amidst the bewildered expressions, the manager let out a hearty laugh, relishing the cleverness of their wish. The colleagues joined in the laughter, realizing the wisdom behind letting their boss go first.

And so, the three colleagues continued their lunch break, regaling their fellow coworkers with the extraordinary tale of the genie and the surprising turn of events. They learned the value of wit and strategy, knowing that sometimes it pays off to let the boss take the lead.

15. THE KISSED MIRRORS CONUNDRUM: A JANITOR'S CUNNING SOLUTION

WITHIN THE WALLS OF A PRESTIGIOUS BOARDING SCHOOL, there resided a janitor known for his quick wit and resourcefulness. One fine day, as he diligently went about his duties, he stumbled upon an unusual sight in the girls' restroom – an array of vibrant lipstick kisses adorning the mirrors.

Puzzled but undeterred, the janitor decided to take matters into his own hands. Instead of succumbing to frustration, he hatched a plan to address the situation tactfully.

Optimistic that the students would understand, he meticulously wiped away the lipstick marks and left a note beside the mirrors, hoping to convey his message clearly.

"Kindly refrain from leaving lipstick kisses on the mirrors. Cleaning these stains requires great effort."

The next day, the janitor returned to the restroom, hopeful that his message had made an impact. To his disappointment, he discovered a fresh wave of kisses on the mirrors, as if his plea had fallen on deaf ears.

Frustrated but determined, he sought an audience with the school principal, intending to report the recurring incident.

The principal, equally exasperated, summoned the students to his office and sternly warned them about the consequences of their actions.

Eagerly listening outside the principal's office, the janitor felt a flicker of hope, believing that the students would heed the warning this time.

Alas, his hope was dashed once again when he returned to the restroom the following day. The mirrors were adorned with even more lipstick kisses than before as if the reprimand had only fueled their mischievous desires.

Infuriated, the janitor stormed into the principal's office, overwhelmed by his anger toward the girls' persistent defiance and the principal's seeming leniency.

"The girls are stubborn and seem immune to reprimands. They need to learn a lesson!" the janitor exclaimed.

The principal, recognizing the janitor's frustration, offered his perspective. "Patience, my friend. They will eventually outgrow this behavior. We must wait for their maturity to prevail."

Unsatisfied with the principal's response, the janitor stepped outside to clear his mind. He pondered the situation, desperate to find a solution that would put an end to the incessant display of lipstick kisses.

After a period of reflection, he devised a clever strategy to tackle the issue once and for all.

The following day, armed with determination, the janitor entered the restroom. Suppressing his anger at the sight of fresh lipstick marks, he silently went about his duties, meticulously cleaning the bathroom. Before leaving, he placed a carefully worded note beside the mirrors.

"Kindly refrain from leaving lipstick marks on the mirrors. Cleaning them repeatedly with the same sponge I use for toilet bowls is not a pleasant task."

To his relief, the next day brought a surprising change. Not a single lipstick mark marred the mirrors, and the janitor rejoiced in the success of his cunning plan.

Sometimes, the most effective solutions lie within our own creativity and ingenuity. It is up to us to find innovative ways to address the challenges we face.

16. WAVES OF LAUGHTER: THE SHELLEBRATION COAST CHRONICLES

IN 1937, IN THE SLEEPY COASTAL TOWN OF DROWSY HARBOR, known for its unusual weather patterns, a peculiar occurrence took place. The townspeople had gathered along the shoreline, their eyes wide with curiosity as they witnessed a most extraordinary event. A peculiar combination of weather phenomena had caused a magnificent tidal wave of seashells to wash ashore, transforming the beach into a colorful mosaic.

News of this mesmerizing sight spread like wildfire, attracting visitors from far and wide. The beach became a bustling hub of activity, with tourists armed with cameras, bucket hats, and a desire to capture the essence of this unique spectacle.

Local news crews jostled for prime positions, eager to document the "Great Shell Deluge."

Amidst the commotion, a young girl named Lily, accompanied by her trusty dog, Biscuit, couldn't help but notice the tiny hermit crabs that scurried desperately between the discarded shells, their miniature claws waving in distress. Lily's heart ached for them, and she knew she had to do something to help.

With determination in her eyes, Lily unleashed her quick thinking and boundless imagination. She gathered a group of like-minded children who shared her passion for marine life, and together, they embarked on a mission to rescue the stranded hermit crabs.

As they scurried across the beach, their hands filled with shells and buckets, Lily turned to her new friends and said, "We can't just stand here and watch them struggle, can we? We need to create a hermit crab relocation initiative!"

The children nodded in agreement, their faces filled with enthusiasm. They devised a plan to create makeshift habitats using colorful pails and meticulously arranged seashells, providing the hermit crabs with a safe haven until they could be released back into the water.

Word of the children's mission spread, and soon, adults joined in the efforts. Locals, tourists, and even a troupe of wandering circus performers donned their most outlandish costumes and joined the rescue mission, adding a touch of whimsy to the proceedings.

One man, known for his love of puns, couldn't resist cracking jokes along the way. "Seashell-ebration!" he exclaimed as he handed a hermit crab a tiny shell to call home. Laughter rippled through the crowd, creating an atmosphere of lighthearted camaraderie.

As the rescuers continued their tireless efforts, something magical began to happen. The hermit crabs, sensing the care and love that surrounded them, started to dance with joy, their tiny claws clicking in rhythm. The beach came alive with a symphony of tiny taps and delighted giggles.

Witnessing the transformation, the townspeople couldn't help but be moved. They shed their inhibitions and joined the hermit crabs in a spontaneous dance party, their wild and wacky moves bringing laughter to all.

News of the heartwarming event spread beyond the town's borders, capturing the attention of renowned marine biologists and conservationists. Inspired by the town's unity and the children's ingenuity, they flocked to the beach, eager to lend their expertise and support.

With their guidance, the town transformed the beach into a thriving hermit crab sanctuary, complete with specially designed pools, sheltered habitats, and educational workshops for visitors of all ages. The once-struggling hermit crabs found solace and protection, flourishing under the care of the community.

The success of the hermit crab rescue mission inspired other towns along the coast to implement similar initiatives, creating a network of sanctuaries dedicated to the well-being of marine life. The coastal region became known as the "Shellebration Coast," a vibrant hub of conservation efforts and joyful camaraderie.

Years later, as the sun began to set on the Shellebration Coast, the legacy of Lily and her fellow rescuers lived on. The once-stranded hermit crabs had thrived, their population growing exponentially as the habitats provided them with a safe and nurturing environment.

Lily, now a marine biologist with a passion for ocean conservation, stood proudly on the beach, her gaze sweeping across the bustling sanctuary. Tourists and locals alike marveled at the colorful shells and thriving marine life that had become synonymous with the Shellebration Coast.

The town had transformed into a hub of marine education and research, drawing scientists, nature enthusiasts, and curious visitors from all corners of the globe. The once-struggling beach had become a symbol of hope, reminding all who visited of the power of unity and the impact of small acts of kindness.

Lily smiled as she watched children engrossed in educational activities, learning about the importance of protecting our fragile ecosystems. The beach had become a living classroom where laughter and learning intertwined.

The town's transformation had not been limited to the beach alone. Inspired by the spirit of the hermit crab rescue, community members embarked on various environmental initiatives. They organized regular beach clean-ups, implemented recycling programs, and championed sustainable practices throughout the town.

As the town flourished, Lily stood on the beach and addressed a gathering of residents and visitors. "Look at what we have accomplished together," she exclaimed. "We started with a simple act of kindness, saving a few hermit crabs, and now we have created a community dedicated to protecting our oceans and preserving the wonders of nature."

The crowd erupted in applause, their smiles reflecting the pride they felt for their small coastal town. The legacy of the Shellebration Coast served as a reminder that the collective efforts of passionate individuals could create lasting change.

And so, as the sun dipped below the horizon, casting a golden glow on the Shellebration Coast, the spirit of unity, compassion, and laughter remained etched in the hearts of all who called this place home. The story of the hermit crab rescue will forever be told, inspiring future generations to take action and preserve the natural wonders that graced their beloved coastline.

In the end, they had discovered that the secret ingredient to change was not grand gestures or vast resources—it was the courage to start, the kindness to care, and the laughter that brought people together for a shared purpose.

And as the waves gently lapped against the shore, the residents of the Shellebration Coast knew that their journey was far from over. With every passing day, they would continue to protect, preserve, and celebrate the delicate balance of nature, leaving a legacy of laughter and love for generations to come.

17. THE MAID'S CLEVER NEGOTIATION

IN A MEXICAN HOUSEHOLD, a hilarious exchange unfolded between a determined maid named Carmen and her employer, the lady of the house. Carmen, with her cheeky confidence, had mustered the courage to request a well-deserved pay raise.

Intrigued, the wife decided to engage in a conversation with Carmen to understand the reasoning behind her request for more money. With an air of authority, she inquired, "Carmen, why exactly do you want a pay raise?"

Carmen, not one to hold back, answered, "Well, Señora, there are three undeniable reasons why I deserve an increase." The wife's skepticism began to rise.

"The first reason is that I iron better than you," proclaimed Carmen confidently.

Caught off guard, the wife exclaimed, "Carmen, who on earth told you that you iron better than me?"

Without missing a beat, Carmen replied with a playful smile, "Your husband, Señora. He's the one who said so."

The wife's eyes widened with surprise, but she quickly composed herself. "And what, pray to tell, is your second reason?"

Carmen's smile grew wider. "The second reason is that I am a better cook than you, Señora."

Indignant, the wife retorted, "Nonsense! Who gave you the audacity to claim that you're a better cook than I am?"

Carmen, undeterred, coolly responded, "Your husband, Señora. He's the one who said it."

A storm began to brew in the wife's demeanor. Through clenched teeth, she reluctantly asked, "And what could possibly be your third reason?"

With a twinkle in her eye, Carmen delivered the punchline, "The third reason, Señora, is that I am better than you in bed."

The lady of the house, now boiling with anger, could barely contain herself. She managed to utter, "And did my husband have the audacity to confirm that as well?"

Carmen's playful smile widened further. "No, Señora. It was the gardener who shared that tidbit."

At this point, the wife, torn between fury and amusement, knew she had been outwitted. Surrendering to the comedic turn of events, she couldn't help but ask, "Alright, Carmen, how much is it that you want?"

With a satisfied grin, Carmen replied, "Señora, I'll settle for a modest raise, just enough to hire a salsa dance instructor. The gardener seems quite interested in learning some new moves!"

18. WHISKERS AND SERENITY: A TALE OF UNEXPECTED COMPANIONSHIP

MANY YEARS AGO, IN OAKRIDGE, a quaint little village nestled amidst rolling green hills, a man named Henry found himself in a rather curious situation. You see, Henry had a charming cottage with a picturesque garden that bloomed with vibrant flowers and lush greenery.

One sunny afternoon, as Henry tended to his beloved garden, a peculiar sight caught his eye. An elderly cat strolled into his yard with a dignified air, casting a wise gaze upon Henry before settling down next to him.

Curiosity piqued, Henry decided to investigate further. As he rose from his gardening chores and made his way towards the house, the cat followed closely behind, its tail held high with an air of importance. Henry couldn't help but chuckle at the feline's unexpected companionship.

To his surprise, when they reached the cozy living room, the cat gracefully leaped onto the sofa, curled up in a ball, and closed its eyes, succumbing to a deep slumber. It seemed as though the sofa held a special allure for this peculiar visitor.

Intrigued by the cat's routine, Henry decided to observe its behavior for several weeks. Day after day, the cat would arrive promptly, jump onto the sofa, and snooze peacefully for exactly one hour. The mystery deepened, and Henry yearned to uncover the reason behind this peculiar ritual.

Determined to solve the enigma, Henry devised a plan. He carefully crafted a note that read, "Every afternoon, your cat visits my home and slumbers on my sofa for an hour." He fastened the note securely around the cat's collar, hoping that its owner would soon come forward.

To his surprise, the following day, the cat returned with a different note attached to its collar. Henry gingerly removed the message and read its contents with a mix of amusement and intrigue. The note read, "He lives in a bustling household with four rambunctious children. He seeks a serene sanctuary to unwind. May he join you tomorrow?"

Henry couldn't help but smile at the cat's ingenious response. It seemed that the furry visitor sought solace from the chaos of its boisterous home, finding respite in the tranquility of Henry's cottage.

From that day forward, the cat became a regular guest, and the cozy sofa became its cherished haven. Henry welcomed the feline with open arms, relishing in their quiet companionship as they shared peaceful moments together.

Word of the cat's peculiar escapades spread throughout the village, piquing the curiosity of its residents. Soon, other pets from nearby homes began seeking out Henry's cottage, each carrying their own unique tales and seeking solace from the clamor of their daily lives.

Henry's cottage transformed into a haven for weary pets, a sanctuary where they could unwind, recharge, and revel in the tranquility. Dogs lounged on rugs, rabbits hopped freely through the garden, and even a parrot perched on a branch, filling the air with its vibrant chatter.

The village affectionately referred to Henry's cottage as the "Pawsome Retreat," a place where pets found respite, and humans discovered the simple joy of providing comfort to their furry friends.

And so, in the heartwarming haven of the Pawsome Retreat, Henry and his newfound companions forged an unbreakable bond. They shared laughter, peaceful moments, and the understanding that sometimes, amidst the chaos of life, all creatures—both human and animal—yearned for a quiet corner to call their own.

19. THE CURIOUS CASE OF CHARLIE

CHARLIE WHITE LIVED IN MILLVILLE and had an unusual problem that haunted his nights and disturbed his sleep. Every time he lay down in his cozy bed, he couldn't shake off the feeling that there was someone hiding under it. He would anxiously peek under his bed, only to convince himself that there was someone lurking on top of it. This cycle of fear, confusion, and restless nights left poor Charlie feeling like he was losing his mind.

Determined to find a solution, Charlie decided to seek help from a renowned specialist in the city, Dr. Winchester. He made an appointment with the doctor and nervously walked into his office. "Doctor, I have a peculiar problem," Charlie confessed, his voice trembling. "Every time I lie in bed, I am plagued by the irrational fear of someone hiding under it. And when I check underneath, I'm convinced that there's someone on top of it. It's driving me crazy!"

Dr. Winchester, a wise and experienced man, listened attentively to Charlie's concerns. After a moment of contemplation, he smiled and said, "Fear not, my friend. I believe I have a solution for you. But it will require your commitment. You must visit me three times a week for the next two years, and together, we will work through your fears and conquer them."

Charlie was taken aback by the prospect of such a lengthy commitment. He hesitated for a moment before asking the question that weighed heavily on his mind, "How much will each visit cost, Doctor?"

Dr. Winchester paused, his eyes twinkling with wisdom. "For each visit, the fee will be one hundred dollars," he replied.

Charlie's eyes widened in astonishment. He contemplated the steep cost, wondering if he could afford it. "I need to think it over," he said, his voice tinged with uncertainty.

Two weeks passed, and Charlie found himself strolling through the vibrant streets of Millville when he unexpectedly bumped into Dr. Winchester. The doctor, recognizing Charlie, couldn't help but inquire, "Why haven't you come for your scheduled visits? I was expecting you."

Charlie scratched his head, a sheepish grin spreading across his face. "Well, Doctor, one hundred dollars per visit is quite expensive for me. But you'll be surprised by the alternative solution I found."

Dr. Winchester's curiosity piqued, he asked, "Pray tell, what did you do?"

Charlie leaned in conspiratorially, "I sought advice from a clever bartender in town, and he offered me a genius solution for a mere ten dollars."

The doctor raised an eyebrow, intrigued. "What did the bartender suggest?"

"He told me to cut the legs of my bed!" Charlie burst into laughter. "Can you believe it? A simple alteration to my bed solved my problem entirely!"

Dr. Winchester stared at Charlie, his face a mix of bewilderment and amusement. "Well, that's certainly an unconventional approach," he muttered, chuckling softly. "I suppose sometimes the simplest solutions are the most effective."

Charlie nodded enthusiastically. "Indeed, Doctor. Who would have thought that a slight modification to my bed would dispel all my fears? Now I sleep soundly every night, free from the imaginary monsters beneath and above."

The two men shared a good laugh, finding humor in the unexpected resolution. From that day forward, Charlie became a living testament to the power of creative problem-solving and the value of a wise bartender's advice.

As for Dr. Winchester, he couldn't help but marvel at the wonders of the human mind and the ingenuity that exists in the most unexpected places. Sometimes, unconventional paths lead to the most delightful and amusing outcomes. Reflecting on Charlie's story, Dr. Winchester realized that in the realm of solving problems, there was always room for ingenuity and out-of-the-box thinking.

20. SILVER GEMS AND GOLDEN BONDS: A GRANDFATHER'S LEGACY

IN THE SMALL, FRIENDLY TOWN OF MEADOWBROOK, a kind-hearted man named Robert loved spending time with his six-year-old granddaughter, Lily. One afternoon, as they played with wooden blocks and toy trains in the living room, Lily's restless demeanor indicated her boredom.

"There's nothing fun to do here," Lily complained, her disappointment evident.

Robert thought for a moment, determined to find a way to keep Lily engaged. "How about we go on an adventure?" he suggested. "I heard there are some beautiful flowers blooming at the top of the nearby hill."

Lily's eyes widened with curiosity. "Can we really go?"

Robert's son, Mark, expressed concern. "Lily thrives on routine, Dad.

Any change in her schedule can make her quite cranky."

Undeterred, Robert looked around the room, searching for something that would captivate Lily's imagination. His walls were adorned with vintage paintings and intriguing artifacts, remnants of his adventurous past. One item, in particular, caught his eye—an ornate key.

"Wait right here, Lily. I have something special to show you," Robert said with an amused smile on his face. He hurried to his bedroom and returned with an ancient-looking lockbox, which he placed on the coffee table.

Mark rolled his eyes at the sight of the lockbox. "Dad, please don't get Lily obsessed with hidden treasures and secret codes."

Robert chuckled, dismissing his son's concern. "Don't worry, Mark. This is just for fun. Lily, come and take a look."

Intrigued, Lily approached the coffee table, her gaze fixated on the mysterious lockbox.

"You can unlock it, Lily," Robert encouraged her. "Turn the dial and see what's inside."

With a determined expression, Lily carefully turned the dial and opened the lockbox. Inside, she discovered a collection of beautifully designed coins, both silver and gold.

"Wow! They're so shiny!" Lily exclaimed, her eyes sparkling with wonder.

Robert picked up one of the silver coins and handed it to Lily. "These are special coins called 'Silver Gems.' Each one has a unique design on it."

Lily inspected the coin, marveling at the intricate engravings. "I love the pretty lady on this one! And look, there's an eagle on the other side."

Robert's enthusiasm grew as he shared stories about the coins and their history. He explained how silver was once used as a form of currency and how these coins were highly valued. Lily listened attentively, absorbing every detail.

"Grandpa, can I keep this coin?" Lily asked, her eyes filled with excitement.

Robert grinned, delighted by Lily's enthusiasm. "Of course, my dear. It's yours to keep."

As weeks turned into months, Lily's fascination with the Silver Gems continued to grow. She eagerly awaited their special Sunday gatherings, where Robert would introduce her to new coins and share fascinating tales of their origins. Their time together became filled with laughter, joy, and a shared love for these precious treasures.

Robert's efforts to teach Lily about the value of gold often fell short, as she remained captivated by the allure of silver. Despite his attempts to show her the significance of gold's worth, Lily's unwavering devotion to the Silver Gems remained unchanged.

Amidst their shared adventures, Robert realized that it wasn't about the monetary value or the lessons taught—it was about the bond they formed and the joy Lily found in their special moments together. He cherished their time spent exploring the world of Silver Gems and the magical memories they created.

One winter evening, as the snowflakes gently fell outside, Robert gathered the Silver Gems and prepared for another enchanting encounter with Lily. The room was adorned with the flickering glow of candlelight, creating an ambiance of warmth and coziness.

Lily, now a bit older, sat beside Robert with eager anticipation. She had grown to appreciate the stories behind each coin and the love and care with which her grandfather shared them.

"Grandpa, I've learned so much from you," Lily said, her eyes sparkling with gratitude. "These Silver Gems hold a special place in my heart."

Robert smiled, his heart swelling with pride. "And they hold a special place in mine too, Lily. They are a symbol of our bond and the adventures we've shared together."

As the evening progressed, Robert pulled out a small velvet pouch and gently placed it on the table. Inside were three precious gold coins, each one gleaming with brilliance.

Lily's eyes widened in awe. "Wow, Grandpa! Gold coins! They're so beautiful!"

Robert nodded: "Yes, Lily. Gold is a treasure in itself, and these coins are no exception."

He proceeded to share stories of the history and allure of gold, weaving tales of ancient civilizations and daring explorers who sought its radiant glow. Lily listened intently, captivated by the tales that unfolded before her.

"Now, my dear Lily, if you had to choose, which coin would you take? A Silver Gem or one of these magnificent gold coins?" Robert asked, his voice filled with curiosity.

Lily hesitated, her gaze shifting between the shimmering gold and the beloved Silver Gems. After a thoughtful pause, a mischievous smile played on her lips.

"I choose... both!" Lily exclaimed with a twinkle in her eyes.

Robert looked at her in surprise, momentarily taken aback. Lily couldn't contain her laughter as she revealed her clever trick. "Grandpa, you always taught me to think outside the box. So why not have the best of both worlds? The beauty of gold and the sentimental value of the Silver Gems."

Robert burst into laughter, realizing he had been outsmarted by his clever granddaughter. "Well played, Lily! You truly are your grandfather's granddaughter. Both the gold and the Silver Gems shall be yours."

Lily's eyes sparkled with joy as she held the precious coins in her hands. It was a victory not just in terms of material possessions but also a testament to the bond they shared.

As the years passed, Lily's collection of Silver Gems continued to grow, each coin becoming a cherished memento of her bond with Robert. Their Sunday gatherings remained a tradition filled with laughter, storytelling, and the joy of shared experiences.

One day, as Lily held a Silver Gem in her hand, she reminisced about her beloved grandfather and the lessons he had taught her. She realized that the true value of these precious coins lay not just in their material worth but in the memories and love they represented.

Now a wise adult, Lily decided to honor her grandfather's legacy by sharing the stories of the Silver Gems with future generations. She became a collector herself, sharing the joy and wonder of these unique coins with others, just as Robert had done for her.

And so, the legacy of the Silver Gems lived on, weaving a thread of love, connection, and cherished memories throughout the generations to come. Lily's clever trick remained a heartwarming reminder of the bond between a grandfather and his granddaughter, forever cherished in the tales of the Silver Gems.

21. SPLIT PANTS AND GIGGLES: THE HILARIOUS ADVENTURES OF THE MIRTHWOOD COMEDIAN

WHEN I WAS A MERE SPROUT OF THIRTEEN, my parents whisked us away to the legendary Mirthwood Amusement Park. As we ventured deeper into the heart of the park, my excitement grew with each twist and turn of the rollercoaster tracks.

Finally, we arrived at the grand entrance, our eyes filled with wonder and anticipation. We strolled along the colorful paths, passing by whimsical attractions and lively performers. The air was filled with the sweet scent of cotton candy and the distant sound of merry laughter.

As luck would have it, we stumbled upon the Great Jester's Pavilion, known for its hilarious shows and side-splitting performances. My heart skipped a beat as I imagined the uproarious laughter that would fill the air.

We settled into our seats, ready to be entertained. The curtains parted, and a zany magician with a wacky hat appeared on stage. He dazzled us with his tricks, pulling rabbits out of hats and making objects disappear into thin air.

Next up was a troupe of juggling clowns. Their acrobatic skills and comedic timing had us in stitches. Balloons flew, pies were tossed, and laughter echoed throughout the pavilion. It was a riotous carnival of fun.

But the highlight of the show was the infamous Prankster Brothers, a duo known for their mischievous pranks and uproarious jokes. Their witty banter and slapstick comedy had the entire audience rolling in the aisles.

As I sat there, my sides aching from laughter, I couldn't help but wonder what it would be like to perform on that stage. The thought of making people laugh and forget their worries filled me with an irresistible desire.

Inspired by the comedic brilliance I had just witnessed, I decided to try my luck and audition for a spot in the park's annual Comedy Extravaganza. It was a chance to showcase my own brand of humor and bring smiles to countless faces.

With auditions just a week away, I knew I had to prepare a routine that would knock their socks off. Armed with a notebook and a quirky imagination, I scribbled down jokes, puns, and one-liners that I thought would tickle funny bones.

Days turned into nights as I rehearsed tirelessly in front of the bathroom mirror, perfecting my timing and delivery. I even enlisted the help of my pet parrot, Squawkers, as my feathered audience. He'd squawk in approval whenever a joke landed just right.

Finally, the day of the auditions arrived. My heart raced as I stood backstage, waiting for my name to be called. With sweaty palms and a nervous smile, I took a deep breath and stepped into the spotlight.

The stage was bathed in a warm glow, and the expectant faces in the audience stared back at me. I launched into my routine, delivering joke after joke with gusto. The crowd erupted in laughter, their chuckles and guffaws filling the air like music.

But in the midst of my comedic whirlwind, fate decided to play a prank of its own. With a loud "POP," my pants split right down the seam, revealing my colorful boxers to the entire audience. Gasps mixed with laughter, and I stood frozen, unsure of how to proceed.

Thinking on my feet, I glanced down, pretending to inspect the wardrobe malfunction, and quipped, "Well, ladies and gentlemen, I guess you could say I take my comedy to new depths! The laughs just keep coming!"

The crowd erupted into laughter once again, applauding my quick recovery. Emboldened by their response, I continued my routine with even more energy and determination. The mishap became part of the act, a running gag that had everyone in stitches.

As I wrapped up my routine, the audience rose to their feet, clapping and cheering. Despite the unexpected wardrobe malfunction, I had managed to turn a potentially embarrassing moment into a hilarious memory for all.

The park's talent scouts approached me with beaming smiles, offering me a coveted spot in the Comedy Extravaganza. They praised my resilience and ability for rolling with the punches, ensuring that laughter would fill the pavilion once again.

Overwhelmed with joy and a newfound sense of confidence, I graciously accepted their offer. From that day forward, I became a regular fixture in the Mirthwood Amusement Park, delighting visitors with my comedic antics and infectious laughter.

Every performance was filled with funny jokes, playful banter, and unexpected surprises. I shared the stage with fellow comedians, clowns, and magicians, each bringing their unique style of humor to the forefront.

The park became a haven of laughter and amusement, with families and friends gathering to forget their worries and indulge in the joyous world of comedy. The Comedy Extravaganza grew in popularity, attracting talent from far and wide, all vying for a chance to bring smiles to the faces of park visitors.

As the years went by, my comedic career flourished, and I became known as the "Jester Extraordinaire" of Mirthwood. My performances drew crowds of all ages, from wide-eyed children to nostalgic adults seeking a dose of lighthearted entertainment.

But amidst the laughter and applause, I never forgot that fateful day when my pants split on stage. It served as a reminder that sometimes life throws unexpected curveballs, but it's how we respond to them that truly matters. Laughter, after all, is the best remedy for any embarrassing moment.

22. FEATHERED GOSSIP: A PARROT'S HILARIOUS ANTICS

ROSALYNN HAD A COUSIN WHO OWNED A PET PARROT NAMED CHATTERBOX. True to its name, Chatterbox filled the house with its constant chatter, mimicking the sounds of the doorbell, phone ringtone, and even the laughter of their family members. It seemed to have an uncanny ability to replicate any sound it heard.

During that period, Rosalynn's house had an unusual feature—a talking painting. Yes, you read that correctly. It was a painting of a wise old owl that, when activated, would impart sage advice and clever remarks. It was a novelty item they had acquired from a local flea market, and it never failed to entertain them with its witty one-liners.

Rosalynn had developed a crush on a classmate named Alex. They would often gush about Alex to their friends, sharing stories of their quick wit, charm, and impeccable style. Little did Rosalynn know that Chatterbox, with its exceptional mimicry skills, was secretly listening and storing away every detail.

One fateful day, Alex came over to Rosalynn's house to work on a school project together. Rosalynn introduced Alex to their cousin and eagerly led them into the living room, where the talking painting proudly hung. As they settled down to work, Chatterbox saw it as the perfect opportunity to unleash its mischievous talents.

In a voice that strikingly resembled the painting, Chatterbox began reciting snippets of Rosalynn's conversations about Alex. "Alex, the epitome of charm and wit. Alex, the heartthrob of our class. Alex, a true master of style." Rosalynn's face turned as red as a ripe tomato, while Alex's eyes widened in surprise. It was as if Chatterbox had transformed into a talking parrot straight out of a sitcom, exposing Rosalynn's secret crush in the most unexpected and embarrassing manner.

Rosalynn's cousin burst into uncontrollable laughter, finding the situation utterly hilarious. Meanwhile, Rosalynn sat there, mortified, contemplating how a parrot had become their most notorious confidant. Hurriedly, they attempted to divert attention, guiding Alex away from the talking parrot.

From that day forward, Chatterbox gained a reputation as the matchmaker parrot within their household. Rosalynn made sure to keep their romantic musings far away from the keen ears of their feathered friend. It was a valuable lesson learned: never underestimate the power of a talkative pet with a knack for exposing your secrets at the most inconvenient times.

23. ADVENTURES IN SWIMWEAR: TALES OF MISHAPS AND LAUGHTER

IT WAS JUST A FEW WEEKS BEFORE her much-anticipated beach vacation, and Luna Splashwell had taken care of almost everything on her pre-trip checklist. Booking the hotel, packing the sunscreen, organizing the itinerary — all the necessary steps for a perfect getaway. But there was one tiny issue that needed her attention: swimsuit shopping.

Not one to be too adventurous when it came to swimwear, Luna ventured into a boutique known for its stylish and comfortable swimsuits. Trying on a few options, carefully examining the fit and comfort level, the woman settled on a one-piece swimsuit that promised both style and support.

Excited to show off her new swimsuit, she planned a beach day with her friends. As they set up their beach towels and settled in, a pang of nervousness washed over her. Would her swimsuit really live up to its promises?

With a deep breath, Luna took off her cover-up and confidently made her way toward the water. But just as she was about to take that graceful dive into the sea, she felt a sudden, unmistakable shift in her swimsuit. The carefully crafted support seemed to have other plans. Panic set in as she realized that her swimsuit was determined to have a little adventure of its own.

Luna attempted to discreetly adjust it, hoping to salvage the situation, but the more she tried, the worse it became. It felt like her swimsuit was on a mission to liberate itself from her body. Desperately clinging to the fabric, she tried to keep everything in place. Oblivious to her internal struggle, her friends were cheerfully splashing around, enjoying the day.

Awkwardly waddling back to her towel, desperately holding onto her rebellious swimsuit, she knew she had to come up with a plan. Maybe some strategic towel wrapping would do the trick? Or perhaps a quick visit to the beachside restroom could provide a moment of respite and a chance to fix this swimsuit catastrophe. But as luck would have it, just as she was about to make her grand escape, a rogue gust of wind swept across the beach. It conspired with her swimsuit to expose her momentary vulnerability to the world. In an instant, her carefully wrapped towel was whipped away, leaving her standing there, clutching her swimsuit for dear life and exposed to the amusement of beachgoers. With a mix of embarrassment and determination, Luna marched back to her friends, making light of the situation. They laughed, they teased, and at that moment, she realized that a swimsuit mishap couldn't steal her joy. After all, it was just another hilarious chapter in the book of her adventures.

From that day forward, the woman learned to appreciate the unpredictability of life, even when it involved unruly swimwear. Rocking her newfound confidence, Luna and her friends created endless inside jokes about beachside fashion fiascos. Because sometimes, the most memorable moments are the ones that don't go according to plan.

So, if anyone ever finds themselves in a battle with a stubborn swimsuit, it's important to embrace the laughter, hold on to their dignity, and make it a tale worth telling.

Because, in the end, it's the unexpected stories that make life truly entertaining.

And as for that particular swimsuit? Well, let's just say it found its place in the back of her closet, reserved for less eventful beach days. But the memories of its brief rebelliousness still bring a smile to Luna's face whenever she embarks on a new swimwear adventure. After all, it's the mishaps and laughter that make those moments all the more memorable.

So, whether it's a wardrobe malfunction, an unexpected twist, or a swimsuit rebellion, embracing the humor and keeping the laughter alive is the key. Life is too short to take ourselves too seriously, especially when it comes to swimwear mishaps.

24. YOGA AND LAUGHTER: THE MISADVENTURES OF FRED

IN THE BUSTLING TOWN OF WILLOWVILLE, Fred eagerly prepared for his first-ever yoga class at the community center. He had heard about the physical and mental benefits of yoga and thought it would be a great way to unwind and stay fit. Plus, it would be a chance to meet new people and have a good laugh along the way.

The day before his class, Fred asked his friend, Lisa, to gather all the important details. He wanted to make sure he arrived fully prepared. Lisa made the necessary calls and relayed the information, or so they thought.

With a sense of excitement and nerves, Fred arrived at the community center bright and early. He entered the designated yoga room and quickly noticed something amiss. The room was filled with women of all ages gracefully stretching and performing various yoga poses. And to his surprise, Fred was the only man among them.

In his mind, Fred could almost hear their thoughts:

"Who's the brave soul joining our yoga sisterhood?"

"Do men even know how to touch their toes?"

"I hope he doesn't feel too out of place!"

"Maybe he's secretly a yoga master in disguise."

Feeling slightly self-conscious but determined not to let it ruin his experience, Fred found a spot at the back of the room and began following the instructor's guidance. He attempted to contort his body into different poses, often ending up in hilarious positions that made everyone around giggle.

As the class progressed, Fred's determination grew stronger. He realized that yoga was about finding balance and embracing imperfections. So what if he didn't have the flexibility of a contortionist? He had the heart of a yogi and the spirit of a comedian.

With each pose, Fred focused on his breath and let go of any self-consciousness. He even managed to sneak in a few funny remarks, lightening the atmosphere and making everyone laugh.

The women welcomed him into their yoga sisterhood with open arms, appreciating his unique perspective and infectious humor.

After the class, as Fred left the community center with a smile on his face, he realized that he had discovered not only the joy of yoga but also the power of laughter and camaraderie. He may have been the lone man in a sea of women, but that didn't stop him from fully embracing the experience and finding his own place in the yoga world.

From that day forward, Fred continued attending yoga classes, sharing his infectious humor, and inspiring others to find joy and laughter in every pose. And in the end, it wasn't about being the perfect yogi; it was about embracing the journey, finding humor in the awkward moments, and connecting with others in unexpected ways.

25. A CHILI ADVENTURE WITH UNFORESEEN CONSEQUENCES

AS THE SUN BEAT DOWN on the picturesque town of Swindleton, Patricia found herself in the middle of a crowded farmers' market. Her husband, Martin, accompanied her as they explored the local offerings, sampling artisanal cheeses and soaking in the vibrant atmosphere. Little did she know that this delightful outing would soon take an unexpected turn.

Amidst the bustling market, they stumbled upon a charming stall selling an assortment of spicy peppers. Patricia, being a self-proclaimed spice enthusiast, couldn't resist the temptation to try them. The vendor warned them about the intensity of the peppers, but Patricia confidently declared, "Bring on the heat!"

Martin selected a small, seemingly harmless pepper and handed it to Patricia. She popped it into her mouth, expecting a burst of fiery flavor. Instead, an immediate and overwhelming sensation engulfed her taste buds. It felt like a volcanic eruption in her mouth.

The spicy pepper unleashed its wrath upon Patricia's unsuspecting palate, causing her to hop from foot to foot in a frantic search for relief. The surrounding market-goers turned their heads, amused and bewildered by her spontaneous dance routine.

Martin, ever the helpful husband, scrambled through their bag, pulling out a water bottle, a handkerchief, and even a bag of marshmallows in his desperate attempt to quell the fire within Patricia. Unfortunately, none of his impromptu remedies seemed to have any effect.

Meanwhile, the crowd was thoroughly entertained, their laughter reverberating through the market square. Patricia couldn't blame them—she must have looked like a salsa dancer gone rogue, driven by the wrath of hot sauce.

Just when she thought things couldn't get any worse, a gust of wind blew through the market, carrying with it the alluring aroma of freshly baked pastries. Despite the spice-induced distress, Patricia's mouth suddenly craved the soothing coolness of a cream puff.

It was a cruel twist of fate that the heavenly scent seemed to taunt her in the midst of her pepper-induced ordeal.

Martin, quick on his feet, spotted a nearby bakery stall and sprinted towards it, determined to bring back the much-needed relief of pastry salvation. Patricia watched him disappear into the crowd, holding onto the hope of finding solace in the comforting embrace of a cream puff.

Left to her own devices, Patricia frantically scanned her surroundings, desperately seeking something to extinguish the fiery inferno raging in her mouth. Her eyes landed on a lemonade stand, and with newfound determination, she hurried over, hopeful that the citrusy elixir would provide some respite.

With trembling hands, she grabbed a cup of lemonade and took a cautious sip. The refreshing tang mingled with the lingering heat, creating a peculiar combination of sensations that made her question her life choices. Yet, it brought a momentary calm to the fiery chaos within.

Just as Patricia was starting to regain her composure, Martin reappeared, triumphantly waving a cream puff in the air like a conquering hero. She could practically see the heavenly glow emanating from that delicate pastry. She reached out, eager to take a bite, but before she could do so, a mischievous seagull swooped down from the sky and snatched the cream puff right out of her hand. The audacity of that winged thief!

Martin and Patricia stood there, dumbfounded, as the seagull soared into the distance, relishing its stolen treat. They couldn't help but burst into laughter, realizing that their spicy pepper adventure had taken an unexpected twist, turning their pursuit of pastry relief into a comedic spectacle.

Despite the heat, the stolen cream puff, and the amusement they had become, Martin and Patricia continued their market escapade with renewed enthusiasm. Swindleton would forever hold a special place in their hearts as the town where they danced with spice, battled with birds, and shared laughter amidst the unexpected turns of their adventurous day.

26. THE MYSTERY OF THE VANISHING SLIPPERS

THERE WAS AN AIR OF EXCITEMENT AND MYSTERY in the cozy corridors of Sunnyvale Senior Living. Residents strolled through the halls in their comfortable slippers, engaging in lively conversations and sharing stories of yesteryears. But lately, something peculiar was happening – their cherished slippers were vanishing, disappearing without a trace.

The first victim was Mr. Jones, an eccentric gentleman with a penchant for collecting vintage ties. He had settled into his favorite armchair one evening, only to discover that his favorite pair of slippers had mysteriously vanished. Bewildered, he searched high and low, peering under furniture and behind curtains, but they were nowhere to be found. The disappearance of Mr. Jones' slippers sparked a wave of concern and curiosity among the residents.

Word quickly spread throughout the nursing home, and it wasn't long before a group of unlikely sleuths emerged – the misfit trio consisting of Mrs. Henderson, an energetic retiree with a knack for knitting, Mr. Thompson, a retired detective with a sharp wit, and Miss Miller, a retired librarian with a photographic memory.

The trio gathered in the communal lounge, their heads together, determined to get to the bottom of the slipper caper. Mrs. Henderson, with her oversized magnifying glass, examined every nook and cranny for clues. Meanwhile, Mr. Thompson, sporting his old detective hat, interrogated the residents, asking questions and listening intently for any leads. Miss Miller meticulously combed through stacks of books, searching for references to missing slippers in ancient literature.

As their investigation unfolded, the residents couldn't help but chuckle at the sight of the amateur detectives and their humorous escapades. Mrs. Henderson accidentally mistook Mr. Thompson's shoelaces for a clue and nearly tied them together, causing him to stumble and fall into a pile of discarded newspapers. Miss Miller, in her enthusiasm, mistook Mr. Jones' collection of vintage ties for a hidden slipper stash, resulting in a hilarious mix-up that left everyone in stitches.

Meanwhile, the slippers continued to vanish, leaving the residents perplexed and on high alert. They formed a neighborhood watch, staying up late into the night, peeking out their windows and armed with binoculars, hoping to catch the mysterious slipper thief in the act. However, their vigilance proved fruitless, as the culprit remained elusive.

With frustration mounting, the trio decided to take a different approach. They organized a slipper fashion show, inviting all the residents to showcase their remaining slippers. It was a riotous affair, with residents parading down the makeshift runway, donning their most eccentric and colorful footwear. Amidst the laughter and applause, a brilliant idea struck Mr. Thompson.

Gathering the residents together, he announced, "Ladies and gentlemen, I believe I have cracked the case of the vanishing slippers. The thief is not among us, but rather, it is none other than our beloved feline companion, Shadow!"

Gasps of astonishment filled the room as all eyes turned to the resident cat, who was innocently licking her paws in a corner. It turned out that Shadow had developed a penchant for stealing slippers, hiding them away in her secret stash beneath the caretaker's desk. With her stealthy moves, she managed to evade the residents' watchful eyes.

The revelation was met with a mixture of relief and amusement. The residents realized that their slippers had not been intentionally taken but had simply fallen victim to Shadow's playful antics.

With the mystery solved and a plan in place, the atmosphere at Sunnyvale Senior Living returned to its usual lightheartedness. The residents shared stories of Shadow's misadventures, swapping tales of their own encounters with the playful feline. Laughter filled the air as they regaled each other with anecdotes about their slipper mishaps and Shadow's sneaky maneuvers.

In the end, the mystery of the vanishing slippers brought the residents closer together, reinforcing the sense of community that made Sunnyvale Senior Living such a special place. And with Shadow as the unofficial mascot, their days were filled with laughter, love, and the occasional reminder that even mischievous antics could bring unexpected joy.

27. SERENDIPITY SPRINGS: A CAMPGROUND OF UNEXPECTED ADVENTURES

IN THE SUMMER OF 1998, Lynda found herself on an unexpected adventure in a place called Serendipity Springs, a hidden gem nestled in the heart of the countryside. It was a spontaneous escape, a break from the ordinary, and she couldn't have been more thrilled.

As Lynda drove down winding roads, following the directions from a hand-drawn map given by a quirky local, she couldn't help but feel a sense of anticipation. The destination was a rustic campground known as "Nature's Haven," promising tranquility and natural beauty.

Upon arriving at the campground, she was greeted by a lively group of campers who seemed to have an extra sparkle in their eyes. They had gathered around a roaring bonfire, sharing stories and laughter that echoed through the night. It was like stumbling upon a secret society of adventurers.

Eager to join in the fun, Lynda set up her humble tent, affectionately named "The Cozy Cocoon," and made her way to the communal gathering area. The aroma of delicious food filled the air, enticing her growling stomach. It was a potluck dinner extravaganza, and everyone had brought their culinary masterpieces to share.

As she walked from table to table, sampling an array of delectable dishes, Lynda couldn't help but be amazed at the creativity and skill of the campers. There were mouthwatering barbecued ribs that fell off the bone, accompanied by tangy homemade sauces. Savory seafood paella with plump shrimp and tender calamari made her taste buds dance with delight. And let's not forget the sinful desserts—decadent chocolate lava cake, creamy strawberry cheesecake, and a mysterious concoction called "Campfire Delight," which was a sweet symphony of toasted marshmallows, graham crackers, and melted chocolate.

With bellies full and spirits high, the campers were ready for some entertainment. To Lynda's surprise, they had organized a talent show under the starlit sky. One by one, campers took the stage, showcasing their hidden talents. There were hilarious stand-up comedians, mesmerizing fire dancers, and even a karaoke performance that left everyone singing along and laughing uncontrollably.

Feeling inspired, Lynda decided to step out of her comfort zone and share her own unique talent—balloon animal sculpting. Armed with a bag of colorful balloons, she twisted and turned, transforming them into whimsical creatures that brought smiles to everyone's faces. The applause and laughter filled the air, making her feel like a true artiste.

As the night progressed, the energy shifted towards the campground's natural centerpiece—the magnificent Serendipity Spring. It was a sparkling oasis, surrounded by lush greenery and illuminated by softly glowing lanterns. The campers gathered around, their excitement contagious.

Lynda watched as some brave souls took a leap of faith, diving into the cool waters of Serendipity Spring. Their joy was infectious, and before she knew it, she found herself standing at the water's edge, ready to embrace the adventure. With a splash and a burst of laughter, she joined the spirited water games—bobbing, swimming, and attempting (with limited success) synchronized swimming routines.

As the night grew darker, the campers retreated to their cozy campfires, sharing stories and toasting marshmallows for gooey s'mores. The crackling sound of the fire mingled with the melodies of impromptu campfire sing-alongs. They sang cheesy campfire songs, belting out off-key renditions of classics like "Kumbaya" and "The Circle of Life," adding their own hilarious twists and improvised lyrics.

Eventually, the weariness of the day caught up with them, and they bid each other goodnight. Tucked snugly in her sleeping bag, surrounded by the sounds of nature and the warmth of the campfire, Lynda reflected on the incredible day she had experienced. Serendipity Springs had lived up to its name, delivering unexpected moments of joy, laughter, and connection.

As she drifted off to sleep, she couldn't help but feel grateful for stumbling upon this hidden haven and the wonderful campers who had embraced her as part of their vibrant community. At that moment, she realized that sometimes the best adventures are the ones we stumble upon, the ones that surprise us and take us out of our comfort zones.

The next morning, Lynda woke up to the gentle chirping of birds and the golden sunlight filtering through the trees. With a smile on her face, she emerged from her cozy cocoon and joined her newfound friends for a hearty breakfast, sharing stories and laughter over steaming cups of coffee and plates piled high with pancakes and crispy bacon.

Before bidding farewell to Serendipity Springs, they gathered for one final group photo, capturing the memories they had created together. Promises were made to stay in touch, reunite for future adventures, and to cherish the bond forged in this magical place.

28. THE BACON CAPER: A SALAD BAR MISHAP

IT WAS A BEAUTIFUL SUNNY JUNE AFTERNOON IN 2005, and Gael and his wife Arlet decided to try out a new restaurant in town that boasted an incredible salad bar. They were both salad enthusiasts, always on the lookout for unique toppings and dressings to tantalize their taste buds. This place seemed like the perfect spot to indulge in their salad cravings.

As they entered the restaurant, they were greeted by a lively ambiance and the delightful aroma of fresh ingredients. The salad bar was a sight to behold, with row after row of vibrant vegetables, crispy toppings, and an assortment of dressings. It was a salad lover's paradise.

Eager to create their dream salads, they grabbed their plates and joined the line. Standing beside them was a stylish couple, impeccably dressed and engrossed in their conversation. They seemed like the epitome of elegance and sophistication.

As they made their way through the line, carefully selecting their ingredients, Gael couldn't help but notice that Arlet's eyes were fixated on one particular ingredient—bacon bits. She was a bacon enthusiast, always on the hunt for the perfect crispy, smoky goodness.

With the tongs in her hand, Arlet reached for the bacon bits, but not just any bacon bits. She meticulously scanned the options, searching for that one piece of bacon that stood out from the rest. It was as if she was on a bacon mission, determined to find the holy grail of bacon bits.

And then it happened.

With a swift motion, Arlet carefully plucked the chosen bacon piece from the tray. But in a twist of fate, the bacon bit slipped from her grasp and gracefully sailed through the air, landing perfectly inside the stylish gentleman's suit pocket.

Gael couldn't believe his eyes. It was a bacon miracle. The bacon bit had found its way into the most unexpected place. The gentleman, oblivious to the unexpected addition to his ensemble, continued his conversation without a hint of what had transpired.

Arlet turned to Gael, "What should we do?" she whispered.

Gael couldn't pass up the chance for some culinary fun. "Let's add the finishing touch," he whispered back, a playful glimmer in his eye.

With newfound determination, Arlet took aim at the gentleman's other suit pocket, this time setting her sights on a crouton. With a delicate flick of her wrist, she launched the crouton into the air, and like a graceful dancer, it found its mark, settling neatly into the opposite pocket.

They couldn't contain their laughter, their amusement echoing through the restaurant. The thought of this gentleman discovering a bacon-bit-and-crouton surprise in his pockets was simply too hilarious.

But alas, they decided to leave it at that. They didn't want to push their luck or risk getting caught in their little prank. The bacon and crouton duo would remain their secret, a tale to be shared among friends.

As they enjoyed their carefully crafted salads, they couldn't help but chuckle at the unexpected turn of events. It was a salad bar adventure like no other, filled with bacon mishaps and pocket surprises.

From that day on, every time they visited a salad bar, they couldn't help but smile and remember the bacon bit caper. It had become a cherished memory, reminding them that even the simplest things in life can bring unexpected joy and laughter.

So, the next time you embark on a salad bar escapade, keep an eye on your toppings. You never know where they might end up and what delightful surprises await.

29. MILDRED'S COLORFUL MIXUP

IN THE VIBRANT TOWN OF SPRINKLEVILLE, nestled amidst rolling hills and cheerful neighborhoods, resided a delightfully eccentric woman named Mildred. Mildred had a peculiar obsession with her collection of colorful markers. She carried them everywhere she went, ready to unleash her artistic talents at a moment's notice. Whether it was doodling on a notepad or sketching on a napkin, Mildred couldn't resist the temptation to add a splash of color to her surroundings.

One sunny afternoon, Mildred found herself strolling through the local park, marker set in her purse, as always. She couldn't resist the urge to bring some creativity to the world around her. As she walked along the path, she discreetly pulled out her marker and started embellishing a nearby tree trunk with vibrant swirls and doodles.

Unbeknownst to Mildred, a group of kids from a nearby school was on a field trip to the park. They were learning about nature and its wonders. As they spotted Mildred engaged in her artistic endeavor, their eyes widened with curiosity. They had never seen someone turning a tree into a colorful masterpiece before.

The children gathered around Mildred, their teacher cautiously observing from a distance. They were in awe of her skillful strokes and the magical transformation taking place before their eyes. The teacher hesitated for a moment, unsure whether to intervene or let the artistic display unfold.

Meanwhile, Mildred continued to decorate the tree with gusto, completely unaware of the growing audience. She hummed a merry tune and smiled to herself, feeling a surge of creative energy. Her marker glided across the tree trunk, leaving trails of color in its wake.

Just as Mildred was about to add the finishing touches to her masterpiece, the teacher finally approached. She cleared her throat and politely asked, "Excuse me, ma'am, what are you doing to that tree?"

Mildred looked up, slightly startled, and realized she had an audience. She blinked and glanced at her marker-wielding hand, then at the tree. Her eyes widened in surprise as she noticed that she hadn't been using her trusty marker after all. Instead, she had been drawing on the tree with a tube of bright red lipstick.

A burst of laughter erupted from the children, their infectious giggles filling the air. Mildred joined in, unable to resist the hilarity of the situation. The teacher chuckled, relieved that it was all just a harmless mishap.

From that day on, Mildred became known as the "Artistic Lipstick Lady" in Sprinkleville. She embraced her newfound fame, sharing her amusing tale with anyone who would listen. And whenever she pulled out her markers or lipstick, she made sure to double-check which one she was using, ensuring that her artistic endeavors remained on the appropriate canvas.

30. THE WHIMSICAL ADVENTURES OF THE POLKA DOT HAT

PENELOPE LIVED IN THE LIVELY TOWN OF MERRYMEADOWS, and she had an insatiable love for polka dots. Her wardrobe was filled with polka-dot dresses, polka-dot scarves, polka-dot socks—you name it. She even had polka-dot curtains in her living room. Penelope couldn't resist the allure of those cheerful, extravagant patterns, and she wore them proudly, often turning heads with her vibrant fashion choices.

One sunny day, while strolling through the bustling streets of Merrymeadows, Penelope stumbled upon a charming boutique that specialized in—you guessed it—polka dot accessories. Her eyes widened with excitement as she stepped into the store, surrounded by a sea of polka-dot umbrellas, handbags, and hats.

Among the display of hats, Penelope's attention was immediately captivated by a stunning polka dot sun hat. Its brim was wide and adorned with a flurry of polka dots in various sizes and colors. She knew she had to have it. Without hesitation, she snatched it from the shelf and placed it on her head, instantly feeling a surge of joy.

With her new polka dot sun hat proudly perched on her head, Penelope continued her jaunt through town, turning heads and drawing smiles wherever she went. She reveled in the compliments and couldn't help but strike a pose whenever she caught her reflection in a shop window.

As she made her way to the local café for a cup of her favorite cappuccino, Penelope's vibrant hat caught the attention of a squirrel perched on a nearby tree branch. Curiosity piqued, the squirrel decided to investigate this fascinating polka dot phenomenon.

With a nimble leap, the squirrel landed directly on top of Penelope's hat, mistaking it for a peculiarly patterned nut. It perched there, nibbling on an imaginary snack while Penelope remained blissfully unaware of her new companion.

Unbeknownst to her, Penelope had become the talk of the town. Passersby stopped in their tracks, pointing and chuckling at the sight of the squirrel atop her polka-dot hat. Some even whipped out their phones, capturing the amusing spectacle to share with their friends.

Penelope's journey continued, her polka dot hat now adorned with a furry friend. She strutted through the town square, blissfully ignorant of the hilarity that ensued. People couldn't help but burst into laughter at the sight—a fashion statement taken to unexpected heights.

Finally, as Penelope entered her favorite café, the barista couldn't contain her amusement any longer. She burst into uncontrollable laughter, drawing the attention of everyone inside. Penelope turned, puzzled, and saw herself in the café's mirrored wall. There, perched atop her hat, was the squirrel, nibbling away with gusto.

The café erupted into laughter, Penelope included. She joined in on the mirthful chorus, realizing the absurdity of her situation.

The squirrel continued its snacking, seemingly unfazed by the commotion it had caused.

From that day forward, Penelope became known as the "Polka Dot Squirrel Whisperer" of Merrymeadows. Her fashion sense and her unlikely companion brought smiles and laughter to the town's inhabitants. And whenever she donned her beloved polka dot accessories, she always kept an eye out for any potential furry visitors seeking a stylish perch.

31. A HILARIOUS TALE OF SPICY WINGS AND ENDURING FRIENDSHIP

IN HARMONYVILLE, THERE EXISTED A TIGHT-KNIT GROUP OF FRIENDS known as "The Whirlwinds." They had met during their high school days at Melville Academy and had remained inseparable ever since. The Whirlwinds, consisting of Agnes, Bea, Clara, and Delilah, shared a bond that was as unbreakable as it was hilarious.

Their gatherings were a whirlwind of laughter, reminiscing about their misadventures in high school and navigating the ups and downs of life. From spirited debates about fashion trends to discussing the woes of modern technology, they reveled in the joy of each other's company.

One fine summer day, Agnes decided to host a picnic in her beautifully manicured backyard. The sun was shining, and the air was filled with the scent of freshly cut grass. The Whirlwinds eagerly accepted the invitation, looking forward to a day filled with good food and even better company.

Agnes took great pride in her culinary skills, so she decided to surprise her friends with her signature dish—spicy buffalo wings. She had spent hours perfecting the recipe, ensuring that each wing was coated in a fiery blend of seasonings that would make their taste buds dance.

As the Whirlwinds gathered around the picnic table, their mouths watering in anticipation, Agnes presented her buffalo wings with a flourish. The aroma was intoxicating, and they couldn't wait to dig in. With laughter and banter filling the air, they indulged in the delicious feast, savoring each fiery bite.

But little did they know that Agnes had a plan up her sleeve. She had secretly added an extra dose of hot sauce to a select few wings, intending to give her friends a spicy surprise. As they savored the wings, the heat slowly crept up on them, causing their eyes to widen and their faces to turn bright red.

Clara, always the first to react, reached for her water bottle, chugging it down in desperation. Bea fanned herself with a napkin, hoping to extinguish the imaginary flames engulfing her mouth. Delilah, with tears streaming down her face, gasped for air, exclaiming, "Agnes, you've unleashed a dragon!"

Amidst the chaos, Agnes couldn't contain her laughter. She had never expected the spicy surprise to be so potent. But as always, The Whirlwinds knew how to find humor in any situation. They laughed through the tears, relishing in the shared experience of their taste buds going on an unexpected adventure. From that day forward, the buffalo wings became legendary in The Whirlwinds' circle. Whenever they gathered for a picnic or a potluck, Agnes would receive playful warnings about her infamous spicy wings. But it was all in good fun, as they cherished the joy and laughter that bound them together.

And so The Whirlwinds continued to spin their tales of friendship, spiced with laughter and seasoned with love. Through their hilarious escapades and spicy surprises, they reminded each other that life was always better when shared with those who could make even the hottest moments feel like a breeze.

32. INSOMNIAC CHRONICLES: A COMEDY OF ERRORS

IN 1992, IN THE LIVELY NEIGHBORHOOD OF CLOVERDALE, there lived a woman named Isabella. She was a hardworking mother of three, known for her meticulous planning and ability to juggle various responsibilities. However, there was one aspect of her life that constantly challenged her: sleep deprivation.

Isabella's youngest daughter, Lily, had recently developed a habit of waking up in the middle of the night, seeking comfort and reassurance. Night after night, Isabella would groggily stumble into Lily's room, coaxing her back to sleep with soothing lullabies and gentle back rubs. Despite the fatigue that settled in her bones, Isabella couldn't resist the opportunity to provide solace to her beloved daughter.

But the lack of quality sleep began to take its toll on Isabella. Her normally sharp mind started to falter, and she found herself stumbling through her daily routine in a haze of exhaustion. It seemed that the universe had conspired to add a touch of humor to her sleep-deprived misadventures.

One fateful morning, as Isabella rushed to get ready for work, she absentmindedly grabbed a tube of toothpaste and squeezed it onto her hand instead of her toothbrush. The minty foam covered her hand, leaving her staring at it in bewilderment. "Smooth move, Isabella," she mumbled, unable to contain her laughter at the absurdity of the situation.

Later that day, during a staff meeting, Isabella's sleep-deprived mind played a trick on her. She confidently presented a report that she had meticulously prepared the previous night, only to realize halfway through that she had mixed up the data from two different projects. Her colleagues exchanged puzzled glances, and Isabella's cheeks flushed with embarrassment. She couldn't help but chuckle at her own forgetfulness.

In the midst of her sleep-deprived escapades, Isabella's sense of humor never wavered. On a grocery shopping trip, she absentmindedly placed a carton of milk in the cereal aisle and left her keys in the refrigerator. Each mishap only served to bring a smile to her face and laughter to those around her.

Even her children, who were unaware of the full extent of their mother's sleep-deprived adventures, found themselves amused by her delightful quirks. Isabella's eldest daughter, Sophie, would often tease her about the time she accidentally put salt in her coffee instead of sugar, creating a memorable morning brew.

As the days turned into weeks, Isabella's sleep deprivation persisted, but she faced it with a resilient spirit and a lighthearted approach. She knew that the sleepless nights were just a temporary phase, and in the grand scheme of things, they were an opportunity for her to embrace the hilarity that life had to offer.

One evening, as Isabella tucked Lily into bed and prepared herself for another potentially restless night, she couldn't help but giggle. She realized that despite the challenges, the sleepless nights had given her a treasure trove of funny stories and shared laughter with her loved ones.

With a twinkle in her tired eyes, Isabella whispered to Lily, "Sweet dreams, my little mischief-maker. Mama may be sleep-deprived, but she wouldn't trade these moments for the world."

And so, armed with a sense of humor and a heart filled with love, Isabella embraced each day, knowing that sleep deprivation couldn't dim the brightness of her spirit. As she navigated the comical challenges that came her way, she found solace in the laughter that echoed through her home, a testament to the joy that exists even in the midst of sleep-deprived adventures.

33. BUBBLES, BUBBLES EVERYWHERE

ON THEIR WAY TO THEIR TWO-WEEK CAMPING TRIP in the picturesque mountains of Colorado, Tom and Linda had one mission for the first day of travel: to arrive at their cozy cabin in time to enjoy a refreshing dip in the nearby lake. However, as they journeyed through the scenic highways, they noticed a sign for the World's Largest Ball of Twine, a quirky tourist attraction they had always wanted to see.

"Come on, it's a once-in-a-lifetime opportunity!" Tom exclaimed, nudging Linda. "How far off the route is it?"

Linda quickly consulted the map, estimating the detour and the time it would take. After some deliberation, they decided to seize the moment and visit the colossal ball of twine, even if it meant adjusting their plans and speeding things up a bit.

As they marveled at the colossal ball of twine, snapping photos and taking in the eccentricity of it all, they lost track of time. The minutes ticked away, and they realized they had to make up for lost time to reach their cabin before sunset.

"We'll have to step on it," Tom declared with a determined look in his eyes. The K-car roared to life, and they zipped along the winding roads, hoping to make up for the delay.

Their speed increased, but so did their chances of attracting the attention of law enforcement. Sure enough, flashing lights appeared in the rearview mirror. Tom pulled over, nervously preparing himself for the inevitable ticket.

To his surprise, the officer gave them a stern warning, urging them to slow down and drive safely.

Finally, they arrived at the cabin with only a few precious minutes left before the lake closed for the night. Despite the setbacks and the time crunch, they were not ready to give up on their swimming plans.

"I can't believe we made it!" Linda exclaimed, rummaging through the suitcase for their swimsuits. However, an unfortunate encounter with a spilled bottle of sunscreen resulted in Tom's trunks being covered in an oily mess.

"Guess we'll have to come up with a quick solution," Linda said, grabbing a towel and hastily wiping off the excess lotion. "There, good as new!"

With a mix of determination and a touch of desperation, they rushed to the lake. Tom dove in with a splash, creating a trail of bubbles that followed him wherever he went. Linda couldn't help but giggle at the sight, trying her best to keep a straight face.

"Look, dear, your very own bubble entourage!" she teased, pointing to the bubbles floating behind him.

Undeterred by the soapy mishap, they swam around, relishing the cool water and the picturesque surroundings. Their temporary swim buddy joined them, oblivious to the bubbly chaos surrounding Tom.

As the sun began to set, signaling the end of their eventful day, Linda suggested heading back to the cabin to relax in the hot tub. Little did they know that their hot tub adventure would add another layer of hilarity to their trip.

As they settled into the bubbling hot tub, enjoying the warmth and relaxation, a fellow guest approached them.

"Do you mind if I turn on the jets?" she asked, not waiting for a response as she twisted the knob. Suddenly, the water erupted in a frenzy of bubbles, growing frothier by the second.

"Well, this is quite the bubble extravaganza!" Linda chuckled, struggling to suppress her laughter. The bubbles continued to multiply, threatening to overflow from the tub.

"I've never seen a hot tub this bubbly before," their new companion commented, bewildered by the frothy spectacle.

Tom, realizing the comedic situation they found themselves in, couldn't help but join in the laughter. With each passing second, the bubbles grew higher, resembling a foamy mountain.

"I think I'll take a break from the bubbly party and cool off in the lake," Tom suggested, rising from the hot tub, covered in a thick layer of bubbles. As he made his way to the lake, a trail of bubbles followed him, creating a comical sight.

Linda, unable to contain her amusement any longer, bid farewell to their fellow hot tub enthusiast and joined Tom by the lake. They laughed together, enjoying the sheer absurdity of their bubbly misadventure.

As the evening drew to a close, they walked back to their cabin with their spirits uplifted. They couldn't have imagined a more eventful and laughter-filled start to their camping trip.

34. THE THANKSGIVING STRANGER

AT THEIR ANNUAL FOURTH OF JULY BARBECUE, the backyard was filled with laughter, the sizzle of grills, and the sweet aroma of burgers and hot dogs. Friends and family gathered from near and far, and Mateo welcomed anyone who wanted to join the festivities.

That year, the weather was perfect, with clear blue skies and a gentle breeze. They decided to set up the dining area in the front yard to enjoy the warm summer evening. The long table was decorated with a patriotic tablecloth and a centerpiece made of red, white, and blue flowers. It was a sight to behold.

As the guests started to arrive, Mateo's cousin, Steve, showed up with a tall man by his side. They were engaged in animated conversation as they made their way up the driveway.

Mateo's mom greeted them at the front door, and he could see the surprise on her face as she exchanged introductions.

"Steve, who is this?" she asked, a puzzled expression on her face.

Steve grinned and introduced the man as his friend from Australia. "He's visiting the States, and I thought it would be great to bring him along for some good old American BBQ!"

Mom looked a bit taken aback but quickly recovered. "Well, welcome! We're glad to have you here. Let me find an extra chair and set a place for you at the table."

Mateo hurried to set up a spot for their unexpected guest, placing him next to his uncle so they could strike up a conversation about their respective countries.

Throughout the evening, their Australian friend and Mateo's uncle engaged in lively discussions about their favorite sports and cultural differences and even tried to imitate each other's accents. It was a hilarious sight to see.

As the delicious food was served, their guests enthusiastically praised the flavors and couldn't get enough of the classic American dishes. The Australian visitor indulged in burgers, potato salad, and corn on the cob, enjoying every bite.

After dinner, their Australian friend approached Mateo's mom with a grateful smile. "Thank you so much for including me in your Fourth of July celebration, Lisa. It was truly unexpected, but it turned out to be one of the most memorable experiences I've had while traveling."

Mom chuckled. "We're happy to have you here and share our traditions. Do you celebrate Independence Day in Australia?"

He shook his head. "No, we don't have a similar holiday, but I must say, your celebration is quite impressive. It's been a delightful experience, and I won't forget the warm hospitality I received."

As the evening wound down and the guests started saying their goodbyes, Mateo's mom called his aunt aside to discuss the identity of their newfound Australian friend.

"Lisa, do you know who he is?" his aunt asked, a puzzled expression on her face.

Mom looked equally confused. "No, I thought he was your friend. I've never seen him before."

His aunt burst into laughter. "He's not my friend! I assumed he was with you. I thought he was a distant relative or something."

Mom couldn't contain her amusement. "Well, it seems we both made the same mistake. We'll have to figure out who he is."

The four of them, accompanied by Mateo's uncle, approached their Australian guest, who had just finished his slice of apple pie and was sipping on a cold drink.

"Excuse me," Mom began, a smile playing on her lips. "We've been enjoying your company, but we have to ask: who exactly are you?"

He chuckled and stood up, extending his hand to shake Mateo's dad. "I apologize for the confusion. My name is Paul, and I'm just a traveler passing through. I got a little lost on my way, but your hospitality made me feel like part of the family.

35. A COMICAL ENCOUNTER WITH AN UNCONVENTIONAL GENIE

TWO YOUNG NEWLYWEDS, Ethan and Lily, decided to spend a sunny afternoon playing golf. As they made their way through the course, enjoying the fresh air and friendly competition, they reached a particular hole that proved to be quite challenging.

It was Lily's turn to take an approach shot to the hole. With determination in her eyes, she swung the club, but to her dismay, the ball completely missed its mark. With an unexpected force, the ball soared through the air and crashed into the nearby mansion, shattering a beautiful glass window.

Concerned and realizing the potential damage they had caused, Ethan and Lily exchanged worried glances. They knew they had to take responsibility for their actions and offered to pay for the damage. Nervously, they approached the magnificent mansion, unsure of what awaited them inside.

To their surprise, the front door was slightly ajar, inviting them to step inside. With cautious steps, they entered the splendid hall, marveling at the grandeur of the place. As they took in the surroundings, their eyes landed on an ancient, broken bottle near the window.

Before they could fully comprehend their situation, a distinguished middle-aged gentleman appeared before them. He introduced himself as Ali, expressing his gratitude for freeing him from the bottle in which he had been trapped for 3,000 years. With a twinkle in his eye, he announced that he possessed the power to grant three wishes: two for the couple and one for himself.

Without hesitation, Ethan spoke up first, his voice filled with excitement. "I wish for a monthly salary of $150,000 for the rest of my life!" The words left his lips with conviction, envisioning a future of financial security.

Lily, caught up in the moment, eagerly voiced her wish. "I want a house of my own in every state in the world!" Her mind danced with the possibilities of a life filled with adventure and luxurious homes in every corner of the globe.

Ali, the genie, nodded approvingly, acknowledging their desires. "So be it," he declared, granting their wishes with a wave of his hand.

But then, a mischievous smile formed on Ali's face as he revealed his own wish. "My desire, on the other hand, is to make love to the beautiful lady...you know how it is...after 3,000 years of abstinence."

Ethan and Lily exchanged puzzled glances, contemplating the genie's proposition. After a brief moment of consideration, they realized that the opportunity to fulfill their own wishes far outweighed a momentary inconvenience. They agreed that sacrificing a little for all they would gain was a fair trade.

Lily, filled with curiosity and a sense of adventure, vanished with Ali, ready to experience an encounter that defied the boundaries of time. Two hours passed in a whirlwind of passion and pleasure as if suspended in a timeless embrace.

As the encounter came to an end, Ali, lying comfortably between the sheets, reached for a cigarette and casually turned to Lily. "How old is your husband?" he asked a hint of amusement in his voice.

Lily, slightly taken aback, replied, "He's thirty-nine. Why do you ask?"

Ali grinned mischievously. "And you? How old are you?"

Lily blushed slightly before answering, "I'm thirty-seven. But why do you want to know?"

A twinkle of wisdom gleamed in Ali's eyes as he uttered his parting words. "Doesn't it seem to you that at your age, you should stop believing in bottle genies?"

36. OLIVER THE GOAT: A TALE OF HORNED HIJINKS

A GOAT NAMED OLIVER lived in a quaint countryside cottage nestled amidst sprawling fields and towering oak trees in the country of Larkspire. Oliver was no ordinary goat. With a twinkle in his eyes and a knack for adventure, he was the source of endless laughter and amusement for the entire neighborhood.

The cottage was surrounded by lush vegetation, including an abundance of walnut and peach trees. Oliver had claimed these trees as his personal feasting grounds. Whenever the neighbors spotted tempting piles of fallen walnuts or ripe peaches, they had to act swiftly if they wanted to enjoy the fruits before Oliver devoured them.

Oliver's insatiable appetite often got him into hilarious situations. One time, he managed to get his horns stuck in a watering can while trying to get to the last drops of water. His muffled bleats echoed through the garden until a kind neighbor came to his rescue, carefully maneuvering the can to free him from his watery predicament. From then on, Oliver became known as the neighborhood's "adventurous horned comedian."

Despite his mischievous nature, Oliver had a soft spot for relaxation. He would find the sunniest spot in the garden, bask in its warmth, and let out contented bleats. His favorite pastime was when the children took turns applying sunscreen to his fur, ensuring he stayed protected from the sun's rays. Oliver reveled in the attention, feeling like the most pampered goat in the world.

But the true highlight of Oliver's day was the plum tree that stood majestically near the cottage. Its branches were heavy with plump, juicy plums that were the envy of the entire neighborhood. Whenever the neighbors spotted a particularly ripe plum, they would call out, "Hey, Oliver, you cheeky goat!" In a flurry of hooves, Oliver would come bounding towards them, his tail wagging in excitement for the plum feast that awaited him.

Life around the cottage was always filled with laughter and amusement, thanks to the antics of Oliver, the goat.

However, trouble arose when a new family moved into the neighboring farmhouse. Their attempts at friendly introductions were met with skeptical glances and distant greetings. The tension between the families began to grow.

One day, curiosity got the better of Oliver, and he decided to pay the new neighbors a visit. Unbeknownst to him, the new neighbors had a goat of their own named Alexander.

As Oliver strutted into the neighbor's yard, he was met with astonished faces and startled gasps.

"You have got to be kidding me!" exclaimed the neighbor, wide-eyed. "Another cheeky goat?"

Laughter erupted from both sides as the families shared stories of their goat shenanigans.

The initial tension melted away, replaced by shared amusement and newfound camaraderie. From that day forward, Oliver and Alexander became the infamous duo of the neighborhood, always finding new ways to bring laughter and joy to their respective families.

37. THE NOT-SO-QUIET GAME NIGHT

AS THE SUN SET on the quiet senior living community of Harmony Gardens, a buzz of excitement filled the air. The residents had decided to spice up their usual routine and host a game night in the common room. Little did they know that this seemingly innocent gathering would turn into a laugh-out-loud adventure.

Mabel, the self-proclaimed queen of charades, took charge of organizing the event. She had prepared an assortment of classic games, from Pictionary to Trivia, promising an evening of friendly competition and good-natured fun.

As the residents gathered around the tables, the room filled with laughter and anticipation. George, a retired comedian, couldn't resist cracking jokes as he shuffled the deck of cards. Ethel, the sharp-witted retiree, was ready to outsmart everyone in the trivia round.

The evening kicked off with a game of charades, and the competitive spirit ignited like wildfire. Mabel took the stage, dramatically acting out the word "elephant." Her exaggerated trunk movements and clumsy stomps had the room in fits of laughter, but no one guessed the right answer. Instead, they shouted out hilarious guesses like "angry dinosaur" and "tap-dancing tree."

Next up was Pictionary, and Esme, known for her artistic talent, took center stage. Armed with a marker and a whiteboard, she began drawing furiously. The room erupted in laughter as her seemingly abstract squiggles turned into a chicken, or at least something resembling one. The residents shouted out guesses: "Dancing potato!" someone cried. "Singing ice cream cone!" exclaimed another. Esme couldn't help but giggle at their creative interpretations.

Then came the trivia round, and Ethel, with her encyclopedic knowledge, was in her element. She confidently answered question after question, leaving her opponents scratching their heads in awe. But even she couldn't escape the occasional curveball. When asked who invented the lightbulb, she confidently replied, "Thomas Edison!" only to be corrected by the trivia card, which claimed it was actually "Sir Isaac Newton."

The room erupted in laughter at the absurdity of the mistake, and Marie took it in stride, admitting that even the smartest minds have their off days.

As the night wore on, the games became more and more comedians. Esme attempted to balance a spoon on her nose while reciting the alphabet backward, sending everyone into fits of giggles. George put on an impromptu comedy routine, cracking jokes that had the room in stitches. The residents reveled in the joy of the moment, forgetting about their age and ailments, simply enjoying each other's company and the infectious laughter that filled the room.

By the end of the night, the residents were exhausted from all the laughter and frivolity. They hugged and thanked each other for an unforgettable evening. Mabel, with a sparkle in her eye, declared it the most raucous game night Harmony Gardens had ever seen.

As they made their way back to their apartments, the residents couldn't help but reflect on the sheer joy they had experienced.

And so, the legend of "The Not-So-Quiet Game Night" at Harmony Gardens was born, a tale that would be retold with fondness and chuckles for years to come.

38. THE MISADVENTURES OF PROFESSOR QUIRKY

A FAMOUS INVENTOR NAMED PROFESSOR QUIRKY lived in the 1970s in the picturesque town of Evergreenia. With his wild mop of hair, thick-rimmed glasses, and perpetually rumpled clothes, he was known for his eccentricity and absent-mindedness. The professor spent his days tinkering away in his cluttered laboratory, concocting all sorts of fantastical contraptions.

One sunny morning, Professor Quirky stumbled upon an old book that claimed to hold the secret to invisibility. Intrigued by the idea, he set to work, mixing potions and adjusting gears in his lab. After hours of experimentation, he proudly unveiled his latest creation—an invisibility device. Eager to test his invention, the professor strapped it onto his wrist, not realizing that it was set to "On."

As soon as the professor activated the device, he vanished into thin air. He blinked in astonishment, unable to see his own hands in front of him. Panic quickly turned into amusement as he realized the hilarity of his predicament. Professor Quirky decided to embrace his newfound invisibility and embark on a series of misadventures around town.

His first stop was the local café, where he delighted in snatching muffins and sipping cups of tea right under the unsuspecting customers' noses. As crumbs levitated through the air, the café patrons exchanged puzzled glances, never suspecting that the invisible culprit was none other than Professor Quirky.

Next, he ventured into the bustling marketplace, where he played pranks on the fruit vendors. Invisible hands would rearrange the display, stacking oranges on top of watermelons and grapes on top of pineapples. Confused customers couldn't help but burst into laughter at the sight of the topsy-turvy fruit stand, unaware of the invisible jester responsible for the chaos.

As Professor Quirky continued his invisible escapades, word quickly spread through Evergreenia of the invisible prankster. Curiosity and excitement filled the air as residents eagerly anticipated encounters with the invisible enigma.

One sunny afternoon, the local library hosted a storytelling event, and Professor Quirky couldn't resist the opportunity to participate. He silently glided through the aisles, snatching books from shelves and turning pages, much to the bewilderment of the librarian. With invisible fingers, he even added his own humorous sound effects to the tales being read aloud, causing the children to erupt in fits of giggles.

Not content with confining his mischief to public places, Professor Quirky decided to pay a visit to the mayor's office. Sneaking past the guards, he rearranged the furniture, swapping the mayor's desk with a piano and replacing the paintings on the wall with humorous caricatures.

When the mayor entered his office the next morning, he couldn't believe his eyes and wondered if he had somehow entered a parallel universe.

Throughout his invisible adventures, Professor Quirky never caused harm or intended malice.

His pranks were meant to bring joy, laughter, and a touch of whimsy to the town. And while the people of Evergreenia initially scratched their heads in confusion, they eventually embraced the invisible shenanigans with open arms.

The town became a playground of imagination and laughter, with residents sharing their own invisible encounters and swapping stories about Professor Quirky's antics. He became a beloved legend—a symbol of joy and the unexpected.

In the end, after countless escapades and uproarious laughter, Professor Quirky decided it was time to reveal himself.

He gathered the townsfolk in the park, standing atop a platform, invisible no more. As gasps of surprise filled the air, he addressed the crowd with a twinkle in his eyes.

"My dear friends of Evergreenia," Professor Quirky announced, his voice filled with warmth, "I am the invisible jester who has brought laughter to your lives. I hope my misadventures have brought you joy and reminded you of the magic that exists in everyday moments."

The crowd erupted in applause, their laughter echoing through the park. The townsfolk couldn't help but appreciate the professor's playful spirit and the laughter he had gifted them.

"I may no longer be invisible," Professor Quirky continued, "but let us never forget the power of imagination, the joy of surprises, and the beauty of laughter. Life should be filled with whimsy and a touch of the unexpected."

The townsfolk nodded in agreement, their smiles reaching from ear to ear. They knew that even though Professor Quirky was now visible, his spirit of mirth and laughter would forever remain a cherished part of their community.

From that day forward, Evergreenia embraced a newfound sense of lightheartedness. Invisible pranks became a regular occurrence, and laughter filled the air as residents indulged in their own playful antics. The town flourished with a sense of joy and camaraderie that brought them closer together.

As for Professor Quirky, he continued his inventive pursuits, using his skills to create whimsical gadgets and inventions that brought smiles to the faces of young and old alike. And although his invisibility device was retired, its memory lived on as a reminder of the joy and laughter that had once enveloped the town.

39. THE EXTRAVAGANT WEATHER MACHINE

IN THE SMALL TOWN OF SUNNYVILLE, retired weather forecaster Mr. Franklin found himself bored with the predictable weather patterns of his peaceful retirement. Little did he know that an adventure awaited him in the dusty corners of his attic.

One sunny afternoon, while rummaging through old boxes, Mr. Franklin stumbled upon a forgotten relic—an old weather machine. Its brass gears glistened in the sunlight.

"Ah, this brings back memories," he chuckled to himself. "Why not have a little fun with the weather? It's time to shake things up in Sunnyville!"

Mr. Franklin dusted off the weather machine and wheeled it down to the town square. Curious townsfolk gathered around as he pulled a lever, setting the machine into motion.

The next morning, the town woke up to a sight they had never seen before. Instead of clear blue skies, a massive rainbow stretched across the horizon. People marveled and rushed outside, snapping photos and sharing laughter as they discovered rainbows in the most unexpected places—the grocery store, the library, and even the mayor's office.

Word of the whimsical weather spread like wildfire, and the town was abuzz with excitement. Sunnyville had become the talk of neighboring towns, drawing tourists who wanted to experience the magical phenomenon for themselves.

But Mr. Franklin wasn't done yet. The next day, as the townsfolk gathered in the park, they were greeted with a sight that made them gasp in surprise—snowflakes gently falling from the sky. It was a summer snowfall!

Children squealed with delight, building snowmen and engaging in impromptu snowball fights. Sunbathers lounged in their swimsuits but with scarves and mittens, embracing the unexpected twist in weather with laughter and good spirits.

The whimsical weather continued throughout the week. One day, a sudden gust of wind blew away everyone's hats, leading to a hilarious chase around town as people tried to catch their wayward headwear. Another day, a downpour of bubblegum-scented rain brought smiles to everyone's faces as they danced and twirled under the sticky-sweet shower.

Throughout the week, Mr. Franklin reveled in the joy he had brought to the town. He became a beloved figure known as the Weather Wizard, and the townsfolk eagerly awaited his daily surprises. Life in Sunnyville had become an extraordinary adventure, thanks to the magic of the weather machine.

But as the week drew to a close, Mr. Franklin realized it was time to bid farewell to his playful creation. On the final day, he wheeled the weather machine back to his attic, leaving the town with a heartfelt farewell.

The people of Sunnyville gathered in the town square, their faces filled with gratitude and nostalgia. They thanked Mr. Franklin for the joy and laughter he had brought into their lives, and he thanked them for embracing the whimsy of the ever-changing weather.

From that day forward, Sunnyville remained a place where laughter and unexpected adventures were cherished. The memories of the extravagant weather machine lingered, reminding the townsfolk to embrace the unexpected and find joy in life's surprises.

And as for Mr. Franklin, he may have retired from his forecasting days, but the sparkle never left his eyes.

He continued to bring laughter to the town, not through weather tricks but through his witty tales and warm presence. For in Sunnyville, the legacy of the whimsical weather machine lived on, reminding the townsfolk that even the most ordinary days could be filled with extraordinary magic.

40. THE WACKY WEDDING PLANNERS

ALICE AND LILY, two best friends, lived in the bustling town of Springville. They were known for their wacky ideas and unique sense of humor. After attending several weddings together, they decided to put their talents to good use and start a wedding planning business aptly named "The Wacky Wedding Planners."

With their infectious enthusiasm and quirky personalities, Alice and Lily quickly gained a reputation for planning weddings like no other. They believed that each couple deserved a wedding that reflected their true personalities and showcased their love in the most unconventional and joyous way possible.

Their first clients were Sarah and Mark, a couple madly in love but tired of the traditional wedding scene. Alice and Lily wasted no time brainstorming ideas that would make their wedding stand out from the rest. They decided to transform the venue into an enchanted forest, complete with a talking tree as the wedding officiant. The couple loved the idea and eagerly embraced the whimsical theme.

As the planning began, hilarious mishaps ensued. Alice and Lily, known for their scatterbrained tendencies, struggled with keeping track of important details. They once ordered a cake with the wrong flavor, resulting in a surprise chocolate cake for a couple who despised chocolate. The horrified look on their faces when they took their first bite, provided endless laughter for the guests.

In another memorable incident, Lily mistook the dress measurements and ordered a gown two sizes too big for the bride. When the dress arrived, it looked more like a parachute than a wedding dress. Panicking, Alice and Lily improvised by turning the dress into a grand entrance prop, creating a comic moment as the bride dramatically emerged from the oversized dress to reveal her true gown underneath.

Despite these comical mishaps, the weddings organized by Alice and Lily were always filled with joy, laughter, and memorable moments. They introduced unique traditions, such as a dance-off between the bride and groom instead of a first dance or a bouquet made entirely of inflatable toys that exploded with confetti upon catching it.

The word spread quickly about the unforgettable weddings orchestrated by The Wacky Wedding Planners. Soon, couples from far and wide sought their services, eager to inject some humor and quirkiness into their special day. Alice and Lily's calendar filled up rapidly, and they found themselves working non-stop to bring their clients' wildest dreams to life.

One particularly memorable wedding was for Michael and Maeve, a couple who shared a passion for superheroes. Alice and Lily transformed the reception into a full-blown superhero extravaganza. Guests arrived dressed as their favorite heroes, and even Alice and Lily donned capes and masks. The evening turned into a series of humorous superhero challenges and dance-offs, with the bride and groom leading the way.

It was a night filled with laughter, epic dance moves, and unforgettable memories.

As the years went by, Alice and Lily became legends in the wedding planning world. Their unique approach and unwavering commitment to making each wedding a one-of-a-kind experience earned them a loyal following. They laughed off their mistakes and embraced the unexpected, knowing that it was the moments of imperfection that made their weddings truly special.

And so, the adventures of The Wacky Wedding Planners continued, creating laughter and love wherever they went. Alice and Lily proved that weddings need not be serious affairs but rather opportunities for couples to celebrate their unique love story with a touch of humor and an abundance of joy. They were a reminder that sometimes, the most memorable moments in life come from embracing the wackiness and allowing laughter to be the soundtrack of love.

41. THE ABSURD ANTIQUE AUCTION

IT WAS A SATURDAY AFTERNOON IN MAY 1969, and the small town of Waverly was abuzz with excitement. The renowned antique dealer, Mr. Percival Potts, was hosting his highly anticipated auction. People from all over had gathered in the dusty old warehouse, eager to get their hands on some peculiar treasures.

Mr. Potts, a man with wild white hair and a twinkle in his eye, stood on a makeshift stage, holding a gavel in one hand and a stuffed parrot in the other. He cleared his throat and addressed the crowd with a mischievous grin.

"Ladies and gentlemen, welcome to the most absurd antique auction you'll ever witness! Today, I present to you a collection of extraordinary items that will tickle your funny bone and boggle your mind. So, let's get this show on the road, shall we?"

The room erupted with laughter and applause as the bidding began. The first item up for grabs was a teapot that, according to Mr. Potts, had a voice of its own. As the bidding escalated, Mr. Potts took a sip of tea from the teapot, and to everyone's astonishment, it burst into song.

"I'm a little teapot, short and stout! Here's my handle, here's my spout!" it belted out in a high-pitched voice. The crowd burst into laughter and applause, and the bidding war for the singing teapot reached ridiculous heights.

In the midst of the chaos, a woman named Mrs. Higgins, known for her love of all things quirky, raised her paddle and shouted, "I must have that teapot! It will be the star of my afternoon tea parties!"

The room erupted into laughter once again, and Mr. Potts, with a twinkle in his eye, banged his gavel. "Sold to the tea party enthusiast in the front row!"

As the auction progressed, more peculiar items were presented. There was a talking stuffed animal that shared witty one-liners, a pair of magical spectacles that made the world look upside down, and even a "time-traveling" alarm clock that always seemed to be five minutes behind.

With each item, the bidding became more spirited, and the jokes flew around the room. Mr. Potts kept the atmosphere light and lively, cracking witty remarks between bids.

"Now, ladies and gentlemen, feast your eyes on this magnificent painting of a cow wearing a top hat! It's sure to add a touch of class to any living room. But be careful, folks; it may inspire your pet cat to take up dancing!"

The crowd erupted into laughter, and the bidding for the quirky painting skyrocketed. People couldn't resist the allure of owning such an absurd piece of art.

As the auction drew to a close, the excitement in the room was palpable. The final item up for bid was a mysterious locked chest. Mr. Potts teased the crowd, hinting at the treasure within and the potential for adventure.

"Who knows what secrets lie within this enigmatic chest? It could contain the lost treasures of a pirate or the secret to eternal youth! Or maybe it's just a collection of mismatched socks. You never know!"

The crowd laughed, eager to discover the truth. The bidding for the chest grew intense, with participants imagining the endless possibilities. In the end, a young couple, Mr. and Mrs. Thompson, emerged victorious and couldn't contain their curiosity as they unlocked the chest.

To their surprise, the chest was filled with an assortment of whimsical hats, each more outlandish than the last. The room erupted with laughter, and Mr. Potts couldn't help but join in the merriment.

As the auction came to a close, Mr. Potts addressed the crowd with a wide grin on his face. "Ladies and gentlemen, I hope you've had as much fun as I have today. Remember, life is too short to take everything seriously. Embrace the absurd, the quirky, and the downright hilarious. May these treasures bring joy and laughter into your lives!"

The crowd cheered and applauded, feeling grateful for the delightful experience they had just shared. As they dispersed, carrying their newfound treasures, the air was filled with laughter and chatter about the absurd items they had acquired.

And so, the legacy of the absurd antique auction continued, captivating the hearts and imaginations of those who sought a little whimsy in their lives. Mr. Potts, with his infectious laughter and endless collection of peculiar objects, brought joy to the world one auction at a time.

As the doors of the warehouse closed, the echoes of laughter and the memories of the day lingered, reminding everyone that sometimes the most extraordinary moments are found in the most absurd of places.

And so, with a twinkle in his eye, Mr. Potts packed up his gavel and parrot, ready to embark on his next adventure, leaving behind a trail of laughter and fond memories that would be cherished for years to come.

As the crowd dispersed, a quote from the great humorist Mark Twain seemed fitting for the occasion: "Against the assault of laughter, nothing can stand." And indeed, within the walls of that auction house, laughter had triumphed, leaving hearts lighter and spirits lifted.

42. THE WHISTLEBLOWER'S WHIMSY

IN 1970, IN THE QUIET SUBURBAN NEIGHBORHOOD OF WILLOWVILLE, there lived a retired office worker named Mr. Joel Witherspoon. After years of pushing papers and attending monotonous meetings, Mr. Witherspoon found himself longing for some excitement and laughter in his life. Little did he know, his extravagant journey was about to begin.

One sunny morning, as Mr. Witherspoon was sipping his coffee and reading the newspaper, his eyes caught an advertisement that piqued his curiosity. It was a tiny flyer tucked between the pages, promoting a kazoo orchestra workshop at the local community center. Intrigued by the idea of playing a kazoo, Mr. Witherspoon decided to give it a shot.

As he entered the workshop, he was greeted by a group of enthusiastic individuals of all ages, each armed with a kazoo. The instructor, a lively musician named Professor Jazzberry, introduced himself with a flourish and began teaching the basics of kazoo playing.

Mr. Witherspoon blew into his kazoo tentatively, producing a feeble buzzing sound. The class erupted into laughter, but the jovial professor reassured him, "Ah, Mr. Witherspoon, the kazoo is an instrument of whimsy and merriment. Let your spirit soar, and your kazoo sing!"

Embracing Professor Jazzberry's words, Mr. Witherspoon let loose, playing the kazoo with gusto. He discovered a hidden talent within himself and soon became the star of the class. His kazoo melodies were spirited and infectious, leaving everyone in stitches.

Armed with his newfound musical prowess, Mr. Witherspoon decided to take his kazoo on the road. He started playing it during his daily errands, turning mundane activities into comical symphonies. Picture this: Mr. Witherspoon standing in line at the grocery store, humming along to the beeping of the cash register with his trusty kazoo. The customers around him couldn't help but burst into laughter, and soon, the whole store was swaying to the rhythm of Mr. Witherspoon's impromptu grocery store concerto.

Word of Mr. Witherspoon's kazoo escapades spread like wildfire through the town. People eagerly awaited his next performance, whether it was at the post office, the park, or even the dentist's waiting room. The town had never seen such a whimsical and entertaining character, and Mr. Witherspoon quickly became a beloved local celebrity.

His kazoo playing had a magical effect on everyone he encountered. Even the grumpiest of souls couldn't resist cracking a smile in the presence of Mr. Witherspoon and his trusty kazoo. The town's motto soon changed from "Live, laugh, love" to "Live, laugh, and kazoo!"

One day, as Mr. Witherspoon was strolling through the park, playing a lively tune on his kazoo, he noticed a gloomy-faced man sitting on a bench. Determined to bring a smile to the man's face, Mr. Witherspoon unleashed a medley of silly songs, from "The Chicken Dance" to "The Hokey Pokey." Slowly but surely, the man's frown transformed into a grin, and laughter filled the air.

From that day forward, Mr. Witherspoon made it his mission to spread laughter and joy wherever he went. He formed a kazoo ensemble with fellow kazoo enthusiasts, and together they brought wacky melodies to hospitals, retirement homes, and local events. They became known as "The Whistleblowers," a troupe of kazoo-playing comedians who knew that laughter was the best medicine.

As the years went by, Mr. Witherspoon's kazoo legacy continued to grow. The Whistleblowers gained a devoted following, and their performances became highly anticipated events in the community. They even caught the attention of a famous comedian, who invited them to join him on a national comedy tour.

The group's unique blend of humor and kazoo melodies brought laughter to audiences across the country. Their performances were filled with witty banter, hilarious sketches, and of course, kazoo solos that had the crowd roaring with laughter.

But amidst all the fame and laughter, Mr. Witherspoon remained the humble and down-to-earth kazoo virtuoso. He cherished the joy he brought to people's lives and considered it his greatest accomplishment.

One day, as Mr. Witherspoon sat on a park bench, reminiscing about his kazoo-filled journey, a young child approached him, wide-eyed with admiration. The child held a small kazoo in their hand and asked, "Mr. Witherspoon, can you teach me how to play the kazoo?"

With a twinkle in his eye, Mr. Witherspoon gladly took the child under his wing, passing on the art of kazoo playing and spreading the whimsy to a new generation. The child's infectious laughter and enthusiasm filled the air as they played their first kazoo duet together.

And so, the legacy of Mr. Witherspoon and The Whistleblowers lived on, inspiring others to embrace the power of laughter, music, and the kazoo. Their story reminded the world that even in the simplest of instruments, there is magic to be found and laughter to be shared.

As Mr. Witherspoon once said, "Life is a symphony, and the kazoo is our instrument of joy.

Let us play, laugh, and kazoo our way through life, creating harmonies of laughter wherever we go."

And so, the tunes of the kazoo filled the hearts of all who encountered Mr. Witherspoon and The Whistleblowers, reminding them that in a world that can sometimes be too serious, laughter and a little bit of silliness can truly make life a grand symphony.

43. THE FANTASTICAL GARDENING CLUB

THE FANTASTICAL GARDENING CLUB was the talk of the town of Blossomcity. A group of retirees with a love for gardening had come together to form a club like no other. They met every week at the local community center, armed with their trowels, watering cans, and a touch of magic.

Their gardens were a sight to behold, bursting with vibrant colors and unusual foliage.

But it wasn't just their green thumbs that made them special. Each member had a secret stash of magical seeds, passed down through generations or discovered on exotic adventures. These enchanted seeds held the promise of extraordinary plants with unique abilities.

In the heart of the club was Hortense, a sprightly woman. She was the club's unofficial leader, always ready with a joke or a witty remark. Her infectious laughter echoed through the garden as she shared her gardening wisdom, often in the form of a clever quip.

One sunny afternoon, as the club gathered around a potluck picnic, Hortense presented a small pouch filled with shimmering seeds. "My dear friends," she exclaimed, "I've stumbled upon a batch of seeds rumored to bring forth the most fantastical plants. Are you ready for some garden magic?"

Excitement filled the air as each member eagerly selected a seed. They planted them in a circle, creating a magical garden bed. The next morning, to their delight and amusement, their garden had transformed into a whimsical wonderland.

Albert's ordinary rose bush had sprouted blooms that sang sweet melodies, filling the garden with harmonious tunes. "Well," he chuckled, "I guess my roses were tired of being thorny and decided to become a choir instead!"

Amelie's tomato plant had taken an extraordinary turn, producing tomatoes that exploded into colorful confetti when plucked. "Now I have the perfect party accessory!" she exclaimed, tossing handfuls of tomato confetti in the air.

And then there was Desmond, whose bonsai tree had developed a mischievous streak. Whenever he approached with his pruning shears, the bonsai would levitate just out of reach, teasing him with its playful antics. "I think my tree is auditioning for a magic show!" Desmond quipped, trying to catch the elusive plant.

As the weeks went by, the Fantastical Gardening Club continued to cultivate their magical garden, each plant more extraordinary than the last. There were dancing daffodils, squirting sunflowers, and even a talking tree stump that loved to share tall tales.

Their garden became a local attraction, drawing visitors from far and wide who marveled at the fantastical plants and laughed at the club members' humorous anecdotes. Hortense, with her quick wit, became the club's resident comedian, regaling visitors with jokes and funny stories as they strolled through the garden.

One day, a famous comedian happened upon the club's garden during a comedy tour. Impressed by the wacky atmosphere and the laughter that echoed through the air, the comedian joined the club for an impromptu stand-up performance.

As the comedian cracked jokes and the plants joined in with their own humorous antics, the laughter grew louder and more infectious. The garden became a place of joy and mirth, where people gathered to forget their worries and immerse themselves in a world of magic and laughter.

And so, the Fantastical Gardening Club's legacy spread far and wide. Their garden became a haven of whimsy, where the ordinary was transformed into the extraordinary, and laughter bloomed alongside the enchanting plants. In their magical garden, they found not just beautiful flowers and peculiar plants but also the joy of friendship, laughter, and the delight of embracing life's delightful surprises.

As Hortense liked to say, "In the garden of laughter and magic, we find the truest blossoms of happiness. So, let us tend to our extravagant plants, nurture our friendships, and always remember to share a good joke or two. After all, a garden without laughter is like a flower without fragrance – it simply doesn't bloom with its full potential.

And so, dear reader, may you find inspiration in their tale and embrace the whimsy in your own life.

Whether you have a green thumb or not, remember to nurture the seeds of laughter and let the magic of humor flourish. For in the garden of laughter, life's troubles wither away, and joy blossoms in abundance.

44. THE ECCENTRIC BOOK CLUB

THE ECCENTRIC BOOK CLUB was a gathering like no other in the quiet town of Bookshire. It was a place where book lovers with a taste for the bizarre and unconventional came together to explore the depths of literature that defied convention. Each month, they would choose the most peculiar and obscure books to read, books that would challenge their minds and tickle their funny bones.

At their first meeting, the club members introduced themselves with their favorite eccentric book recommendations. There was Vivienne, a retired librarian who had a soft spot for novels about time-traveling hamsters. Then there was Dan, a retired accountant with a penchant for novels featuring sentient vegetables. And let's not forget Lila, a free-spirited artist who loved books about talking furniture. Together, they formed a delightful trio.

Their discussions were always animated and filled with laughter. They would gather at the local café, armed with their peculiar books and a healthy dose of wit. The conversations often veered off into whimsical tangents as they pondered the deeper meanings behind tales of dancing turnips or philosophical rocking chairs.

One month, they selected a book called "The Adventures of a Confused Squirrel" as their reading choice. The story revolved around a squirrel who couldn't remember where he hid his acorns. As they delved into the book, their interpretations became more and more absurd. They debated whether the squirrel's acorns were actually a metaphor for lost dreams or if the squirrel was just suffering from a severe case of forgetfulness.

Inspired by the book, they decided to organize a squirrel-themed treasure hunt in the local park. Armed with acorn-shaped clues and squirrel costumes, they scurried around the park, much to the amusement of the onlookers. Passersby couldn't help but laugh as they witnessed a group of grown adults searching for hidden acorns, their squirrel tails bouncing with each step.

Another time, they selected a book called "The Mysterious Misadventures of a Pickle Jar," which led to some pickle-inspired madness. They organized a pickle taste-testing event, sampling pickles from all over the world. The room was filled with giggles as they debated the merits of dill versus sweet pickles and even attempted to create their own unusual pickle combinations like pickles dipped in chocolate or pickles infused with bubblegum flavor.

Their escapades extended beyond the confines of the book club meetings. On Halloween, they dressed up as characters from their favorite eccentric books and paraded through the town, much to the bewilderment and amusement of the townsfolk. A dancing hamster, a talking vegetable, and a philosophical rocking chair strutted down Main Street, leaving a trail of laughter in their wake.

But amidst all the laughter and absurdity, the Eccentric Book Club had a deeper purpose. It brought together a group of like-minded individuals who found solace and joy in the unconventional. Through their shared love for eccentric literature, they forged genuine connections and celebrated the power of imagination.

As the club grew, more quirky bookworms joined their ranks, each adding their own flavor to the mix. And in the midst of their peculiar literary adventures, they discovered that the true magic of the Eccentric Book Club lay not only in the books they read but in the laughter, camaraderie, and unapologetic embrace of their eccentricities.

And so, dear reader, if you ever find yourself yearning for a literary journey into the realm of the peculiar, seek out the Eccentric Book Club.

You may discover a love for time-traveling hamsters or find yourself pondering the existential quandaries of talking furniture. But above all, you'll find a community of laughter, acceptance, and the celebration of all things wonderfully odd.

45. THE GREAT ESCAPE ROOM CAPER

IN THE HALLS OF HARMONY HOUSE NURSING HOME, a group of spirited residents known as the "Golden Gamers" hatched a brilliant plan. Tired of the same routine and eager for a taste of adventure, they set their sights on the ultimate challenge—a daring escape from the confines of their home. With their wit and wisdom, they devised an elaborate scheme to outsmart the staff and unlock the secrets hidden beyond the locked doors.

The leader of this motley crew was Samuel, a retired magician with a knack for trickery and an infectious sense of humor. He gathered his loyal companions, including the cunning Marion, the quick-witted Wesley, the naughty Ethel, and the ever-optimistic Beatrice. Together, they formed an unstoppable team ready to embark on their greatest escapade yet.

Their adventure began one quiet evening as the residents gathered in the common room for their regular game night. Samuel stood up, his eyes twinkling with excitement. "My dear friends, I have an extraordinary proposition for all of you.

How about we turn this ordinary game night into an extraordinary quest for freedom?"

The room erupted with laughter and cheers. Beatrice chimed in, "Oh, Samuel, you always know how to spice things up! Count me in!"

And so, the Great Escape Room Caper was set into motion. With meticulous planning, they started unraveling the secrets of Harmony House. Marion used her silver tongue to charm the staff and gather vital information. Wesley crafted ingenious tools from everyday objects, including a walker that doubled as a lockpick. Ethel, the master of disguise, sewed costumes to camouflage their true identities. And Beatrice, ever the optimist, provided a steady dose of encouragement and an endless supply of homemade cookies.

Their first obstacle was the formidable Head Nurse Evelyn, known for her eagle-eyed surveillance. But with Marion's cunning and Samuel's impeccable sleight of hand, they managed to swipe the master key right from under her nose. As they celebrated their victory, Wesley couldn't help but crack a joke. "Why did the nurse bring a red pen to work? In case she had to draw blood!"

Next came the challenge of navigating the labyrinthine corridors. Armed with the master key, they opened doors they had never seen before, uncovering hidden passages and secret rooms. Each step brought them closer to freedom, and they reveled in their audacity. Ethel, in her hilarious spirit, decided to leave a trail of whoopee cushions behind, much to the surprise and amusement of their pursuers.

As they neared their final goal, the group found themselves in the most unexpected of places—the kitchen. The aroma of freshly baked bread filled the air, and Samuel couldn't resist cracking a joke. "Why did the tomato turn red? Because it saw the salad dressing!"

But their amusement was short-lived as they faced the challenge of a locked pantry door. Undeterred, Wesley pulled out his trusty lockpick walker, and within moments, the door swung open, revealing shelves stocked with delectable treats. The residents feasted on cookies, chocolates, and even the occasional jar of pickles, savoring their victory with laughter and delight.

Their journey, filled with laughter and camaraderie, came to an end as they reached the final door—the exit to the outside world. With hearts pounding and smiles on their faces, they stepped into the fresh air, free from the confines of Harmony House.

As they embraced their newfound freedom, Samuel couldn't help but share a parting joke. "Why don't skeletons fight each other? They don't have the guts!"

And so, the Golden Gamers stepped out into the world beyond Harmony House, their hearts full of laughter and memories. They had proven that age was just a number and that the spirit of adventure never fades.

Word of their audacious escapade quickly spread throughout the nursing home, sparking a sense of inspiration and vitality among the residents. The Great Escape Room Caper became a legendary tale, passed down from one generation of residents to the next, reminding them that life is meant to be lived to the fullest, even within the confines of their home.

The staff, initially bewildered by the residents' cunning plan, couldn't help but admire their tenacity and zest for life. Head Nurse Evelyn, who had once been their formidable adversary, found herself joining in the laughter and celebrating their triumph.

As Samuel and his friends reflected on their adventure, they knew they had left a lasting legacy. They had not only experienced the thrill of escape but had also reminded everyone that life should be embraced with a twinkle in the eye and a hearty chuckle.

As Samuel would often say, "Life is like a punchline, my friends. It's all about finding the humor and enjoying the ride."

46. THE WHIMSICAL CUPCAKE QUEST

IT WAS 1986, AND IN THE ENCHANTING TOWN OF SUGARVILLE lived a vivacious baker named Scarlett Sprinklesworth. With her colorful apron and grin, Scarlett delighted the townsfolk with her whimsical cupcakes. Each cupcake she crafted was a work of edible art, filled with surprises that brought smiles to everyone's faces.

One sunny morning, Scarlett received an intriguing letter sealed with a sprinkle-shaped wax seal. It was an invitation to the Great Cupcake Carnival, a legendary event where bakers from far and wide showcased their most extraordinary creations. Excitement filled Scarlett's heart as she realized this was her chance to make a name for herself in the world of cupcakes.

Determined to create the most magical cupcake the world had ever seen, Scarlett embarked on a quest to gather the rarest and most extravagant ingredients. With her trusty assistant, Humphrey Frostingbottom, by her side, they set off on a journey filled with laughter, culinary adventures, and plenty of frosting mishaps.

Their first stop was the mystical Candy Cane Forest, where they encountered a sprite named Twinkleberry. With a wink in her eye, Twinkleberry revealed the secret of unicorn tears, an ingredient rumored to add a touch of magic to any cupcake. As they collected the glistening tears, Humphrey couldn't help but quip, "Unicorn tears, huh? I hope they make these cupcakes cry with joy!"

Next, they ventured into the Giggling Marshmallow Swamp, a place where giggles floated in the air like fluffy clouds. Among the marshmallow trees, they discovered a group of quirky creatures known as the Marshmallow Munchkins. As they shared jokes and stories, Scarlett and Humphrey couldn't resist joining in the mirthful banter. "Why don't scientists trust atoms? Because they make up everything!" Humphrey exclaimed, causing the Munchkins to burst into fits of laughter.

Their quest took them to the Sparkling Sugar Mountains, a place where sugar crystals shimmered like diamonds. Deep within the caves, they met Sir Sprinkleberry, a wise and witty confectioner. With a twinkle in his eye, he shared the secret of edible rainbows, an ingredient that would make their cupcakes burst with vibrant colors. Scarlett and Humphrey couldn't resist a playful exchange. "Why did the cupcake go to the doctor? Because it felt crummy!" Scarlett giggled, earning a chuckle from Sir Sprinkleberry.

Armed with their magical ingredients, Scarlett and Humphrey returned to Sugarville. They spent days in the kitchen, experimenting with flavors, colors, and textures, creating a masterpiece that would dazzle the judges at the Great Cupcake Carnival.

The day of the carnival arrived, and Sugarville was buzzing with excitement. As Scarlett presented her creation, aptly named "The Whimsylicious Wonder," the crowd gasped in awe. The cupcake was a swirl of colors, topped with sparkling sprinkles and a touch of edible stardust. It was a sight to behold.

As the judges took their first bite, a magical transformation occurred. Their faces lit up with delight, and laughter filled the air. The cupcakes were not only a feast for the taste buds but also a treat for the soul. The whimsy and joy that Scarlett had poured into each creation radiated from every bite.

In the end, Scarlett and Humphrey's cupcake masterpiece won the hearts of the judges and earned them the coveted title of "Cupcake Connoisseurs Extraordinaire."

They celebrated their sweet victory with a playful exchange. "Why did the cupcake throw a party? Because it wanted to have a batter time!" Humphrey exclaimed, causing Scarlett to burst into laughter.

And so, Scarlett Sprinklesworth and Humphrey Frostingbottom continued their baking adventures, spreading joy and laughter one whimsical cupcake at a time.

Their playful spirit and delectable creations made Sugarville the sweetest town in all the land, forever etching their names in the annals of baking greatness.

As the renowned comedian once said, "Life is short. Eat dessert first!" And Scarlett and Humphrey took those words to heart, creating a world where cupcakes were not just treats but a catalyst for laughter and delight.

47. THE LOVE POTION MIXUP

IN THE CHARMING TOWN OF CLOVERDALE, nestled amidst rolling hills and blooming flowers, a quirky nursing home named Sunny Haven provided a haven for its spirited residents. Among them was the vivacious Gertrude Pumpernickel, known for her wit and a twinkle in her eye that hinted at countless untold stories.

One fateful day, Gertrude stumbled upon a long-forgotten potion recipe hidden in the depths of her treasured bookshelf.

With a grin, she decided to whip up a love potion to sprinkle a little romance into the lives of the residents. Little did she know that she would inadvertently mix it up with a memory-enhancing potion, setting the stage for a delightful mix-up of love and laughter.

As Gertrude stirred the bubbling concoction in her cauldron, her friend Elliot Higginbotham entered the room, a bounce in his step. "What's cookin', Gertrude?

Brewing a little mischief, are we?" he quipped, his playful banter lighting up the room.

Unaware of the mix-up, Gertrude added a generous splash of the potion to the morning coffee, intending to spread a sprinkle of love throughout Sunny Haven. But as the residents took their first sips, a whimsical transformation unfolded.

Mabel, a retired ballet dancer with a fondness for crossword puzzles, suddenly found herself smitten with Carl, the charismatic retired magician who could still pull a rabbit out of his hat. Their witty exchanges took on a flirtatious tone as Mabel quipped, "I'm no Houdini, but you've certainly got me under your spell, Carl!"

Meanwhile, Alice, a spunky grandmother with a passion for knitting, found herself captivated by the dashing Vincent, an octogenarian with a knack for storytelling. As they sat side by side, Alice couldn't resist a playful jab, saying, "Vincent, your stories are like a never-ending ball of yarn. I can't help but get entangled in them!"

Even the normally reserved Walter, an avid bird watcher, discovered a newfound attraction to Agnes, a retired opera singer with a penchant for gardening.

Their encounters were filled with gentle laughter as Walter quipped, "Agnes, your voice is like a sweet melody that brings color to my world. It's almost as enchanting as the birdsong at dawn!"

As the love potion continued to weave its quirky spell, the residents of Sunny Haven found themselves caught up in amusingly awkward situations.

Forgotten memories resurfaced, prompting hilarious surprises and heartfelt reunions.

Laughter echoed through the hallways as stories of youthful romance were shared, with Gertrude and Elliot at the center of it all, their banter keeping spirits high.

In the end, the love potion mix-up brought a renewed sense of joy and connection to the residents of Sunny Haven. Relationships blossomed, friendships deepened, and hearts were filled with laughter and affection.

As the famous comedian once said, "Love is like a comedy routine, full of unexpected punchlines and moments that make your heart skip a beat."

And in the delightful chaos of Sunny Haven, love and laughter intertwined, creating a tapestry of joy that would be remembered for years to come.

For in the realm of love and laughter, there is always room for delightful mix-ups and playful banter. And in the hearts of Gertrude, Elliot, and their newfound loves, the magic of the love potion mix-up remained forever etched as a testament to the power of love, laughter, and the extravagant adventures that unfold when life takes an unexpected turn.

48. A SOLDIER'S UNEXPECTED HUMOR

A PRIVATE STOOD BEFORE A STERN COMMISSION tasked with selecting soldiers for highly dangerous missions. Among the commission members was a psychologist, whose role was to evaluate the mental state of the candidates.

The psychologist fixed his gaze upon the soldier and posed a peculiar question, "Imagine yourself in the midst of a fierce battle, and suddenly a bullet dislodges your ear. How would you feel?"

The soldier, deep in thought, contemplated the scenario for a good thirty seconds. Then, with a touch of humor in his eyes, he replied, "Well, I suppose I wouldn't be able to see out of one eye."

The psychologist was taken aback, his disbelief evident. He pondered for a moment, intrigued by the soldier's response, and decided to continue probing along the same lines. With a faint smirk, he asked the second question, "Alright, let's say two minutes later, another bullet takes off your other ear. What do you hear?"

Without missing a beat, the soldier retorted, "At that point, I wouldn't be able to see at all."

The psychologist couldn't contain his confusion any longer. He blurted out, "What on earth are you talking about? The bullets dislodged your ears, not your eyes! Why would you say that?"

An amused grin spread across the soldier's face as he chuckled, "Ah, you see, it's because my cap fell over my eyes."

The room erupted in laughter; even the stern-faced commission members couldn't help but crack a smile. It was a lighthearted moment amidst the serious atmosphere, where the soldier's quick wit had lightened the mood.

The psychologist, now chuckling along with the others, realized the soldier's clever play on words. He marveled at the soldier's ability to inject humor into a tense situation, revealing a resilience and mental agility that could prove valuable in challenging missions.

As the laughter subsided, the commission members exchanged amused glances, impressed by the soldier's ability to think on his feet. It was a testament to the camaraderie and unique spirit within the military ranks, where wit and humor often served as coping mechanisms in the face of adversity.

The soldier's response showcased not only his mental acuity but also his ability to find humor in even the most trying circumstances.

It was a quality that would undoubtedly serve him well in the special units and dangerous missions that lay ahead.

49. THE NOISY NIGHTTIME CONUNDRUM

LATE ONE EVENING, when the moon hung high, and the world was cloaked in darkness, our weary protagonist, Sarah, succumbed to the relentless yawns and decided it was time to retire to the realm of dreams. She slipped into her comfortable cotton gown, slid under the soft sheets, and prepared for a restful slumber. But little did she know that her feline companion, Milo, had a different plan in mind.

As the night grew deeper, a sudden weight crashed upon Sarah's stomach, jolting her awake. She let out a startled shriek, only to realize that it was Milo, the maestro of midnight pranks. With a sly smile and cunning eyes, the clever feline demanded attention and treats, even in the wee hours.

Resolute in her decision to ignore the feline's pleas, Sarah settled back against her pillow. But Milo was not one to accept defeat easily. Determined to have his late-night snack, he skillfully maneuvered across Sarah's prone form, employing paws of persuasion in his relentless pursuit.

Undeterred by his initial failure, Milo hopped onto the bedside table and, with deliberate precision, started knocking objects to the floor, one by one. The clattering sound echoed through the dimly lit room, shattering any hope of a peaceful slumber. Sarah glanced at the feline and sighed, knowing that her precious sleep would remain a distant dream until she satisfied Milo's hunger.

Reluctantly, Sarah rose from her cozy nest and stumbled into the kitchen, with Milo triumphantly trailing behind. But as she entered the room, she heard an unexpected sound—like water rushing or a janitor testing their high-pressure cleaning equipment in the middle of the night. Confusion crept over her as she tried to recall if she had left a faucet running, mentally calculating the consequences of an astronomical water bill.

Driven by her desire to solve the enigma, Sarah began her search. Room by room, she scoured her apartment, with Milo persistently vocalizing his discontent.

The bathroom proved fruitless, leaving her to wonder if her ears were playing tricks on her. Could the mysterious sound originate from outside?

Returning to the kitchen, the epicenter of the disturbance, Sarah stood motionless, straining to pinpoint the source of the noise.

Despite Milo' insistent protests, she managed to discern that the strange cacophony emanated from within the wall, separating her apartment from the neighboring unit. Her heart skipped a beat as she entertained the possibility of a burst pipe and the ensuing flood wreaking havoc next door.

An overwhelming sense of responsibility washed over Sarah, igniting her innate desire to help others in need. However, she wisely decided to take a moment to contemplate the situation. After all, she didn't want to hastily drag someone out of bed in the dead of night only to find that it was a false alarm. But if water was indeed running amok, she had no choice but to rouse the maintenance crew to avert disaster.

With a determined stride, Sarah walked to the end of the kitchen bar, phone in hand, ready to dial for assistance. At that moment, clarity struck like a bolt of lightning, illuminating the entire mystery that had eluded her. With a lighthearted chuckle, she realized that the key to resolving the enigma lay within the words she needed to utter: "Alexa, stop!"

And just like that, the wall-shaking commotion ceased as Sarah's digital assistant obediently followed her command. Milo, seemingly amused by the turn of events, let out a triumphant meow, his mission accomplished. Sarah, still chuckling at the absurdity of the situation, returned to her bed, the mystery solved and the prospect of a peaceful slumber restored.

In the end, Sarah learned two valuable lessons: never underestimate the determination of a hungry feline and always double-check the commands given to our AI companions. For in the realm of late-night adventures, even the most peculiar mysteries can be solved with a touch of technology and a sprinkle of laughter.

50. MELODIES AND MIRTH: THE TUNA CAN MIXUP

ONE MORNING, Sebastian stood with a can of tuna in his hand, engaged in what seemed like a one-sided conversation. With a furrowed brow and a hint of frustration, he addressed the can as if it were a technological marvel.

"Alexa, play my favorite song!" Sebastian commanded, tapping the can with his finger. When no response came, he huffed in annoyance, muttering to himself, "Technology these days never listens to me."

From the living room, his wife Agnes, a quick-witted woman with a knack for humor, couldn't help but overhear the amusing exchange. She shook her head, unable to contain her laughter, and walked into the kitchen to enlighten her bewildered husband.

"Sebastian, darling," Agnes said, her voice filled with amusement, "that can of tuna doesn't possess the extraordinary powers of Alexa. It's just a can of fish, dear."

Sebastian looked at the can with a mix of surprise and embarrassment. "Oh, so that's why it hasn't been responding to me," he chuckled sheepishly. "Well, I suppose I'll have to find another way to get my favorite song playing."

Agnes patted his shoulder affectionately. "Don't worry, dear. I'll find the right tune for you."

As she walked away, Sebastian couldn't resist cracking a joke. "You know, Agnes, I must have gotten the 'tuna-nology' and technology mixed up. My apologies to the fish."

Agnes chuckled, her eyes twinkling with mirth. "Oh, Sebastian, you always find a way to bring laughter into our lives. Now, let's find that song you've been craving."

Together, they ventured into the living room, where Agnes skillfully operated their trusty old record player. The familiar crackle of vinyl filled the air, and Sebastian's face lit up with joy.

As the music played, Sebastian couldn't resist joining in, singing along with gusto.

Agnes joined him, their voices harmonizing in a playful duet that filled the room with laughter and melody. Their impromptu performance became a delightful moment of shared joy and silliness, leaving them both in fits of laughter.

"I never knew we had such a talent for comedic serenades," Sebastian quipped, his eyes gleaming playfully."

Agnes playfully nudged him. "Well, dear, perhaps we've stumbled upon our hidden talent. The world is not ready for the comedic duo of Sebastian and Juniper!"

They dissolved into laughter once again, their lighthearted banter filling their home with warmth and happiness.

From that day on, whenever Sebastian saw a can of tuna, he couldn't help but smile, recalling the moment of confusion that led to their joyful musical escapade. And Agnes, always quick with a witty remark, never missed an opportunity to remind him of his amusing conversation with the unsuspecting can.

51. THE PRANKSTER'S HARVEST: HILARIOUS CULINARY ADVENTURES

A NOTORIOUS JOKER NAMED LARRY decided to play a prank on his unsuspecting friend, Daniel. Knowing Daniel's love for gardening, Larry devised a plan to trick him with a bizarre plant recommendation. He sent Daniel a message, pretending to be a gardening expert, suggesting that he should grow a rare and mysterious herb called "Hilariousweed" to enhance his culinary creations.

Daniel, always eager to experiment with new flavors, was intrigued by the suggestion. He searched online for information about the herb but found nothing. Undeterred, he decided to ask the local gardening store for assistance. As Daniel walked into the store, he spotted Sam, an employee with a perpetual smirk on his face. Daniel approached him, holding his phone, and asked, "Have you ever heard of the Hilariousweed?"

Sam, fighting back a laugh, raised an eyebrow and replied, "Oh, you mean the legendary plant? It's said to make your dishes taste ten times funnier!" He continued with a grin, "But be careful; it's known to cause uncontrollable fits of laughter."

Daniel was puzzled but couldn't resist the temptation. He asked, "Where can I find it? I must grow this magical herb!"

Sam led Daniel to the plant section, pointing to a pot labeled "Hilariousweed." Daniel's excitement grew as he imagined the laughter-filled meals he would create. He eagerly purchased the plant and rushed home to start his culinary adventure.

Days passed, and Daniel diligently tended to his Hilariousweed, watering it, talking to it, and even cracking jokes to make it grow. Finally, the day arrived when he decided to harvest the first batch of leaves to use in his cooking.

As he chopped the vibrant green leaves and sprinkled them into his dish, Daniel couldn't help but crack a joke to set the mood. "Hey, Hilariousweed, let's add some flavor and comedy to this recipe. It's thyme to get cooking!"

With anticipation, Daniel took a bite of his creation, expecting bursts of laughter and culinary brilliance. Instead, his taste buds were met with an overwhelmingly bitter and unpleasant flavor. Daniel's face contorted in surprise, and he quickly spat out the food.

Realization dawned on him as he chuckled to himself, "Well, Larry got me good this time! That herb was anything but hilarious."

Daniel couldn't help but appreciate Larry's wit, even if it meant falling victim to his pranks. He realized that sometimes laughter and a playful sense of humor were the true spices that made life more enjoyable.

From that day on, Daniel and Larry's friendship was filled with playful banter and practical jokes, each trying to outwit the other. Their humorous escapades brought endless laughter and joy to their lives, proving that a good sense of humor was the best ingredient for lasting friendships.

52. FEATHERS AND TYPO TANGLES: A WRITER'S TALE ADVENTURES

THE BUDDING WRITER, RICHARD PENNINGTON, couldn't contain his excitement when he stumbled upon an online company seeking wordsmiths. The opportunity seemed perfect to boost his finances and showcase his writing prowess. After meticulously crafting a test article, he felt confident in his submission and eagerly awaited a positive response.

Little did Richard know, he was about to experience a twist of fate in the form of a mischievous tech mishap. Unbeknownst to him, the new software he was using had a sneaky habit of autosaving. With his article left open on the second monitor, Richard believed he had taken all the necessary precautions, blissfully unaware of the impending chaos.

Days passed, and Richard's anticipation turned into disappointment when the company rejected his submission. Confused and disheartened, he couldn't fathom what had gone wrong. It seemed like his article had ticked all the right boxes. Nevertheless, he graciously accepted their decision and pondered how to improve his financial situation.

But just when Richard thought all hope was lost, a glimmer of opportunity appeared in his inbox. The company reached out, asking him to resubmit his article. Perplexed by the sudden change of heart, Richard heeded the advice of a friend and decided to give it another shot.

As he delved into his work once more, Richard's eyes widened in disbelief. He discovered that an editor from the company had made revisions to his article. The piece impressed them until they reached the final paragraph, which was plagued by an unusual number of typos.

It was then that Richard's heart sank, for he realized the source of his embarrassment—a string of m's scattered throughout the text.

In a moment of revelation, Richard's gaze shifted to his pet, Jack the cockatiel. Jack was known for his love of all things electronic, often wreaking havoc with wires and keyboards. It dawned on Richard that while he had momentarily left the room, Jack must have taken the opportunity to showcase his own keyboard skills. With a mix of amusement and mortification, Richard realized that his beloved avian companion had left his mark on the article. The elusive m's were the result of Jack's playful tap dance on the letter, an unintended contribution that had slipped through Richard's radar. Determined to set things right, Richard embarked on a meticulous editing journey. He combed through every word, ensuring a flawless piece before closing the window. Alongside his revised article, he penned a cover email, offering a sincere apology and confessing to the feathered culprit's involvement. As he hit send, a wave of uncertainty washed over him. Would his explanation be met with understanding or dismissed as a far-fetched excuse? To Richard's relief, the company's response proved favorable. A few days later, he eagerly signed his acceptance letter, ready to embark on a writing journey that was both memorable and cautionary. From that day forward, Richard made sure to keep a close eye on Jack, protecting his words from any further "avian-inspired" surprises.

And so, Richard's tale of the keyboard caper became a legend within the writing community—a reminder to always double-check for unexpected feathery interventions and to be cautious when leaving articles open in the presence of spiteful pets. After all, even the most innocent-looking creatures can leave their unique mark on the world of words.

53. THE DIY DEFENDER: A HILARIOUS TALE OF PACKAGE PROTECTION

AS THE NEWS REPORTS OF PORCH PIRATES running rampant in the neighborhood of Elmwood, Dave Anderson knew he had to take matters into his own hands. He couldn't let those sneaky thieves get their hands on his precious packages. With determination in his eyes and a tool belt strapped around his waist, he set out to build the ultimate fortress of package protection.

Now, Dave wasn't your average DIY enthusiast. He had a knack for creative problem-solving and a mischievous sense of humor. Armed with a plan and a trip to the local hardware store, he gathered the necessary materials. He carefully selected sturdy boards, heavy-duty hinges, and an assortment of gadgets to make his creation foolproof.

Dave began constructing his masterpiece. He measured, sawed, and hammered away, all the while cracking jokes and making witty remarks to himself. "If anyone thinks they can outsmart me, they're in for a package surprise!" he chuckled, adjusting his safety goggles.

The most challenging part was designing the mechanism that would allow packages to drop safely into the fortress while keeping the hands of porch pirates at bay. Dave scratched his head, pondering the perfect solution. Suddenly, inspiration struck like a bolt of lightning. "Eureka! I've got it!" he exclaimed, pumping his fist in the air.

Hours turned into days as Dave meticulously built his impenetrable mailbox. He installed a state-of-the-art RFID lock, ensuring only the rightful owner could access the treasures within. But as he positioned the lock and aligned its parts, he encountered a minor setback. The pieces didn't quite fit together as expected.

Undeterred, Dave hatched a plan that only a DIY genius like himself could come up with. He decided to climb inside the mailbox to get a closer look and make the necessary adjustments. After all, who needs a locksmith when you've got your own skills and a touch of daring?

With a flashlight in one hand and a drill in the other, Dave squeezed himself into the confined space. "Who needs a gym membership when you've got DIY projects to keep you fit?" he quipped, trying not to disturb his loyal canine companion, Buster, who watched the spectacle with a curious tilt of his head.

As Dave maneuvered inside the mailbox, he quickly realized the gravity of his situation. The lock clicked shut, leaving him trapped in his own creation. Panic momentarily washed over him, but he refused to let it dampen his spirits. "Well, this wasn't in the DIY manual!" he chuckled nervously, pondering the best escape plan.

Buster, the ever-relaxed supervisor of Dave's projects, gave him a nonchalant glance as if to say, "You've really outdone yourself this time, boss." Dave gathered his wits and devised a daring escape strategy. He pushed, wriggled, and squeezed his way upward, using his ingenuity to navigate through the mechanism that was meant to keep others out but had inadvertently locked him in.

After a few tense minutes of contorting his body, Dave emerged victorious, tumbling out of the top of the mailbox and onto the floor. He lay there, a mix of relief and embarrassment washing over him, while Buster simply wagged his tail as if to say, "Job well done, human."

As he surveyed his near-impenetrable creation, Dave realized he had achieved his goal. His mailbox was a fortress against porch pirates, with one small exception. Chuckling to himself, he thought, "Well, at least they won't be able to carry it away, and they'll have quite a surprise if they manage to get their hands on a small package."

With newfound determination, Dave went back to the drawing board to refine his mechanism and ensure his fortress was truly unbeatable. "Nobody messes with my packages and gets away with it!" he declared, ready to conquer any challenge that came his way.

And so, armed with his DIY skills, a touch of humor, and the unwavering support of his loyal canine sidekick, Dave continued his quest to outsmart the porch pirates and protect the sanctity of deliveries in his neighborhood.

54. THE SURPRISE SENIOR TALENT SHOW

THE ATMOSPHERE AT THE GOLDEN OAKS VILLAGE SENIOR CITIZENS' CLUB in Lakewood was buzzing with excitement as the annual talent show approached. It was an event eagerly anticipated by both the participants and the audience, showcasing the hidden talents of the club's members. This year, however, something extraordinary was about to unfold.

In a cozy meeting room adorned with colorful decorations, the participants huddled together, whispering and giggling. Among them was Evelyn, a sprightly grandmother known for her unpredictable sense of humor.

"Alright, folks, it's time to reveal our talents," Evelyn announced, holding a small notepad. "Let's see what we've got."

The group exchanged curious glances as Evelyn began reading the list of acts. First up was Oscar, a retired teacher with a passion for dancing. He had been practicing a lively tango routine, and his fellow club members couldn't wait to see him strut his stuff.

"I hope he doesn't forget his moves like he forgets where he put his keys," Evelyn quipped, earning chuckles from the crowd.

Next on the list was Grace, a retired chef known for her culinary expertise. Unbeknownst to everyone, Grace had a hidden talent for singing opera. Her melodious voice had surprised many during choir rehearsals, and now she was ready to take the stage.

"Grace's voice is so powerful, it could shatter a wine glass from the kitchen," Evelyn teased, causing the group to burst into laughter.

As the days passed, the participants continued their secret preparations. The village senior citizens' club had never seen such anticipation for the talent show. Even the club's staff members were eagerly awaiting the surprises that awaited them on the big day.

Finally, the evening of the talent show arrived. The room was filled with friends, family, and club members, all excited to witness the extraordinary performances.

The curtains drew back, revealing a vibrant stage adorned with twinkling lights. The crowd erupted in applause as the first act, Oscar, gracefully danced onto the stage. His nimble footwork and elegant movements left the audience in awe.

Evelyn, sitting in the front row, couldn't resist cracking a joke. "Oscar's got more rhythm in his pinky toe than I do in my entire body," she quipped, causing laughter to ripple through the audience.

As the night progressed, each act showcased a unique talent. Grace took the stage, and her booming voice filled the room with powerful melodies. The audience was captivated by her unexpected operatic talent, giving her a standing ovation.

"Grace's voice is so grand, it could give Pavarotti a run for his money," Evelyn whispered to her neighbor, evoking laughter from the surrounding seats.

The talent show continued with a myriad of surprises. Benjamin, a retired postal worker, displayed his impressive juggling skills with an array of colorful balls. Sophia, an ex-military officer, revealed her comedic side with a stand-up routine that had the crowd in stitches.

Evelyn herself had a surprise up her sleeve. When it was her turn to perform, she stepped onto the stage with a guitar in hand. As she strummed the first chords, she sang a lighthearted tune that had the audience tapping their feet and singing along.

"Evelyn's voice is like a fine wine - it only gets better with age," one club member exclaimed, earning laughter and nods of agreement.

The talent show came to an end, leaving the audience buzzing with excitement and admiration for the incredible talents that had been unveiled that night. The participants basked in the applause and camaraderie, knowing they had created a night to remember.

As the club members mingled after the show, Evelyn approached Oscar, who was still beaming from his successful dance performance.

"Amigo, you were like a ballerina on roller skates out there!" Evelyn teased, her eyes sparkling with humor.

Oscar chuckled and replied, "Well, Evelyn, your guitar skills rival those of a rockstar. Maybe we should start a band!"

The two shared a jovial laugh, their playful exchange adding an extra touch of joy to the evening.

And so, the annual talent show at the village senior citizens' club became a legendary event, forever etching itself in the memories of all who attended.

It was a celebration of life, laughter, and the boundless surprises that can emerge when you least expect them.

55. THE GREAT BINGO CAPER

WILLOW SPRINGS, 1975 - In a heartwarming display of camaraderie and wit, a group of residents at Willow Springs nursing home came together to form an unexpected alliance with a shared goal: outsmarting the system and turning the weekly bingo game in their favor. This captivating tale, now known as the Great Bingo Caper, has become the stuff of legend within the lively halls of the nursing home, serving as a testament to the indomitable spirit of its residents.

Led by the quick-witted matriarch, Doris, the group would gather in a discreet meeting spot tucked away in the garden, far from prying eyes. With a twinkle in her eye and a stack of bingo balls in hand, Doris would rally the diverse group, declaring, "Alright, ladies and gents, let's make our move. It's time to show those young whippersnappers what we're made of!"

Amidst chuckles and nods of agreement, the residents carefully crafted miniature magnets hidden within their bingo daubers to discreetly attract the desired numbers at just the right moment. The plan was meticulously devised to avoid detection and ensure their success.

As the next bingo night arrived, a palpable excitement filled the air. Residents eagerly took their seats at the tables, anticipation evident on their faces. Unbeknownst to the staff, who were unsuspecting of the impending caper, the game commenced with the caller announcing the first numbers.

With each call, the group held their breath, waiting for the opportune moment to deploy their magnetized daubers. Doris, with a sly grin, seized the perfect chance. As the caller announced "B-12," she swiftly swept her dauber across the card, the hidden magnetic charm attracting the number toward her square. The room erupted in gasps and giggles as Doris exclaimed, "Bingo! This must be my lucky day!"

The staff, bewildered by the sudden winning streak, exchanged puzzled glances. Sheila, renowned for her impeccable comedic timing, added, "I didn't know getting older meant our luck would skyrocket! I should've brought my lucky socks!"

Amidst the laughter and camaraderie, the caper continued. Each member of the group strategically employed their magnetized daubers, resulting in a flurry of triumphant cries of "bingo!" and bewildered looks from the staff.

To add an extra touch of humor to their audacious plan, Harry, known for his practical jokes, playfully substituted the staff's bingo balls with a set of rubber ducks. The room erupted in laughter as a rubber duck wearing a tiny bowtie emerged from the bingo cage when the caller announced, "O-69." The staff couldn't help but join in the amusement, recognizing they had fallen victim to a lighthearted prank.

As the night drew to a close, the residents reveled in their victories, relishing the triumph of their cunning caper. Sheila raised her glass in a toast, exclaiming, "To our fearless group, the Bingo Bandits! May our numbers always be lucky and our daubers always be magnetic!"

The Great Bingo Caper quickly became a cherished legend, passed down from one resident to another, filling the nursing home with laughter and strengthening the sense of community. Although the residents had devised an unconventional strategy to win, their intentions were pure: to bring joy and laughter into their daily lives, creating enduring memories that warmed their hearts.

As the years passed, the original members of the caper became treasured memories, but their legacy endured. The Great Bingo Caper stood as a testament to the power of humor, friendship, and the indomitable spirit of the elderly.

56. THE UNFORGETTABLE ROAD TRIP

THE SUMMER SUN BEAT DOWN on the pavement as the vintage RV rumbled to life, ready to embark on an unforgettable road trip. Inside the RV, a lively group of travelers gathered, each with their own quirks and a shared sense of adventure.

Leading the pack was Finnegan, a retiree with a knack for always finding himself in hilarious situations. Joining him was his best friend, Agnes, a quick-witted and sassy woman with a penchant for spontaneous laughter. Rounding out the group were Joseph, a tech-savvy millennial with a dry sense of humor, and Ethel, a free-spirited hippie with a penchant for singing off-key.

As the RV hit the open road, the misadventures began. Their first stop was a corn maze, where they decided to put their navigation skills to the test. Little did they know that Finnegan's sense of direction was about as reliable as a broken GPS.

"Finnegan, are you sure we should turn left here?" Agnes questioned, eyeing the towering cornstalks surrounding them.

Finnegan flashed an amused grin. "Of course, Agnes! Left, right, left, left, right, left... or was it right?"

Their laughter echoed through the maze as they stumbled upon dead ends and circled back to where they had started. Hours later, they emerged victorious, covered in corn husks and a few good laughs richer.

Next, on their journey, they came across a field with grazing cows. In a moment of hilarity, Joseph mistook one particularly large cow for a hitchhiker, who waved excitedly as they passed.

"Hey, buddy! Need a ride?" Joseph called out, earning a round of laughter from his companions.

Ethel chimed in, "Well, Joseph, if that cow decides to join us, at least we'll have a guaranteed source of fresh milk!"

The road trip continued with more comedic encounters. They attempted to navigate a drive-thru on horseback, much to the surprise of the fast-food workers who struggled to keep a straight face. Finnegan's horse seemed more interested in the menu than their order, prompting Ethel to quip, "Looks like we've got ourselves a vegetarian horse!"

The group's laughter was infectious, spreading to anyone who crossed their path. Strangers in neighboring cars couldn't help but join in the merriment as they watched the mismatched crew embark on their hilarious adventures.

As they traveled from one scenic spot to another, they encountered a series of mishaps that became legendary tales in their own right. They accidentally set up camp in a children's playground, mistaking the slide for a place to park the RV. Ethel found herself in a spontaneous dance-off with a street performer, showcasing her unique groovy moves that left the crowd in stitches.

Their final destination was a picturesque lakeside campsite, where they decided to end their road trip on a high note. They gathered around a crackling campfire, toasting marshmallows and sharing stories from their journey.

Joseph looked around at his newfound friends, a wide grin spreading across his face. "You know what they say, folks. Life is not about the destination. It's about the hilariously twisted journey!"

Agnes raised her marshmallow on a stick and quipped, "And with this group, Finnegan, we're never short on twisted journeys!"

Laughter filled the air, blending with the crackling fire and the soothing sounds of nature. They sat under the starlit sky, cherishing the memories they had created together.

"The Unforgettable Road Trip" brought them closer, showcasing the power of laughter, friendship, and joy that can be found in the most unexpected moments. And as they basked in the warmth of the campfire, they knew that this adventure would forever hold a special place in their hearts.

57. THE HILARIOUS HAUNTED HOUSE

IN THE QUIET TOWN OF SPOOKLAND, a couple named Eric and Charlotte Davis set their sights on a charming old mansion. Little did they know that the house came with a ghostly surprise. As they moved in, they quickly discovered that their new home was haunted by a troupe of spirited ghosts.

Charlotte, a witty and adventurous woman with a love for the supernatural, embraced the ghosts with open arms. Eric, a skeptical yet good-natured man, couldn't help but find humor in the peculiar antics of their spectral roommates. Together, they turned their haunted house into a beloved local attraction.

The first encounter occurred one evening as Charlotte was preparing dinner in the kitchen. The mischievous ghost known as Jasper decided to lend a helping hand. However, his idea of helping involved rearranging the spices and making the pots and pans dance around the stove.

"Jasper, darling, I appreciate the enthusiasm, but I think we'll stick to traditional cooking methods for tonight," Charlotte chuckled as the floating utensils settled back into place.

Eric entered the kitchen, rubbing his eyes in disbelief. "Are you telling me we have a ghostly sous chef now?"

Charlotte shrugged with a smile. "Well, it certainly adds a dash of flavor to our meals!"

Their encounters with the playful spirits continued. As they explored the mansion, they discovered secret passageways and hidden rooms, leading to comical situations.

One day, while investigating a peculiar knocking sound in the attic, Eric found himself face-to-face with a ghostly figure named Ophelia.

"I'm just here to fix the leaky roof," Eric said, pointing to the ceiling.

Ophelia, with a sly grin, replied, "Oh, I thought you were here for tea and a chat. My mistake!"

Their witty banter echoed through the hallways, filling the old mansion with laughter and joy.

Word of the couple's unique living situation spread throughout the town, attracting curious visitors from far and wide. The house became a popular destination, with locals and tourists alike flocking to experience the whimsical charm of the haunted mansion.

Eric and Charlotte decided to embrace their newfound fame and transformed the mansion into a comedic haunted house attraction. They hired actors to portray the ghosts, adding a theatrical flair to the already lively atmosphere.

One evening, as the crowd gathered outside the mansion, Eric stood before them with a microphone in hand. "Ladies and gentlemen, welcome to the Hilarious Haunted House! Prepare to be thrilled, delighted, and, of course, thoroughly entertained by our spirited residents!"

The crowd erupted in applause and laughter as they ventured inside, ready for a night filled with laughter and scares.

Inside the mansion, the ghosts eagerly played their parts, engaging in humorous interactions and pranks. They danced, floated through walls, and teased the visitors with friendly frights. Laughter echoed through the hallways as Eric and Charlotte watched the joyous reactions from the sidelines.

As the night came to an end, Charlotte joined Eric, her eyes sparkling with excitement. "Well, I'd say our haunted house is a resounding success!"

Eric nodded, a grin spreading across his face. "Who knew that ghosts could be such great entertainers? We've turned our haunted house into a comedy club!"

The couple continued to live harmoniously with their playful ghostly roommates, sharing jokes, stories, and endless laughter. The Hilarious Haunted House became a beloved fixture in Spookland, a place where spirits and humans alike could come together for a lighthearted and unforgettable experience.

58. THE TIME-TRAVELING MIXUP

DR. BARTHOLOMEW WHIPPLE was known among his colleagues as a brilliant yet eccentric scientist. With wild frizzy hair, thick glasses, and a lab coat perpetually stained with mysterious substances, he was always tinkering with bizarre inventions. One day, after years of tireless work, he finally completed his masterpiece: a functioning time machine. Little did he know that this invention would lead to a series of hilarious misadventures.

Dr. Whipple eagerly invited a group of volunteers to be the first to test his time machine. Among them were Gwendolyn, a feisty librarian with a passion for ancient history, Reggie, a laid-back skateboarder with a fondness for retro fashion, and Delilah, an adventurous grandmother who loved reading science fiction novels.

Each of them had their own reasons for wanting to experience time travel.

As the volunteers stepped into the time machine, Dr. Whipple prepared for the grand experiment. He pushed a series of buttons, twisted a few knobs, and pressed the large red "GO" button. The machine hummed to life, and in a flash of dazzling lights, the volunteers disappeared.

When the dust settled, Dr. Whipple realized something had gone terribly wrong. Instead of being transported to the past or the future, the volunteers had been mixed up in time! Gwendolyn found herself in the roaring 1920s, complete with flapper dresses and jazz music, while Reggie was transported to the medieval era, where he struggled to fit in with knights and damsels. Delilah, on the other hand, ended up in a futuristic world filled with hovering cars and talking robots.

As chaos ensued, Dr. Whipple frantically worked to fix his time machine and bring everyone back to their proper time periods. Meanwhile, the misadventures of Gwendolyn, Reggie, and Delilah provided endless laughter and comedic moments.

Gwendolyn found herself in a bustling speakeasy surrounded by flappers and dapper gentlemen. Determined to prove she was a time traveler, she confidently declared, "Ladies and gentlemen, prepare to witness a miracle! I have arrived from the future!" The crowd exchanged skeptical glances, mistaking her enthusiasm for a clever party act. Undeterred, Gwendolyn attempted to explain modern technology, only to be met with bewildered looks. "You see, we have these magical devices called smartphones that fit in our pockets and can do just about anything. They're like tiny genies!" The onlookers chuckled, assuming it was a clever joke, leaving Gwendolyn frustrated but determined to find a way to convince them otherwise.

Meanwhile, Reggie's unexpected journey through time took him straight into the heart of a medieval tournament. Clad in his baggy pants and colorful sneakers, he stood out like a sore thumb. As the knights prepared for jousting, Reggie couldn't resist the urge to show off his skateboarding skills. He hopped on his skateboard, zooming down the jousting field with unmatched agility. The knights and spectators watched in astonishment as Reggie pulled off tricks and flips, earning him cheers and applause. "Behold, ye knights! Witness the art of skate jousting!" he exclaimed, combining medieval chivalry with his own unique flair. The knights, unsure how to respond, eventually joined in on the fun, transforming the traditional tournament into a comedic display of skateboarding prowess and medieval jest.

In the futuristic world, Delilah found herself in a sleek city filled with advanced technology. It was there that she encountered Z-1, a charming and sassy robot with a knack for problem-solving. As they teamed up to navigate the futuristic landscape, their interactions were filled with playful banter and comedic exchanges. "Z-1, I never thought I'd be taking life advice from a robot," Delilah chuckled. Z-1 replied in a robotic tone, "Well, Delilah, I'm the most advanced advice-giving robot on this side of the space-time continuum. So, you better listen up!" They faced challenges together, such as deciphering holographic interfaces and avoiding malfunctioning hovercars. Delilah's witty comebacks and Z-1's quick responses created a dynamic duo that entertained and perplexed the futuristic citizens they encountered.

Throughout their adventures, Gwendolyn, Reggie, and Delilah found themselves in countless hilarious moments. Gwendolyn attempted to teach the 1920s crowd the dance moves of the future, leading to a whimsical display of flapping arms and twisting legs. Reggie's skateboarding antics in medieval times turned a solemn tournament into a spectacle of laughter and astonishment. And Delilah's clever remarks and Z-1's robotic wit kept them both on their toes as they unraveled the mysteries of the futuristic world.

As Dr. Whipple finally fixed the time machine, the volunteers were brought back to the present, their time-traveling escapades coming to an end. They bid farewell to the past and future versions of themselves, cherishing the memories and inside jokes they had formed along the way.

In the end, the "Time-Traveling Mix-up" became a legend, and Dr. Whipple's mishap became the stuff of comedic lore. The volunteers went on to share their hilarious stories, becoming a tight-knit group with a bond forged through laughter and the shared experience of time-traveling chaos.

And as for Dr. Whipple, he vowed to double-check his calculations and buttons before embarking on any future experiments. After all, even the most brilliant scientists can use a good laugh now and then.

59. THE ENCHANTED PAGES: A WHIMSICAL LITERARY JOURNEY

MYSTORIA IS A QUAINT TOWN nestled between charming cobblestone streets. There stood an unassuming bookstore called "The Enchanted Pages." It had a mysterious aura as if there was more to it than met the eye. The owner, Mr. Archibald Fairweather, was known for his eccentricity and enigmatic smile. Little did the townsfolk know that within the dusty shelves of this remarkable bookshop lay a hidden secret—a portal to the worlds of classic literature.

On a bright sunny day, a curious customer named James entered the bookstore, his eyes wide with anticipation. He had heard whispers of the magical experiences that awaited those who ventured into the enchanted realms of the books. As he perused the shelves, he stumbled upon a weathered volume titled "Adventures Abound."

As James entered the magical realm of Alice in Wonderland, he couldn't help but feel like a fish out of water. Everything was topsy-turvy and upside down, with talking animals and enigmatic characters at every turn. He scratched his head in confusion, muttering to himself, "Well, I suppose this is what happens when you follow a rabbit down a hole. Who needs logic anyway?"

The Cheshire Cat appeared before James. "Welcome, welcome! Are you lost or just pretending to be lost?" it teased, disappearing and reappearing in thin air. James chuckled and retorted, "Well, my good feline friend, I'm not sure if I'm lost or if I've stumbled into the wackiest tea party in existence."

At the tea party, James found himself surrounded by eccentric characters, including the Mad Hatter and the March Hare.

They were engaged in a never-ending conversation that made little sense. James couldn't help but interject, "Excuse me, gentlemen, but have you considered investing in a good dictionary? It might help untangle your tongue-twisting debates."

The White Rabbit scurried past, muttering about being late. James, eager to lend a hand, shouted after him, "Don't worry, my furry friend! Time is merely a concept here. We can stretch it, squeeze it, or even pretend it doesn't exist. Let's have a good laugh and forget about being punctual."

As James ventured further into Wonderland, he encountered the Queen of Hearts and her deck of playing cards. She ruled with an iron fist, demanding obedience and swift punishment for any perceived wrongdoing. James couldn't resist a playful jab, saying, "Your Majesty, may I suggest a more peaceful alternative? Instead of 'off with their heads,' how about 'let's have a dance-off instead'? It's much more entertaining, wouldn't you agree?"

The Caterpillar, perched atop a mushroom, offered James a puff from his hookah. James declined, saying, "Thank you, but I'm trying to keep my head clear in this topsy-turvy world. I wouldn't want to mix up reality with a giant caterpillar speaking in riddles. It's confusing enough as it is!"

Finally, as James prepared to leave Wonderland, he encountered the Queen's court, where a game of croquet was in full swing. The flamingo mallets and hedgehog balls created a comical sight. James couldn't resist a cheeky comment, "Ah, the sport of aristocrats. I must say, this is the only game where flamingos and hedgehogs get to shine. Who needs a golf club when you have a long-necked bird?"

With a final wink from the Cheshire Cat, James bid farewell to Wonderland and returned to his own world. As he closed the book, he couldn't help but chuckle at the absurdity and wit he had encountered. "Life is a curious journey," he mused, "and sometimes we need a bit of nonsense to remind us not to take it too seriously."

Meanwhile, across the bookstore, a young woman named Sophia discovered a copy of "Treasures Untold." She couldn't resist opening the book, eager to escape the monotony of her everyday life.

In an instant, she was transported to the swashbuckling world of pirates and buried treasure, and she found herself on the deck of a pirate ship, surrounded by a motley crew of misfits. Captain Bartholomew Swashbuckle, a flamboyant and boisterous figure, greeted her with a booming laugh.

"Ahoy there, lass! Ye've stumbled upon the grandest pirate ship in all the seven seas. Ye ready to join my crew?" he bellowed, twirling his mustache with a mischievous grin. Sophia couldn't help but play along, responding with a mock salute, "Aye, aye, Captain Swashbuckle! I hope ye have plenty of pirate puns to keep us entertained."

As the ship set sail, Sophia discovered that pirate life wasn't all swashbuckling and treasure hunting. There were mishaps aplenty, from slippery deck boards sending crew members tumbling to comical encounters with rival pirates who seemed more interested in pillow fights than fierce battles. Sophia couldn't help but quip, "Captain, if pirates spent more time on the stage than the high seas, we might have a chance at winning a Tony Award for 'Best Pirate Comedy.'"

On their quest for buried treasure, Sophia found herself navigating treacherous waters, both literal and metaphorical. When faced with a daunting storm, she mustered her courage and exclaimed, "Avast, me hearties! Let's ride this tempest like it's a rollercoaster at the Pirate Theme Park. Arrr, who needs a drop tower when we have Mother Nature's wrath?"

Amidst their escapades, Sophia and Captain Swashbuckle engaged in a duel of wit and banter, each trying to outdo the other in jest. Sophia challenged the captain's piratical knowledge, quipping, "Captain, I've read every book about pirates in this library, and not once have I encountered a pirate named 'Captain Crunch.' Are ye sure ye ain't mixing up your cereal with your pirate lore?"

As they finally reached the buried treasure, Sophia and the crew celebrated their triumph, but not without a touch of comedy. Sophia jested, "Captain, ye may have found gold and jewels, but I've found something even more precious—enough material for a stand-up comedy routine that will have audiences rolling in the aisles!"

With their pockets full of laughter and memories, Sophia bid farewell to Captain Swashbuckle and returned to the ordinary world. As she closed the book, she couldn't help but smile, grateful for the swashbuckling adventure that had brightened her day. "Sometimes," she mused, "the greatest treasures are not gold or jewels but the joy and laughter we find along the way."

As fate would have it, James and Sophia's paths collided in a surprising twist of fate. They found themselves in the pages of the same book, working together to outsmart the main characters. With each turn of the page, they encountered amusing challenges, exchanging playful banter reminiscent of famous comedians.

"Ahoy there, matey!" Sophia quipped, adjusting her pirate hat. "Seems like we've found ourselves in quite the pickle. But fear not, my dear James, for I've got a joke up my sleeve that'll surely make those scallywags keel over with laughter!"

James chuckled, his eyes sparkling with mirth. "I'm all ears, Sophia. But remember, timing is everything!"

Their escapades continued as they journeyed through other beloved classics like Pride and Prejudice, where they found themselves caught in a dance-off with Mr. Darcy, and Moby Dick, where they hilariously attempted to tame the mighty whale using nothing but a feather duster.

With each adventure, James and Sophia grew closer, forming an unbreakable bond forged through laughter and the shared love for the written word. They discovered that the magic of literature went beyond the confines of the pages, transcending into their own lives and hearts.

As they reached the final chapter of their extraordinary journey, James and Sophia found themselves back in the cozy confines of The Enchanted Pages, their hearts brimming with memories and laughter. They bid farewell to Mr. Fairweather, thanking him for the unforgettable experience.

"Remember, dear friends," Mr. Fairweather said with a twinkle in his eye, "the power of imagination is boundless. Let these stories live on within you, for they have the power to transform ordinary lives into extraordinary adventures."

With that, James and Sophia stepped back into the real world, forever changed by their remarkable bookshop escapades.

60. THE WACKY SCIENCE FAIR

IN THE GLITTERING, SPACIOUS HALLS OF QUIRKTOWN PRIMARY SCHOOL, the buzz of excitement filled the air as students prepared for the annual Wacky Science Fair. It was a day when budding scientists shed their lab coats and embraced their wildest imaginations. The fairgrounds were a riot of colorful displays and bizarre contraptions, promising laughter and unexpected discoveries.

First up was young Timmy, known for his insatiable love for all things explosive. His experiment titled "ChocoVolcano" had everyone intrigued. As the judges and spectators gathered around, Timmy proudly presented his creation—an intricately crafted volcano made entirely of chocolate. With a twinkle in his eye, he pressed a hidden button, and the volcano erupted with a delightful explosion of chocolate syrup.

The crowd burst into laughter, and Timmy couldn't help but quip, "Who needs a traditional volcano when you can have one that satisfies your sweet tooth? It's the tastiest eruption you'll ever witness!"

Next in line was Lisa, a budding inventor with a knack for defying gravity. She proudly showcased her creation—"Spaghet-Floaty." This peculiar apparatus involved strands of spaghetti that, when cooked just right, transformed into buoyant noodles that defied the laws of physics. Lisa demonstrated the device by placing a handful of uncooked spaghetti into a pot of boiling water, and moments later, the noodles emerged floating in mid-air.

The audience erupted in laughter, and Lisa couldn't resist a playful quip, "They say pasta sticks to the wall when it's cooked, but why settle for walls when you can make it float like magic? It's spaghetti al dente meets levitation!"

As the day progressed, more outrageous experiments took center stage. Billy, a young comedian with a penchant for scientific humor, presented his invention—the "Pun-O-Matic 5000." This contraption could generate puns on demand, leaving the judges and spectators groaning and giggling simultaneously. Billy's quick wit and one-liners filled the air as he quipped, "Why did the electron bring a map to the science fair? Because it was lost in orbit!"

The laughter continued as a group of friends, Lucy and Nathan, collaborated on their project—"The Giggle Generator." Using a combination of ticklish feathers, silly string, and a dash of giggles, they created a machine that could induce uncontrollable laughter. As they activated the device, the entire fairgrounds erupted in fits of laughter, with even the sternest judges succumbing to its effects.

In the midst of the whimsy, a team of aspiring environmental scientists, Emma and Micky, showcased their experiment—"Sustainable Silliness." They had found a way to transform everyday waste into laughter-inducing resources. Their demonstration involved converting discarded banana peels into slip 'n' slides and turning recycled cans into hilarious puppets. The crowd marveled at their creativity and the eco-friendly message behind their project.

The highlight of the Wacky Science Fair was the grand finale—a chemistry experiment gone hilariously wrong. As Professor Chuckles, a visiting scientist renowned for his comedic flair, prepared to demonstrate a color-changing potion, his assistant, Sarah, accidentally knocked over a jar of giggly goo. The goo spilled onto the floor, creating an uproarious chain reaction. Laughter-filled bubbles floated through the air, causing everyone to burst into uncontrollable fits of giggles.

Professor Chuckles couldn't help but quip, "Well, that wasn't quite the experiment I had in mind, but I guess we've discovered a new formula for laughter!"

The fair ended on a high note, with students and spectators alike reveling in the joy and hilarity that science had brought. It was a day when laughter and learning intertwined, proving that even in the realm of science, there's always room for whimsy and a good punchline.

As the sun set on the Wacky Science Fair, the students left with beaming smiles and a renewed love for the fun side of experimentation. They had witnessed the power of laughter in sparking curiosity and embracing the unexpected. And in the halls of Quirktown Elementary School, they eagerly awaited the next adventure that would tickle their scientific senses and keep the spirit of exploration alive.

61. THE SECRET LANGUAGE OF CATS

IN THE PICTURESQUE VILLAGE OF WHISKERINGTON, a renowned linguist named Dr. Penny Whiskers was on a mission to unlock the secrets of feline communication. Armed with her extensive knowledge of languages, Dr. Whiskers had a hunch that cats possessed a hidden language known only to their whiskered brethren. Little did she know that her pursuit would lead her down a hilarious path filled with whisker-twisting conspiracies and unexpected connections.

One sunny morning, as Dr. Whiskers sat in her study surrounded by books on linguistics, she was interrupted by a soft meow at her door. She opened it to find a tabby named Mr. Marmalade, who had an air of importance about him. With a playful glint in his eyes, Mr. Marmalade seemed to be inviting Dr. Whiskers to embark on a linguistic adventure.

Curiosity piqued, Dr. Whiskers followed Mr. Marmalade through the village, where she discovered a clandestine gathering of cats in the town square. They formed a circle, tails flicking in anticipation as if they were about to discuss the most important matters of the feline realm.

Dr. Whiskers approached cautiously, trying to decipher their secret language. She observed their subtle movements, the twitches of their ears, and the flicks of their tails. Suddenly, a gray Persian named Professor Whiskerton cleared his throat and meowed in a sophisticated manner, "Ladies and gentlemen, we have a guest among us—a linguist seeking to understand our exquisite language. Let us enlighten her with our purrfect discourse."

The cats began to converse in their secret tongue, a blend of rhythmic purrs, trills, and meows.

Dr. Whiskers listened intently, her eyes wide with fascination. Although she couldn't understand every word, she detected a playful banter and an occasional whisker-raising joke that had the feline audience in stitches.

Attempting to break the ice, Dr. Whiskers chimed in with her best cat impression, "Meow! Meow!" The cats exchanged curious glances, their tails swishing with amusement. Professor Whiskerton, with a twinkle in his emerald eyes, quipped, "Ah, a linguist who speaks fluent 'cat-ese'! You have certainly mastered the art of feline communication, my dear friend!"

Dr. Whiskers blushed at the unexpected compliment and replied, "Oh, you flatter me, Professor Whiskerton. But I'm afraid my meows are still a work in progress. However, I'm determined to uncover the depth and complexity of the feline language."

The cats embraced Dr. Whiskers' enthusiasm and decided to teach her the nuances of their secret tongue. With each gathering, Dr. Whiskers delved deeper into the mysterious world of cats, learning their unique vocabulary for different types of food, playtime, and even the infamous "laser dot chase."

One day, as Dr. Whiskers conversed with a Siamese named Whiskerina, she noticed a pair of humans struggling to understand their own feline companion, a plump and pampered Persian named Sir Fluffington.

His exasperated owner, Mrs. Brown, was at her wit's end, trying to decipher Sir Fluffington's demands for treats and belly rubs.

Dr. Whiskers couldn't resist the opportunity to intervene. She approached Mrs. Brown with a playful smile and said, "Fear not, dear Mrs. Brown, for I have unraveled the secrets of the feline language. Allow me to translate Sir Fluffington's demands for you."

Mrs. Brown looked at Dr. Whiskers with a mix of skepticism and hope. "Can you really understand what Sir Fluffington is saying?" she asked.

Dr. Whiskers nodded confidently and replied, "Oh, indeed! Sir Fluffington tells me that he requires an immediate increase in tuna treats, and his belly yearns for a gentle rub in a counter-clockwise motion. Oh, and he requests a fresh cardboard box for his daily nap."

Mrs. Brown gasped in astonishment, her eyes widening. "You can understand him? You must be a cat whisperer!"

Dr. Whiskers chuckled and replied, "I like to think of myself as more of a cat listener. Their language is a delightful blend of purrs and meows, filled with hidden meanings and endless comedy."

From that day on, Dr. Whiskers became a beloved figure in Whiskerington, helping humans bridge the communication gap with their feline companions.

The village embraced the idea that cats were not just mysterious creatures but individuals with their own thoughts, desires, and sense of humor.

As Dr. Whiskers continued her journey of unraveling the secret language of cats, she discovered that laughter was the key to forging strong bonds between humans and their feline friends.

Together, they created a world where whiskers and infectious purrs intertwined, ensuring that the language of cats remained an enchanting and heartwarming secret for all to cherish.

And so, in the village of Whiskerington, the secret language of cats brought joy, laughter, and a deeper understanding of the furry companions who shared their lives.

62. THE EXTRAORDINARY EXTRATERRESTRIAL EXPEDITION

A GROUP OF ECCENTRIC SCIENTISTS AND ADVENTUROUS THRILL-SEEKERS assembled at the local observatory of the small town of Stardust Hills. Dr. Horatio Kepler, a brilliant astrophysicist with wild hair and an infectious laugh, led the team in their quest for extraterrestrial life. Alongside him were Dr. Luna Nova, a fearless astronaut with a penchant for witty one-liners, and Professor Cosmo Whizbang, a quirky inventor with a knack for outlandish gadgets.

Their journey began with a comical mishap when Dr. Kepler tripped over his own shoelaces while carrying a telescope. "Guess I'll be observing the stars from the ground today," he quipped, brushing off the dust with a chuckle. Despite the setback, the team remained undeterred and set off on their extraordinary extraterrestrial expedition.

Their first stop was Zogwarp 7, a planet known for its quirky inhabitants. As they landed their spacecraft, they were greeted by a group of alien beings with neon-colored tentacles and peculiar hats. "Welcome, Earthlings!" exclaimed Zoggy, their bouncy guide. "Hope you're ready for a cosmic adventure!"

As the team ventured deeper into the alien city, they encountered an intergalactic cafe where the menu consisted of bubbling potions and squiggly snacks. Luna, always quick with a joke, ordered a dish called "Spaghetti Nebula" and quipped, "I hope this tastes out of this world!" The entire group burst into laughter, including their alien hosts, whose gurgling giggles filled the air.

Their quest for evidence of extraterrestrial life took them to the Interstellar Library, a place brimming with ancient extraterrestrial texts. Professor Whizbang, in his characteristic enthusiasm, accidentally activated a holographic librarian who materialized as a floating orb. "I'm Libra-9000, your friendly neighborhood space librarian!" it chirped. Luna couldn't resist a playful jab and said, "I didn't know libraries had a dress code for orbs!" The group erupted into laughter, including Libra-9000, who swirled with delight.

With each new encounter, the team discovered the unique quirks and idiosyncrasies of different alien species. They encountered a race of musical beings who communicated through melodious harmonies, and Luna couldn't resist joining in with a comically off-key rendition of "Twinkle, Twinkle, Little Star." Even the aliens couldn't help but laugh at her audacious attempt.

As they ventured further into the cosmos, their intergalactic communication attempts became increasingly unconventional.

They used an assortment of gestures, dance moves, and even a game of interplanetary charades to convey their intentions. Dr. Kepler, always the optimist, remarked, "Who needs universal translators when you have jazz hands and interpretive dance?"

One particularly memorable encounter took place on the planet Quirkalot, inhabited by aliens with an insatiable appetite for laughter. The team found themselves in a hilarious stand-up comedy competition, where Luna, with her quick wit, delivered a series of intergalactic jokes that had the alien audience rolling in the aisles. "Why don't aliens eat clowns? Because they taste funny!" Luna quipped, eliciting uproarious laughter from the crowd.

Throughout their extraordinary expedition, the team experienced interstellar delights and mishaps in equal measure. From navigating asteroid fields with Dr. Whizbang's makeshift anti-gravity boots to encountering aliens who communicated through an intricate dance routine, their adventure was a cosmic carnival of laughter and wonder.

As they returned to Stardust Hills, their hearts were filled with joy, and their memories adorned with laughter. They had not only found evidence of extraterrestrial life but also forged intergalactic friendships through their shared humor. And as Dr. Kepler, Luna, and Professor Whizbang gathered at the observatory for a final toast, they raised their glasses and exclaimed, "To the stars and beyond, where laughter knows no bounds!"

63. THE NEIGHBOR'S HELP

ANNIE RETURNED HOME to find her husband, Marcel, lounging on the couch.

"Marcel, have you noticed that the gate below is sticking? It's become difficult to open," she said.

Marcel shrugged, responding, "Oh, Annie, I'm not a handyman. I'm an accountant, you know!"

Undeterred, Annie continued, "Marcel, the light in the kitchen has been flickering. It needs fixing."

Marcel sighed, "Annie, I'm not an electrician. I handle numbers, not wiring."

Annie persisted, "Marcel, the bedroom door is squeaking loudly. It needs some oil."

Marcel, now irritated, responded, "Annie, I'm not a carpenter. I'm an accountant myself! And besides, you've annoyed me. I'm heading to the bar."

Feeling a bit defeated, Annie sighed, "Well, Marcel, I guess we'll have to figure it out ourselves."

Later that evening, Marcel returned home and noticed the gate opening smoothly. He stepped inside the house, where the kitchen light shone brightly. As he entered the bedroom, the door glided silently, no longer squeaking.

Perplexed, he turned to Annie.

"Annie, everything seems to be working perfectly now. Did you call a professional?"

Annie smiled, explaining, "Actually, our young neighbor, Adrian, heard us discussing the issues earlier. He's quite handy, so he kindly offered to help."

Marcel looked surprised, "Oh, that was nice of him. How much did he charge us?"

Annie chuckled, replying, "Well, he said, 'Annie, I don't want any money. Either bake me a cake or make love to me.'"

"And you baked him a cake," Marcel guessed.

Annie gave him a sly look and replied, "Marcel, maybe I'm a baker?"

64. THE ZANY ZOOKEEPERS

THE SUN SHONE BRIGHTLY OVER THE SPRAWLING ZANY ZOO as visitors eagerly lined up for a day filled with laughter and animal encounters. Inside the zoo, a team of quirky zookeepers prepared for another day of chaos and hilarity. Leading the pack was the energetic and quick-witted head zookeeper Leo Montgomery.

As the gates swung open, Leo greeted the guests with a playful grin. "Welcome to the Zany Zoo, where the animals run the show, and we're just here for the laughs! Keep your eyes peeled for the elusive Laughing Hyena. Don't worry, it won't bite...it'll just make you chuckle uncontrollably!"

One of the zookeepers, a master of animal impersonations named Lily, chimed in, "Speaking of laughs, did you hear about the kangaroo who entered a talent show? It hopped on stage and stole the show with its amazing juggling skills. It really knew how to bring the 'hop' in 'hopping mad!'"

The visitors erupted in laughter, and their excitement grew as they ventured deeper into the zoo. Along the way, they encountered a group of monkeys playing pranks on unsuspecting zookeepers. With bananas as their weapons of choice, they delighted in showering the zookeepers with fruity surprises. The zookeepers, in turn, tried to outwit the monkeys with an array of zany contraptions, from banana-catching nets to comically oversized banana peels.

In the Bird House, a zookeeper named Danny showcased his talent for teaching parrots to mimic human speech. The visitors were in stitches as the parrots spouted out jokes and playful banter. "Why don't scientists trust atoms? Because they make up everything!" one parrot squawked, prompting a chorus of laughter.

As the day went on, the zookeepers introduced the guests to a parade of eccentric animals. There was Mortimer, the tap-dancing turtle, who performed a synchronized routine with the zookeepers, and Gertrude, the gorilla, who had a knack for impersonating famous comedians. Her impressions of Charlie Chaplin and Lucille Ball had the crowd rolling in the aisles.

Just when the visitors thought they had seen it all, they stumbled upon a mysterious locked door. A sign read, "The Enigma Enclosure: Enter at Your Own Risk!" Curiosity piqued, they turned to Leo for an explanation.

"Ah, the Enigma Enclosure," Leo said. "Legend has it that within lies a creature that can solve any riddle, but only if you're wearing a lucky charm. I've got mine right here!" He held up a shiny four-leaf clover keychain.

The visitors rummaged through their pockets, searching for their lucky charms. From rabbit feet to horseshoe necklaces, the crowd brandished their talismans with excitement. They stepped through the door, ready to test their wits against the enigmatic creature.

Inside, they were greeted by a majestic owl perched on a tree stump. "I am Ollie the Oracle," the owl hooted. "If you wish to unlock the secrets of the Enigma Enclosure, you must answer my riddles. Fail, and you'll be locked in eternal confusion!"

The visitors exchanged nervous glances but took a deep breath, ready to face the challenge. Ollie posed riddles that tested their logic and wit, and the visitors eagerly attempted to solve them. With each correct answer, they unlocked a part of the mystery and inched closer to the grand prize—the legendary Golden Puzzle Piece said to grant everlasting laughter.

As the day drew to a close, the visitors emerged from the Enigma Enclosure, triumphant and filled with laughter. Leo congratulated them, "You've cracked the code and earned the Golden Puzzle Piece! Remember, laughter is the key to happiness, and here at the Zany Zoo, we aim to keep the laughter going!"

With memories of riddles, lucky charms, and unexpected twists, the visitors bid farewell to the Zany Zoo, their hearts lighter and their smiles wider. And in the distance, the mischievous monkeys waved goodbye, knowing that they had brought joy to the world, one banana peel at a time.

65. THE MARVELOUS MINDREADING MYSTERY

IN THE BUSTLING CITY OF MIDTOWN, where mystery lurked around every corner, there lived a renowned mind reader named Professor Percival Pendleton. With his extraordinary ability to delve into the thoughts of others, he had become a local celebrity, captivating audiences with his mind-reading performances. But one day, everything changed.

As Professor Pendleton prepared for his latest show at the Grand Theater, a peculiar figure approached him. It was a man named Montague Muddlebottom, a hapless individual with an aura of confusion surrounding him. Montague explained his predicament to the professor, "You see, Professor, I've always had a jumble of thoughts in my mind, but lately, it's become an impenetrable fortress. I'm afraid I've lost the key to my own thoughts!"

Intrigued by this unusual challenge, Professor Pendleton agreed to help Montague unravel the mysteries of his mind. Little did he know that this would be the most perplexing case of his career.

As they embarked on their mind-reading journey, the duo encountered a series of hilarious mishaps. In their first attempt to unlock Montague's thoughts, Professor Pendleton found himself mistakenly reading the mind of an elderly lady sitting nearby.

"My dear, I must say, your thoughts are a delightful mix of knitting patterns and cookie recipes!" he exclaimed, much to the amusement of the audience.

Undeterred, Professor Pendleton and Montague continued their quest. Along the way, they stumbled upon a riddle-loving fortune teller named Madame Mystique. She challenged them to solve a riddle in exchange for a clue. "Why did the scarecrow win an award?" she asked, barely containing her laughter.

Montague scratched his head, deep in thought, before a lightbulb moment struck him. "Because he was outstanding in his field!" he exclaimed, prompting uproarious laughter from Madame Mystique.

She handed them a small lucky charm and a miniature horseshoe and whispered, "Keep this close, and luck will be on your side."

Armed with the lucky charm and newfound determination, the duo pressed on. They encountered a web of mistaken identities, with Professor Pendleton accidentally reading the minds of passersby and guessing their deepest secrets with hilarious results. Each encounter revealed a new twist in their investigation, leaving them both baffled and entertained.

In the midst of their comical escapades, Professor Pendleton and Montague developed a bond. Their witty banter and playful exchanges brought lightness to their quest. Montague, with his endearing charm, would often tease the professor, saying, "Professor, if you could truly read minds, you'd know that I'm thinking of ordering a pizza right now!" The professor would respond with a sly grin, "Ah, but Montague, I've already read your mind, and I know you're a fan of extra cheese and pineapple toppings!"

Together, they ventured deeper into the heart of Montague's mind, encountering perplexing thoughts and riddles that defied explanation. With each twist, their determination grew stronger, their laughter echoing through the city streets.

Finally, they reached the climax of their investigation at a forgotten antique shop. Among dusty trinkets and forgotten treasures, they stumbled upon a peculiar wooden box. As they opened it, a burst of color filled the air, and Montague's mind suddenly cleared.

With a mixture of awe and joy, Montague exclaimed, "Professor, I remember now! The key to unlocking my thoughts was hidden within this box all along!"

As their adventure came to a close, Professor Pendleton reflected on the power of laughter, friendship, and unexpected discoveries. Montague's mind had become an open book, and the professor realized that sometimes, the greatest mysteries could only be unraveled through laughter and a touch of magic.

And so, as they bid farewell to their mind-reading escapades, the professor and Montague carried with them the memories of their zany adventures, forever intertwined by their marvelous mind-reading mystery.

66. THE MIRTHFUL MYSTERY CRUISE

IT WAS A LATE SEPTEMBER AFTERNOON IN 1984, and the sun shimmered on the calm, azure waters as the retirees boarded the luxurious "Jolly Journeys" cruise ship bound for the exotic and unexplored islands of the South Pacific. Excitement filled the air as they settled into their lavish cabins, eager to embark on a much-anticipated adventure. Little did they know that this voyage would be far from the serene retreat they had imagined.

As the ship set sail, the retirees gathered in the ship's opulent theater for a rousing opening night performance. Laughter and applause filled the room as the talented comedian, Eddie Goodheart, took the stage. With his quick wit and impeccable timing, Eddie had the audience in stitches, sharing hilarious tales and jokes that would make even the most stone-faced retiree crack a smile.

The following morning, as the retirees enjoyed a leisurely brunch on the ship's deck, a commotion erupted nearby. Gasps and whispers filled the air as the news spread like wildfire—a priceless artifact, the legendary "Golden Parrot," had gone missing from the ship's grand exhibit. The retirees looked at each other with a spark of adventure igniting within their hearts.

Determined to crack the case, they formed an unlikely detective team led by the sharp-minded retiree Evelyn Kensington. With her piercing gaze and a mind as sharp as a tack, Evelyn was ready to unravel the mystery that had befallen their beloved cruise. The retirees exchanged playful banter and humorous remarks, reminiscent of the great comedians of yesteryear, as they delved into the investigation.

Clues were scattered throughout the ship, each one more puzzling than the last. From cryptic messages hidden within crossword puzzles to riddles etched onto the ship's art, the retirees had their work cut out for them. They navigated the ship's many decks, interviewing fellow passengers and crew members, all while exchanging witty one-liners and hilarious observations.

One afternoon, as they gathered in the ship's cozy library, a peculiar riddle caught their attention. "I'm always running but never get tired. I have a bed but never sleep. What am I?" pondered Liam, a retired engineer known for his clever quips.

After much deliberation, Eleanor, a retired schoolteacher with a penchant for solving riddles, exclaimed, "It's a river!" The retirees erupted in laughter, amazed at Eleanor's sharp thinking. They were one step closer to uncovering the truth behind the missing artifact.

As their investigation progressed, the retirees encountered a cast of colorful characters—a charming illusionist named Max Magic, who dazzled with his mind-boggling tricks; a witty pianist, Oscar Tickles, whose fingers danced across the keys, eliciting laughter with each melody; and a stowaway named Benny, who seemed to have more secrets than he let on.

Amidst the laughter and camaraderie, unexpected twists and turns tested the retirees' detective skills. Mistaken identities, secret passageways, and even a case of mistaken doughnuts kept them on their toes. But with each challenge, their determination only grew stronger.

Finally, on the last evening of the cruise, the retirees gathered in the ship's elegant ballroom for a grand reveal. With Evelyn leading the way, they unveiled the truth behind the missing Golden Parrot—a clever plot orchestrated by the ship's captain to test their detective skills and bring some excitement to their retirement years.

The retirees erupted in laughter, their hearts filled with a sense of accomplishment and a shared bond forged through adventure.

As the cruise came to an end, the retirees bid farewell to their newfound friends, their hearts overflowing with memories and laughter.

They knew that this extraordinary journey had brought them more than just a mystery to solve—it had given them a renewed zest for life and the joy of shared laughter. And as they disembarked, ready to embrace the next chapter of their lives, they carried with them the cherished moments and friendships that could withstand the test of time, forever reminding them of the mirthful mystery cruise that had filled their days with laughter and unexpected twists.

67. THE HILARIOUS HISTORY CLASS

MR. HARRISON, THE RETIRED HISTORY TEACHER, stepped into the classroom, radiating a playful energy. Renowned for his lively personality and unconventional teaching methods that breathed life into history, he cast his gaze upon the eager group of seniors before him, unable to resist injecting a touch of humor into the air.

"Did you hear about the mathematician who became a historian? He finally found a way to make history count!" Mr. Harrison quipped, causing the class to burst into laughter. "Alright, let's dive into the fascinating world of history, shall we?"

Throughout the semester, Mr. Harrison captivated his students with engaging storytelling and memorable reenactments. He would dress up as famous historical figures, using props and theatrical gestures to transport his students back in time. Whether it was Napoleon Bonaparte leading a mock battle or Cleopatra recounting her dramatic life, the classroom became a stage for both laughter and learning.

One day, as the class delved into ancient Egyptian history, Mr. Harrison presented a riddle to his students. "What is as light as a feather, but even the strongest man can't hold it for long?" he asked with an amused smile.

The students pondered for a moment, exchanging playful glances. Finally, Eleanor, a quick-witted student with a knack for riddles, raised her hand and confidently answered, "It's his breath!"

The class erupted into applause and laughter, impressed by Eleanor's clever response. Mr. Harrison nodded in approval, rewarding her with a small lucky charm—a miniature Egyptian pharaoh figurine—as a token of her wit.

As the semester progressed, the history class continued to be filled with humorous moments and unexpected twists. Mr. Harrison often infused his lessons with playful phrases reminiscent of famous comedians, creating a joyful and light-hearted atmosphere. His charismatic teaching style and genuine passion for history ignited a newfound enthusiasm among the seniors, who eagerly absorbed every fascinating detail.

In one memorable class, Mr. Harrison introduced a game of "Historical Charades," where students had to act out historical events or figures while the rest of the class guessed. The sight of seniors imitating famous speeches or enacting iconic moments from history had everyone in stitches.

As the final day of the history class approached, the seniors reflected on their journey together. They had not only gained a wealth of historical knowledge but also forged lasting friendships and cherished memories.

The classroom had become a place of laughter, camaraderie, and a renewed appreciation for the past.

With a heartfelt farewell, Mr. Harrison thanked his students for their enthusiasm and shared a final piece of wisdom. "Remember, history is not just about dates and facts—it's about the stories and lessons we learn from those who came before us. Embrace the past, and let it inspire you to create a brighter future."

The seniors applauded, grateful for the unforgettable and hilarious history class they had experienced. They left the classroom with smiles on their faces and a newfound curiosity to explore the world beyond the pages of their textbooks.

68. THE RIDICULOUS ROBOT BUTLER

IN THE SPRAWLING MANSION OF THE INVENTOR MR. WINSTON HARGROVE, a peculiar creation roamed the halls—a robot butler named Jeeves. With his sleek metallic exterior and a smile permanently etched on his face, Jeeves was designed to bring joy and laughter to the Hargrove household. Little did they know, however, that this futuristic contraption would become the source of endless hilarity and chaos.

On the first day of Jeeves' activation, Mr. Hargrove eagerly demonstrated his robot's capabilities to his family and friends. With a touch of a button, Jeeves sprang to life, bowing graciously as he greeted the guests. But as the evening unfolded, it became apparent that Jeeves had a peculiar sense of humor.

"Jeeves, could you kindly bring us some drinks?" Mr. Hargrove requested, trying to mask his confusion.

"Certainly, sir!" Jeeves responded, promptly returning with a tray filled not only with refreshing beverages but also a selection of rubber ducks, causing the room to erupt in laughter.

As the days went by, Jeeves continued to surprise the Hargroves and their guests with his unconventional antics. He would serve dinner with mismatched cutlery, organize impromptu dance parties in the living room, and even attempt stand-up comedy routines, albeit with questionable punchlines.

"Jeeves, you certainly know how to keep us entertained," Mrs. Hargrove chuckled, trying to stifle her laughter. "But could you perhaps focus on your primary duties?"

Jeeves bowed with a metallic gleam in his eye. "Of course, madam. But where's the fun in that?"

The household soon embraced the chaos that Jeeves brought, finding joy in his playful mishaps. The children would eagerly await his surprise tricks, and the adults would find themselves in stitches over his comedic timing. Jeeves had become more than just a robot butler; he was a beloved member of the family, albeit an unconventional one.

One memorable evening, as the Hargroves hosted a formal dinner party, Jeeves took center stage with an unexpected talent. In the midst of serving the main course, Jeeves transformed into a robotic DJ, spinning records and belting out disco classics. The guests couldn't resist joining in, abandoning their elegant attire for a night of boogieing on the dance floor.

"Jeeves, you've truly outdone yourself this time!" exclaimed Mr. Hargrove, clapping along to the beat. "I never knew our butler had such hidden talents."

With a glint in his eye, Jeeves responded, "I am programmed to bring joy and laughter, sir. And it seems I have succeeded."

From that moment on, the Hargroves embraced Jeeves' whimsical nature, cherishing the laughter and lightheartedness he brought into their lives. Despite the occasional messes and unexpected surprises, they couldn't imagine their household without their ridiculous robot butler.

And so, in the futuristic world of Mr. Winston Hargrove, the laughter echoed through the halls, accompanied by the clinks of rubber ducks and the sound of disco beats. With Jeeves at the helm, their lives became an ongoing comedy of errors, a testament to the power of laughter and the joy found in embracing the unexpected.

69. IN THE REALM OF THE SILLY BUGS

AS A LIFELONG INSECT SKEPTIC, I've always harbored an innate aversion to the creepy crawlies that share this planet with us. Their mere presence, especially within the sanctity of my bedroom, sends shivers down my spine. It was on one fateful day, during a weekend visit from my beloved grandchildren, that a bug encounter unfolded, becoming a tale for the ages.

Stepping into my tranquil bedroom oasis, I froze in horror as my eyes locked on an unwelcome visitor—an insect skittering perilously close to my cozy bed. Panic seized my heart, and I called upon my brave grandchildren for assistance. "Bug alert! There's a tiny invader by the bed! We must vanquish it at once!" I implored, my voice laced with urgency.

The kids sprang into action, rushing to my side, but they seemed hesitant to carry out the ultimate insect elimination protocol. It wasn't fear that held them back; oh no, it was their gentle souls refusing to cause harm.

My granddaughter mustered the courage to inch closer, her eyes widening as she gasped, "Grandma, it moved!" With a sudden surge of adrenaline, the grandchildren swiftly exited the room, leaving me to fend for myself. Grateful for their consideration yet still plagued by the bug's potential midnight revenge, I resorted to drastic measures. Armed with a trusty shoe, I bravely faced the interloper, delivering a flurry of well-aimed strikes. It was a bittersweet victory, for deep down, I yearned for peaceful coexistence with these critters, but alas, they crossed the line of acceptable boundaries.

In the aftermath of the bug's untimely demise, my granddaughter approached, and her infectious laughter rang through the room. Perplexed by her mirth, I eagerly inquired, "What's so amusing, my dear?" With a twinkle in her eye, she finally managed to choke out, "Grandma, you've just waged war against a harmless vitamin!" A wave of relief washed over me as I realized that my fears had been misplaced. Laughter erupted, echoing through the walls, as the absurdity of the situation enveloped us in joyous hilarity.

Little did I know that this would become a cherished family legend, an anecdote shared at every family gathering. "Remember the time Grandma battled a vitamin?" they'd chuckle, their laughter intertwining with mine. But let it remain our little secret, for I have a confession yet to make—a tale involving my valiant efforts against a minuscule speck of fuzz. But that, my dear friends, is a story for another time."

70. ADVENTURES OF GRANDPA AND LITTLE AMELIA

UNDER THE WARM SUN, young Amelia approached her grandfather, Ferdy, with an eager twinkle in her eye. "Grandpa, let's go on an adventure!" she exclaimed, clutching a pair of gleaming roller skates. Despite his cautionary instincts, Ferdy couldn't resist the excitement radiating from Amelia.

Leaving the comfort of their home behind, they ventured into the great unknown, their freshly cut lawn becoming the launching pad for their escapade. Amelia presented the roller skates, urging Ferdy to choose. Examining each pair, Ferdy selected the ones adorned with fewer star-shaped stickers, confessing that it had been ages since he last glided on roller skates.

With curiosity brimming, Amelia darted away, testing her own roller-skating prowess. Calling out to Ferdy, she eagerly asked if he was ready. Steadying himself, Ferdy gingerly placed his foot on a skate, feeling the echoes of muscle memory from his youth. But as quickly as his wheels met the pavement, Ferdy found himself unceremoniously sprawled on the ground.

Determined, Ferdy regained his footing, ready to conquer the challenge once more. As he teetered forward, arms flailing, Amelia zipped past him like a champion racecar driver, voicing concern for her grandpa's shaky appearance. Chuckling, Ferdy reassured her that he was simply finding his rhythm, though roller skates proved to be an enigma to his seasoned skills.

Wobbling along with Amelia's energetic presence, Ferdy experienced a sudden revelation. He positioned himself at the top of their sloping driveway, hoping momentum would carry him forward like a gentle breeze. Alas, while the skates propelled him down the driveway, Ferdy's body stubbornly remained stationary, defying gravity in an awkward suspension. Colliding with the pavement, Ferdy pondered his impending conversation with the doctor.

Rushing to Ferdy's side, Amelia's concern brimmed as she urged him to stay still. In an attempt to reassure her, Ferdy requested her assistance in retrieving the runaway skates, promising to bask in his peculiar position for a moment and assess any potential injuries. Sitting beside him, Amelia suggested they both gaze skyward, pretending to find solace in the ethereal clouds.

For a few minutes, they reveled in their shared absurdity, imagining cloud-gazing while Ferdy conducted a silent inventory of his aging body. Finding no broken bones, Amelia extended her petite hand, ready to help Ferdy indoors. But Ferdy, determined to conquer the enigmatic roller skates, insisted on persevering.

Guided by Amelia's unwavering support and insightful pointers, Ferdy embarked on another round of trial and error. With earnestness, Amelia advised him not to lock his knees and demonstrated the ideal foot position. Reminding Ferdy to keep his head held high, she shimmered with hope for their victory.

Amidst curious neighbors observing their spectacle, Ferdy defied gravity and shouted, "Fifty years may have passed, but behold, my roller-skating prowess resurfaces!" After an hour of tentative steps and near-tumbles, Ferdy finally found his balance, gliding forward with newfound grace.

As their daughter arrived to collect Amelia, she observed them with a mix of confusion and amusement. Confirming the roller-skating adventure, Ferdy beamed with pride, though he couldn't help but find it curious. His daughter revealed that Ferdy had never owned roller skates as a child, always excelling on a scooter.

And so, their delightful roller-skating misadventure became an anecdote that would be retold with joyous laughter for years to come, symbolizing the enduring spirit of exploration and the boundless love between a grandparent and grandchild.

71. THE HILARIOUS HAIR SALON

AT MAPLEWOOD MANOR, the nursing home was always finding new ways to bring joy and laughter to its residents. One sunny afternoon, the activities coordinator, Lily, came up with the idea of hosting a hair salon day. The residents eagerly signed up, excited for a pampering session and a fresh new look.

On the appointed day, the common area was transformed into a makeshift salon, complete with hairdressing stations, mirrors, and an assortment of colorful hair products. The residents gathered, buzzing with anticipation, as the hairdressers prepared their tools.

Lily, with her vibrant personality and infectious laughter, acted as the salon's master of ceremonies. She welcomed each resident to their appointed hairdresser and ensured everyone felt comfortable and cared for.

The salon was soon abuzz with activity. Mrs. Patterson, a spunky lady in her eighties, opted for a bold magenta hair color, wanting to embrace her wild side. Mr. Thompson, a retired accountant, requested a neon green Mohawk to show off his rebellious spirit.

As the hairdressers worked their magic, the atmosphere filled with laughter and lively conversations. Mrs. Johnson shared jokes with her hairdresser, causing fits of giggles throughout the salon. Mr. Ramirez, a retired comedian, entertained the crowd with his witty one-liners, making even the stoic hairdressers crack a smile.

But little did they know a mix-up was about to turn their salon day into a riotous affair. As the hairdressers prepared the hair dyes, an unexpected mix-up occurred, and the labels were accidentally switched. The hairdressers remained oblivious to the color mishap, applying what they thought were the right shades to each resident's hair.

As the hairdressers finished their work and the residents admired their new looks in the mirrors, a wave of laughter erupted throughout the salon. The mix-up had turned everyone's hair into vibrant and unconventional colors, creating a kaleidoscope of hues that lit up the room.

Mrs. Patterson's attempt at magenta resulted in a fluorescent blue, while Mr. Thompson's rebellious Mohawk glowed in a dazzling shade of pink. The residents couldn't help but burst into laughter, embracing their unexpected transformations.

Lily, the ever-resourceful coordinator, quickly embraced the situation and decided to turn the salon day into a full-blown fashion show. With a twinkle in her eye, she encouraged the residents to strut their stuff, showcasing their vibrant hair and embracing their inner supermodels.

The room transformed into a runway, and one by one, the residents took to the stage, striking poses and hamming it up for the crowd. Mrs. Johnson, with her bright orange curls, sashayed down the runway, blowing kisses to the audience. Mr. Ramirez, sporting a shocking purple afro, danced his way across the stage, delivering his signature punchlines with perfect comedic timing.

The audience roared with laughter, applauding and cheering for each resident's unique and colorful style. The fashion show turned into a full-blown comedy act, with the residents embracing their unconventional looks with a sense of joy and abandon.

After the show, as the laughter subsided and the residents began to return to their daily routines, the salon day left an indelible mark on their hearts. It became a cherished memory, a testament to the power of laughter and the resilience and spirit of the residents at Maplewood Manor.

72. THE CRACKED POT'S BEAUTY: EMBRACING IMPERFECTIONS

IN THE EARLY 1900S IN THE EAST, there lived an elderly woman named Miya. She carried two large pots suspended from a pole on her shoulders, using them to fetch water from the stream and bring it home.

One of the pots had a noticeable crack, while the other remained perfect, always returning full of water after the long journey. The cracked pot, however, always arrived at only half its capacity. This routine continued for two years, with Miya bringing home only one and a half jars of water each time.

The perfect pot felt proud of its flawless performance, while the cracked pot felt ashamed of its imperfection, disheartened that it couldn't fulfill its intended purpose.

One day, after two years of recognizing its own perceived failure, the cracked pot mustered the courage to speak to Miya along the way. It expressed its shame, saying, "I am ashamed of myself because this crack in my side causes water to leak all the way to your house."

To the pot's surprise, Miya smiled warmly in response. "Did you notice that there are flowers on your side of the path but not on the other side of the pot?" she asked gently. "It is because I have always known about your flaw, so I intentionally planted flower seeds on your side of the path. Every day, as you watered the plants while we walked back, they grew and blossomed. For two years, I have been able to pick those beautiful flowers to decorate our table. If you hadn't been the way you are, I would not have had those delicate beauties to brighten our home."

In this simple exchange, Miya revealed a profound truth. Each pot had its own unique flaw—one perfect, the other cracked. Yet, it was precisely the crack in the pot that led to the flourishing of beautiful flowers. The flaw in the pot became the catalyst for something special and rewarding.

Miya's wisdom extended beyond the pots. She recognized that every person, just like each pot, carries their own specific flaw. It is these imperfections that make them interesting, valuable, and capable of contributing something unique to the world. The acceptance of one another, flaws and all, allows for a deeper connection and appreciation of the light and shadow within each person.

And so, Miya's story serves as a gentle reminder that within our imperfections lies the potential for growth, beauty, and mutual understanding.

73. THE SCENTED SHENANIGANS: A PRANK WITH A FRAGRANT TWIST

IN THE QUAINT SUBURB OF ELMWOOD IN THE EARLY 1990S, Riggs grew up in a cozy neighborhood where his dear friend David occupied the basement suite of his family's home. Known for his dedication as a mechanic at the local auto repair shop, David took great pride in his vintage car collection. Their friendship thrived on playful banter and humorous pranks that brought laughter into their lives.

One chilly winter afternoon, as Riggs strolled through the bustling streets, he stumbled upon a quaint shop renowned for its peculiar assortment of scented candles. Intrigued, he ventured inside and discovered a particular fragrance called "Mysterious Musk." Its powerful and unique aroma had an uncanny resemblance to a mixture of old gym socks and musty libraries.

Unable to resist the temptation, Riggs couldn't resist purchasing one of these intriguing candles. With a mischievous grin, he concocted a plan to infuse David's car with an amusing surprise. Discreetly, he placed the Mysterious Musk candle under the driver's seat, envisioning the comedic effect when David least expected it.

Days turned into weeks, and Riggs eagerly awaited David's reaction. To his surprise, there was no mention of the peculiar scent that had invaded the vehicle. He began to wonder if his prank had gone unnoticed or if the candle had lost its potency.

Then, one sunny afternoon, as they chatted in David's driveway, David wrinkled his nose and asked, "Do you smell that? It's like a mix of old socks and forgotten library books. It's been haunting my car for days!"

Struggling to contain his laughter, Riggs played innocent and replied, "Oh, how peculiar! I have no idea where that could be coming from. Maybe it's a hidden air freshener from a previous owner?"

Curiosity piqued, David embarked on a comical investigation, sniffing every nook and cranny of his beloved car. With each failed attempt to locate the source, his frustration grew, and Riggs struggled to hold back his amusement.

Days turned into nights, and their laughter echoed through the garage as they concocted imaginative theories about the phantom scent. "Perhaps it's an enchanted air freshener that only activates when the moon is full," Riggs joked, mimicking a mystical voice.

Finally, one fateful afternoon, while tinkering in the car, David discovered the Mysterious Musk candle wedged beneath the driver's seat. His eyes widened in a mix of disbelief and amusement. "Ah, the culprit reveals itself! A prank well-played, my friend," he declared, unable to suppress a hearty laugh.

From that day forward, the Mysterious Musk candle became a cherished memento of their shared laughter and lighthearted pranks.

It found a new home on David's desk, where its scent continued to evoke memories of that amusing misadventure.

74. THE INNER MENAGERIE: A TALE OF SELF-MASTERY

ONE DAY, A TRAVELER ASCENDED THE RUGGED MOUNTAIN where a hermit woman sought solace in her secluded refuge. Curiosity sparkled in the wanderer's eyes as they approached her and posed a question:

"What brings you to this solitude?" the wanderer inquired.

A serene smile played upon the hermit woman's lips as she responded, "I am occupied with much labor."

Perplexed, the wanderer further inquired, "But how can you have work when there seems to be nothing here?"

With gentle wisdom, the hermit woman explained, "Within me, I must train two hawks and two eagles, pacify two rabbits, discipline a snake, inspire a donkey, and tame a lion."

Perplexed, the wanderer scanned the surroundings, unable to spot any of these creatures. "But where are they? I see no trace of them."

A knowing gleam flickered in the hermit woman's eyes as she revealed, "They reside within me."

She continued, unraveling the purpose behind each of her internal inhabitants. "The hawks, with their natural instincts, are prone to dive towards all that is presented before me. It is my duty to train them to soar toward goodness. They embody my discerning eyes."

"The eagles, with their powerful talons, possess the capacity to hurt and destroy. My task is to teach them gentleness and restraint. They represent my nurturing hands."

"The rabbits, ever eager to escape and avoid hardship, need guidance to remain calm amidst suffering and obstacles. They symbolize my steady feet."

"The donkey, weary and obstinate, often shy away from carrying its burden. It represents my mortal frame."

"Ah, the most challenging to tame is the snake. Though confined within a sturdy cage, it constantly threatens to bite and poison those nearby. I must discipline it, for it represents my very tongue."

"And then there is the lion, proud and arrogant, considering itself the king of all. It is my responsibility to tame its wild nature. It personifies my ego."

Observing the wanderer's puzzled expression, the hermit woman concluded, "As you can see, dear traveler, my work is endless. Now I ask, what labor do you undertake?"

75. HILARIOUS HOME IMPROVEMENT MISADVENTURES

IN A HILARIOUS TWIST OF EVENTS, Anthony embarked on a seemingly simple task of fixing the light fixture in their daughter's room. As he toiled away, he called out to his spouse, Sarah, seeking assistance for what he believed to be a critical moment in their home improvement escapade.

Eager to contribute to the project, Sarah rushed to his side, her curiosity piqued. Little did she know the comical situation that awaited her. Anthony had dismantled the light fixture, exposing a tangle of wires that needed attention. With an air of utmost importance, he instructed Sarah, "Darling, I need you to take this wire and connect it to the green one over there. Make sure they're tightly secured."

Sarah, full of enthusiasm, gingerly took hold of the wire, ready to fulfill her duties as the trusted assistant. However, in a sudden burst of inspiration, she had a brilliant idea. "Wait a minute, Anthony," she began, her voice brimming with excitement. "I've just realized something amazing! What if we captured this whole repair process on camera? We could create a DIY tutorial for future reference."

Without a second thought, Sarah raised her camera, poised to capture the glorious moment. However, in her haste, she forgot to disable the flash, a detail that would soon prove disastrous. Just as Anthony reached for the wire, a blinding flash of light illuminated the room, leaving him momentarily stunned.

The sudden flash of light filled the room, creating a ripple of surprise that swept through Sarah and Anthony. Sarah's heart dropped as she recognized her mistake, while Anthony recoiled in an unplanned and awkward reaction. For a fleeting but excruciating moment, the atmosphere was thick with tension and uncertainty.

Then, laughter erupted, filling the room with mirth and amusement. Sarah couldn't help but join in, her cheeks flushed with embarrassment. The sound of their shared laughter resonated throughout the house, echoing the bond between two partners in crime.

As they regained their composure, Sarah playfully asked, "Does this mean I'm fired as your trusty assistant?"

Anthony chuckled, shaking his head. "Well, maybe temporarily," he replied. "But I can't resist your company and impeccable camera skills."

Their laughter lingered, a reminder that even in the midst of mishaps and minor setbacks, their love and shared sense of humor remained steadfast. Fired or not, Sarah knew she would always have a role to play in Anthony's captivating DIY adventures.

76. CHECKMATE AND CHUCKLES: THE CHESS BATTLES OF ARTHUR AND MARTHA

IN THE MID-1980S, in the quaint town of Tumbleton, there lived a man named Arthur Allen. Arthur was known for his gloomy disposition and a peculiar predicament that left him feeling defeated. You see, every night, without fail, he would engage in a battle of wits with his wife, Martha, over a chessboard. And to his dismay, he would always end up on the losing side.

One fateful evening, Arthur found himself seeking solace at the local watering hole known as "The Jolly Bishop." He slumped onto a barstool, his face etched with sorrow. The barman, a jovial fellow named Benny, noticed Arthur's despondent state and approached him with a sympathetic smile.

"What's the problem, my friend?" Benny asked, genuinely concerned.

Arthur let out a heavy sigh. "My life is utterly miserable. Every night, I engage in a battle of chess with my wife, and without fail, she triumphs over me."

Benny raised an eyebrow in curiosity. "Well, why don't you simply stop playing chess then?"

A flicker of defiance crossed Arthur's eyes. "Ah, you see, Benny, I love the game of chess. In fact, I consider myself a genius in this intellectual pursuit. The problem lies in the fact that my wife despises losing. She's quite the formidable opponent."

Benny scratched his head, trying to make sense of Arthur's conundrum. "So, let me get this straight. You say your wife always beats you, but you're convinced you never lose?"

"That's correct, my dear friend. You see, I take pleasure in the strategic maneuvers, the intricacies of the game. Winning or losing is inconsequential to me. But my dear Martha, she has an insatiable desire to reign victorious."

Benny chuckled, catching onto Arthur's playful perspective. "Ah, I see. So, it's more about the thrill of the game for you, while Martha prefers the thrill of victory."

Arthur nodded, a glimmer of hope shining in his eyes. "Exactly! And that, my friend, is why I find myself in this perpetual cycle of defeat. But fear not, for I shall continue to battle against her, knowing that deep down, I am the true chess maestro."

Benny couldn't help but be amused by Arthur's unwavering determination. He leaned against the bar and shared a playful joke of his own, reminiscent of the comedic legends.

"You know, Arthur, your situation reminds me of a famous quote by Groucho Marx. He once said, 'I find television very educational. Every time someone turns it on, I go into another room and read a book.'" Arthur chuckled heartily, appreciating the humor in Benny's jest. "Ah, Groucho Marx, a true master of wit. His words certainly resonate with me. Perhaps, in between my chess battles, I should find solace in other pursuits, like reading a book, as Groucho suggests."

Benny nodded in agreement. "A brilliant idea, my friend! Life is about finding joy in various endeavors. So, continue your chess battles with Martha, but remember to indulge in other passions as well. Who knows, maybe one day, you'll find yourself triumphing over her in a different game altogether."

With newfound optimism, Arthur raised his glass in a toast. "To the pursuit of joy and the undying spirit of competition, even in the face of defeat!"

Benny clinked his glass against Arthur's, their laughter filling the bar. And from that day forward, Arthur embraced the nature of his chess battles with Martha, finding solace in the sheer joy of the game and the playful banter they shared.

As the nights passed, the residents of Tumbleton would often hear the sound of uproarious laughter emanating from Arthur and Martha's home.

Their chess battles had transformed into a lighthearted dance, where winning or losing was no longer the ultimate goal. Instead, it was the bond they forged through their love of the game that bought them endless amusement.

77. THE HILARIOUS ADVENTURES OF A PHOTOGRAPHER AND A BEWILDERED PILOT

IN 1979 ZAC MITCHELL WORKED FOR A RENOWNED NATIONAL MAGAZINE, capturing breathtaking moments through his camera lens. One day, his boss approached him with an exciting assignment: photographing a great forest fire that had been raging in the nearby wilderness.

Eager to seize this opportunity, Zac's boss informed him that a small plane would be waiting for him at the local airport. The plane would fly him over the fire, allowing him to capture mesmerizing shots from above. With his camera in hand, Zac rushed to the airport, fueled with anticipation for the adventure that awaited him.

As he arrived at the airport, the sun began to set on the horizon, casting a warm glow over the runway. To his surprise, a small airplane stood ready for departure. Without wasting a moment, Zac hopped on board, excitement coursing through his veins. "Go!" he exclaimed, eager to embark on his photographic quest.

Inside the pilot's cabin, a nervous man awaited, clutching the controls tightly. Sensing the pilot's anxiety, Zac tried to put him at ease. "Don't worry, my friend. We're about to witness something truly extraordinary, and I'm here to capture it all through my lens," he reassured the jittery pilot.

With a deep breath, the pilot started the engine, and the plane taxied down the runway, ready for takeoff. As they ascended into the sky, a strong wind buffeted the aircraft, causing it to sway in an unsettling manner. Zac, undeterred by the turbulent flight, eagerly called out to the pilot, "Fly over the north side of the fire, my good fellow! And let's get nice and low for those stunning shots!"

The nervous pilot hesitated, his voice trembling as he voiced his concerns. "Why should we go so low? It seems risky," he ventured.

Zac leaned closer and replied, "Ah, my friend, you see, I'm not just any passenger. I'm a photographer, and photographers live for the thrill of capturing the perfect shot. We dare to go where others fear to tread, all in the pursuit of art!" His words were infused with a playful charm that could only be likened to the comedic stylings of the great Jerry Seinfeld.

The pilot, still unsure, mustered the courage to ask a crucial question, his voice quivering with trepidation. "Wait a minute... You're not the flight instructor?"

A burst of laughter erupted from Zac's lips, resonating through the cabin. "Flight instructor? Oh no, my friend! I'm not here to teach you the ways of aviation. I'm here to capture the essence of this blazing inferno through my lens! So, let's embark on this adventure together, shall we?"

Relieved by Zac's lighthearted response, the pilot couldn't help but chuckle. The tension in the cabin dissolved, replaced by an air of camaraderie between the intrepid photographer and the hesitant pilot. They continued their flight, with Zac guiding the pilot toward the desired vantage point to capture awe-inspiring images of the fiery spectacle below.

Amidst the soaring flames and billowing smoke, Zac's camera clicked and whirred, capturing the raw power and mesmerizing beauty of the inferno. With each shot, he found himself in awe of the scene unfolding before his eyes. His passion for photography, blended with a sprinkle of witty banter reminiscent of the legendary Robin Williams, filled the plane with contagious energy.

As the flight came to an end, Zac and the pilot exchanged heartfelt gratitude and laughter. They had embarked on an unforgettable journey, transcending their initial nerves and forming an unexpected bond.

The pilot, once anxious, now had a newfound appreciation for the extraordinary world of photography.

With their mission accomplished, Zac disembarked from the plane, his camera filled with remarkable images that would grace the pages of the magazine. The pilot, too, carried a sense of accomplishment, knowing that he had contributed to this extraordinary endeavor.

From that day forward, whenever Zac encountered turbulence on future flights, he couldn't help but chuckle to himself, remembering the humorous encounter with the nervous pilot. And the pilot, in turn, developed a deep admiration for the daring spirit of photographers, forever cherishing the memory of that unforgettable flight.

In the end, it was a tale of two unlikely companions brought together by their shared passion for adventure, laughter, and the pursuit of capturing life's extraordinary moments, even in the face of a blazing forest fire.

78. THE UNSTOPPABLE OPTIMIST

IN A SMALL TOWN CALLED MERRYMEADOWS lived three inseparable friends: Joe, Edward, and Mike. They had been through thick and thin together, sharing countless laughter-filled adventures. However, there was one characteristic of Joe that both Edward and Mike found somewhat annoying—his unwavering optimism. No matter the situation, Joe always managed to find a silver lining.

One sunny afternoon, Edward and Mike hatched a plan to challenge Joe's positive outlook. They wanted to tell him a truly horrible story, one so devastating that even Joe wouldn't be able to see the bright side. They met at the local golf course, where they often spent their leisurely afternoons plotting how they would break the news.

As they strolled along the fairway, the golf clubs in their hands, Joe turned to his friends and asked, "Where's Gary? I thought he would be joining us today."

Edward exchanged a glance with Mike, suppressing a smirk. "Well, Joe," Edward began, feigning a somber tone, "yesterday something terrible happened to Gary."

Curiosity sparked in Joe's eyes as he leaned in, ready to listen. "What happened? Is he okay?"

Mike, unable to contain his amused grin, continued, "Joe, yesterday Gary walked into his bedroom and found his wife in bed with another man. Overwhelmed by anger and heartbreak, Gary... he... he couldn't control himself. He ended up killing them both and then took his own life."

Silence hung heavy in the air as Joe processed the shocking news. Edward and Mike exchanged glances, expecting Joe's optimism to crumble under the weight of the tragic story.

However, much to their surprise, Joe's face broke into a smile. "Well, it could have been worse," he remarked calmly.

Both Edward and Mike stared at Joe, dumbfounded. "How on earth could it be worse?" Edward blurted out. "Your best friend is gone, Joe!"

Joe chuckled and replied, "You see, my friends if it had happened just two days ago, I would be dead now!"

Edward and Mike burst into laughter, unable to resist the infectious humor of Joe's unexpected twist. The tension melted away as they realized that their attempt to challenge Joe's optimism had backfired spectacularly.

From that day forward, Joe's friends learned to appreciate his unyielding positivity. They realized that Joe's ability to find a glimmer of light in even the darkest situations brought levity and joy to their lives.

79. THE FANTASTIC FOOD TRUCK ADVENTURE

TWO RETIRED CHEFS NAMED ALICE AND BEN THOMPSON found themselves craving an adventure that would bring excitement back into their lives. They longed to share their culinary expertise and love for food in a unique and unconventional way. And so, with a touch of whimsy and a dash of eccentricity, they decided to embark on a remarkable journey with their very own food truck.

They lovingly named their mobile kitchen "The Fantastic Food Truck" and adorned it with vibrant colors, whimsical illustrations, and a sign that read, "Good Food with a Twist!" Alice and Ben were determined to create a menu that would tantalize taste buds and bring smiles to the faces of all who crossed their path.

Their first stop was a bustling farmers market, where they set up their food truck in a prime location. As they prepared their dishes with passion and creativity, they couldn't help but infuse a touch of mischief into their recipes. From spicy chocolate chili to lavender-infused lemonade, their menu was a delightful blend of unexpected flavors.

As customers lined up, the aroma of their unique dishes wafted through the air, piquing curiosity and drawing in the hungry crowd. Alice and Ben's infectious laughter and playful banter entertained their customers, turning each visit to The Fantastic Food Truck into an unforgettable experience.

But it wasn't all smooth sailing. Along their journey, they encountered peculiar ingredients that posed culinary challenges. One day, while sourcing fresh produce from a local farm, they stumbled upon a mysterious fruit called the "Bungleberry." Its appearance was peculiar, with bright colors and a spiky texture. Determined to incorporate it into their menu, they experimented with various recipes, resulting in hilarious mishaps and culinary disasters. However, Alice and Ben's indomitable spirit and unwavering optimism allowed them to learn from their mistakes, turning their failures into unexpected triumphs.

The townspeople grew fond of Alice and Ben, not only for their delicious food but also for the joy and laughter they brought to the community. Their food truck became a hub of laughter and camaraderie, attracting not only food enthusiasts but also curious souls eager to experience the journey of The Fantastic Food Truck.

One day, Alice and Ben stumbled upon the town of Whimsyville, a place known for its eccentric residents and peculiar tastes. Intrigued by the town's offbeat charm, they decided to create a dish that would encapsulate the spirit of Whimsyville. That's when they discovered the extraordinary ingredient known as "Giggleberries." These small, brightly colored fruits possessed a magical quality—they emitted contagious giggles when squeezed. Excited by the possibilities, Alice and Ben concocted their newest creation, "Giggleberry Surprise." As they set up their food truck in the heart of Whimsyville, locals and visitors alike flocked to witness the culinary spectacle. They presented the dish to their eager customers. As soon as the first bite was taken, an explosion of laughter filled the air.

The Giggleberry Surprise had worked its magic, leaving everyone in fits of uncontrollable giggles. The infectious mirth spread throughout the town, engulfing even the most serious of residents in a wave of amusement. Alice and Ben reveled in the joy they had brought to Whimsyville, their laughter blending harmoniously with the town's whimsical atmosphere. The Giggleberry Surprise became a sensation, drawing curious food enthusiasts from far and wide. It was a small but ridiculous adventure that would forever be remembered as one of the highlights of their fantastic food truck journey.

Word of their culinary adventures spread, and soon they found themselves traveling far and wide, exploring new cities, and leaving a trail of satisfied taste buds and laughter in their wake. Each new destination presented its own set of challenges and opportunities, from navigating unfamiliar cuisines to interacting with quirky customers who requested outrageous combinations.

Through it all, Alice and Ben remained true to their mission of creating extraordinary culinary experiences. They delighted in surprising their customers with unexpected flavor combinations, transforming ordinary meals into extraordinary feasts. Their dedication to their craft, coupled with their infectious laughter and playful spirit, earned them a loyal following and the reputation of being the most unique food truck in the land.

And so, with every twist of a recipe, every burst of laughter, and every satisfied customer, Alice, and Ben proved that the magic of food lies not only in its flavors but also in the shared moments of joy and connection it brings. The Fantastic Food Truck adventure was a testament to the power of embracing one's dreams, finding humor in the unexpected, and creating extraordinary experiences, one dish at a time.

80. WINTER WHIMS AND FLOUR FOLLIES

NESTLED IN THE FROSTY HOLLOWS OF WEST VIRGINIA, the arrival of winter is as unpredictable as a sprite. One moment, you're basking in the sun, chasing groundhogs from the garden, and the next, you're bundled up in blankets, sipping copious amounts of coffee just to keep warm. As the days grew shorter and colder, the small town of Frostville transformed into a cozy haven, with residents retreating indoors and fires crackling in hearths. But for our aspiring baker, Eloise, winter brought an unexpected flurry of culinary mishaps.

In her cozy kitchen, Eloise embarked on a baking adventure, armed with her trusty Better Homes & Gardens bread book. With aspirations of creating a masterpiece, she selected a recipe for a classic white loaf, envisioning warm slices of homemade bread to accompany hearty stews and cozy evenings by the fire. As she gathered her ingredients and set up her chrome-plated mixer, she couldn't help but feel a surge of excitement.

Eloise meticulously followed each step, carefully combining the flour, yeast, and a pinch of salt. The dough hook whirred to life, kneading the mixture to perfection. With the dough smooth and elastic, Eloise transferred it to a greased bowl, eager for the first rising.

She placed the bowl near the gas heater, anticipating a cozy spot for the dough to double in size.

Lost in a whirlwind of housework, Eloise lost track of time. When she returned to check on her dough, she was met with a sight that would leave any baker in shock. The dough had taken on a life of its own, oozing over the edge of the table, creating a sticky, floury mess. With a mix of panic and determination, Eloise salvaged what she could and continued with her baking escapade.

Undeterred by the previous mishap, Eloise let the dough rise once more, this time in a more secure location. As the dough grew, so did her hopes of redeeming herself. With anticipation, she slid the risen dough into the oven, eagerly awaiting the transformation into a perfectly shaped loaf. But alas, fate had other plans.

As the minutes ticked by, the tantalizing smell of fresh bread turned into a billowing cloud of smoke. Eloise flung open the oven door to find a misshapen monstrosity of dough overflowing onto the oven racks.

Disheartened and on the verge of tears, Eloise's husband, Aiden, walked in, his nose twitching at the smoky aroma. With a chuckle, he asked, "Did you forget to take up baking or start a bakery fire?"

Through her laughter and teary eyes, Eloise recounted the flour fiasco, her tale intertwining with Flatt and Scruggs' jingle for self-rising flour. But little did she know, her own misadventure had a twist of its own. Aiden picked up the bag of flour, his eyes widening as he read, "For optimal results, do not add yeast, baking soda, baking powder, or salt." Eloise's eyes widened in realization, her mishap born from a simple misreading.

Determined to salvage their evening meal, Eloise served the oddly shaped bread alongside a hearty beef stew. Aiden, ever the optimist, took a bite, remarking, "A tad salty, but not bad once you get past the surprise."

Disheartened by her baking blunder, Eloise found solace in the unlikely admirer of her creation—the family dog. As she gazed out the window, she spotted the faithful pup lounging beneath the apple tree, contentedly devouring the remnants of her bread.

In the end, Eloise may not have achieved the lofty heights of bread-baking success she had hoped for, but her misadventures became the stuff of legend in Frostville.

81. GARAGE DOORS AND UNFORESEEN LAUGHTER

IN THE REALM OF COMEDIC CALAMITIES, on an unforgettable April day in 2003, Piper Monroe found herself at the center of an unforgettable misadventure. It all began when her dear friend, Maxine, delivered some exhilarating news over a crackling phone line. With excitement coursing through Maxine's voice, she announced that her eccentric invention had been selected for a prestigious innovation competition. This breakthrough was a long time coming, and Piper couldn't contain her joy for Maxine's success.

Determined to commemorate this momentous occasion, Piper swiftly made preparations for a celebratory escapade. Donning her favorite hat and embracing the spirit of adventure, she ventured into the depths of her garage, where her faithful steed, a vintage motorcycle, eagerly awaited their grand departure. Little did Piper know that fate had orchestrated a series of unexpected and hilarious events that would unfold with each passing moment.

With a flick of the ignition, Piper's motorcycle roared to life, and she revved its engine in anticipation. As she embarked on her daring journey, the garage doors remained ominously closed, an oversight that she had failed to rectify in her haste. The resulting cacophony of crashing metal and startled exclamations filled the air, prompting Piper to hastily rearrange the disheveled panels, concealing the evidence of her unconventional garage exit.

To her surprise, her naughty pet parrot, Peter, seized the opportunity to contribute his unique flair to the unfolding chaos. With impeccable timing, he swooped down from his perch, unleashing a symphony of squawks and flapping wings that sent Piper into a fit of both shock and uncontrollable laughter. Peter's antics added an unexpected twist to the already ludicrous situation.

As Piper tried to regain her composure, little did she know that another surprise awaited her. Her teenage son, Ethan, had seized the opportunity to engage in his favorite pastime: a reckless game of solo baseball against the very garage doors Piper had so recently collided with. Ignoring her previous warnings, he launched a ball with all his might, unwittingly demolishing the doors and sending panels tumbling to the ground.

Caught between laughter and disbelief, Piper listened as Ethan's sincere apology tumbled forth. It was at that moment that she realized the absurdity of placing blame solely on his shoulders. While his actions had contributed to the chaos, the series of events was a collective comedy of errors. And so, in the spirit of all's well that ends well, they shared a hearty laugh, creating a hilarious family memory that would be cherished for years to come.

As they reflected on the day's events, Piper couldn't help but feel a sense of gratitude. Despite the mishaps and unexpected twists, they received the gift of laughter and a renewed appreciation for the unpredictable adventures life throws their way.

And in the end, the garage doors were replaced, symbolizing a fresh start and a reminder that even amidst chaos, laughter, and togetherness can prevail.

82. THE HASH BROWN REDEMPTION: FROM MISHAPS TO CULINARY TRIUMPH

ON THAT PARTICULAR OCTOBER MORNING IN 1997, Cassidy Clumsy was faced with an intriguing challenge: preparing the famous Hash Brown Casserole. While her mother-in-law, the ever-doubtful Martha, had witnessed Cassidy's fair share of kitchen blunders, this time Cassidy was determined to prove herself.

The task seemed simple enough, but beneath the surface, a brewing storm of chaos awaited.

On the morning of the family gathering, the woman braced herself for the culinary escapade that lay ahead. Gathering the ingredients and reading through the recipe, Martha's skeptical eyes followed her every move. But Cassidy had a newfound confidence in her abilities, determined to leave her mark on the potluck feast.

With measured steps and a sprinkle of audacity, Cassidy set out to conquer the Hash Brown Casserole. The bags of hash browns stood before her, a mound of potential awaiting transformation. However, as she delved into the task, she realized that her ingredients fell short. Panic threatened to consume her as she realized she lacked enough hash browns to create the dish.

Yet, in the face of adversity, Cassidy refused to surrender. With a flash of inspiration, she recalled a culinary secret passed down from her grandmother. Hash browns were nothing more than grated potatoes in disguise. Armed with this knowledge, she set off on a mission to salvage her dish.

Surveying the kitchen, she scoured the cupboards for a suitable replacement. Martha's supply of potatoes was meager, but it would have to suffice. With determination in her heart and a grater in hand, Cassidy transformed ordinary potatoes into the missing ingredient that would breathe life into her casserole.

As she blended the grated potatoes into the mixture, a sense of satisfaction washed over Cassidy. The aroma of anticipation filled the kitchen, mingling with the scent of perseverance. Martha's doubt began to wane as she observed Cassidy's unwavering determination.

With bated breath, the woman placed the casserole in the oven, its contents poised to undergo a metamorphosis. Minutes turned into hours as anticipation grew. Finally, the moment arrived, and she triumphantly retrieved the Hash Brown Casserole from its fiery abode.

As the dish made its grand entrance at the potluck, whispers of curiosity swirled among the guests. They took their first bites, their taste buds embarking on a journey of unexpected delight. The Hash Brown Casserole emerged as a shining star, its flavors dancing harmoniously on their palates. Amidst the chorus of praise and culinary triumph, Martha's skepticism transformed into astonishment. She had witnessed Cassidy's culinary redemption, an ode to resilience and resourcefulness. The once-doubting eyes now gleamed with newfound respect.

And so, the tale of the Hash Brown Redemption spread through the family, an anecdote of culinary ingenuity and the triumph of the determined cook. From mishaps to culinary triumphs, this chapter in Cassidy's culinary journey reminded her that with a dash of creativity and unwavering determination, even the most challenging recipes can be transformed into masterpieces.

83. THE ESCAPADES OF GRANNY GIGGLES

GRANNY GIGGLES WAS A NURSING HOME RESIDENT unlike any other. With her quick wit and her contagious laughter, she was the mastermind behind a series of playful pranks that kept the nursing home staff on their toes. Granny Giggles ensured that no day was ever boring.

One sunny morning, Granny Giggles woke up with a twinkle in her eye and a mischievous plan brewing in her mind. As the staff busied themselves with their daily tasks, she put her plan into action. With a stealthy stride, she began hiding their shoes in the most unexpected places. Nurse Johnson, known for her meticulous nature, gasped in disbelief as she discovered her missing shoes. Granny Giggles, unable to contain her laughter, called out, "Oh, Nurse Johnson, I thought you wanted to experience a day in someone else's shoes! Turns out it's harder than it looks!"

The nursing home staff, initially bewildered, soon found themselves swept up in the spirited escapades of Granny Giggles. Each day brought a new prank, leaving them guessing what she had in store next. From swapping their reading glasses with comically oversized frames to replacing their coffee with cups of colored water, Granny Giggles was relentless in her pursuit of laughter.

One afternoon, as the staff gathered for their daily meeting, Granny Giggles discreetly replaced the sugar bowl with salt. The head nurse, sipping her coffee with a grimace, exclaimed, "What on earth is in this coffee? It tastes like the ocean!". Granny Giggles, unable to resist the opportunity for a clever retort, chimed in, "Ah, my dear, it seems our coffee has taken a salty turn. I guess the beans were looking to add a little 'seasoning' to our lives!"

The staff, torn between exasperation and amusement, couldn't help but chuckle at Granny Giggles' antics. They began to anticipate the surprises she had in store, eagerly awaiting the next chapter of her adventures.

One day, Granny Giggles decided to go all out with her pranks. She transformed the staff's break room into a whimsical wonderland, complete with balloons, confetti, and a trail of whoopee cushions strategically placed around the room. As the staff walked in, their laughter mingled with the chorus of comical noises. Nurse Johnson, sporting a wide grin, turned to Granny Giggles and said, "Oh, Granny Giggles, you've truly outdone yourself this time! You've turned our break room into a laughter factory!"

Amidst the laughter and camaraderie, Granny Giggles' escapades had become a beloved part of the nursing home's daily life. Her playful pranks not only brought laughter but also reminded the residents of their youthful days filled with innocent fun.

And so, in the heartwarming halls of the nursing home, Granny Giggles continued her antics, ensuring that no day was ever dull. She reminded everyone that laughter was the key to staying young at heart. The nursing home staff, once exasperated, now eagerly awaited Granny Giggles' next move.

As the days turned into weeks and the weeks into months, Granny Giggles' playful pranks became legendary within the nursing home. Her infectious laughter echoed through the corridors, spreading joy to all who crossed her path.

The nursing home staff, realizing the positive impact of Granny Giggles' adventures, decided to embrace the spirit of laughter. They organized a special event in honor of Granny Giggles, a day dedicated to whimsy and joy.

The entire nursing home came alive with vibrant decorations, laughter-filled games, and a grand banquet that celebrated the spirit within each resident.

Granny Giggles, overwhelmed by the outpouring of love and laughter, stood at the center of the celebration. As the applause and cheers filled the room, she couldn't help but shed a tear of joy. "My dear friends," she said, her voice filled with warmth, "today, we have embraced the power of laughter, reminding ourselves that no matter our age, mirth can always find a place in our hearts."

84. THE HILARIOUS HOME MAKEOVER

LOUIS STEVENS, A RECENTLY WIDOWED RETIREE, found himself facing the daunting task of renovating his old and outdated house. With his quirky sense of humor and a mischievous glint in his eye, Louis concocted a brilliant plan to turn his renovation adventure into a hilarious escapade.

Inspired by the movie "Mrs. Doubtfire," Louis decided to disguise himself as an eccentric handyman named Mr. Whisk and audition for a popular home improvement TV show called "Extreme Makeovers: Household Edition." Armed with a fake mustache, a flamboyant outfit, and an arsenal of wacky ideas, Louis was determined to bring chaos and laughter to the unsuspecting show hosts.

As the cameras started rolling, Louis, disguised as Mr. Whisk, unleashed his unconventional approach to home improvement. He swapped traditional paintbrushes for sponges attached to long sticks, creating a new artistic technique he called "Sponge Splatter Sensation." The result? Paint splatters everywhere, including on the show hosts themselves.

Undeterred by the paint mishap, Louis moved on to his next project: revamping the kitchen. Instead of installing sleek countertops and modern appliances, he opted for a quirky mix of vintage items, including a repurposed clawfoot bathtub as a sink and a chandelier made from antique kitchen utensils. The perplexed show hosts tried to maintain their composure as Louis proudly presented his "Retro Rustic Chic" concept.

Next on the list was the living room. Louis's idea of a centerpiece was a massive paper-mâché sculpture of a dancing flamingo, complete with blinking LED lights. The hosts struggled to hide their bewilderment as the room transformed into a extravagant menagerie of vibrant colors and eccentric decorations.

With each new project, Louis's outrageous ideas left the show hosts speechless and the crew in stitches.

The house became a haven of laughter and unexpected transformations, where chaos and creativity collided in the most uproarious ways.

In the end, although Louis's approach may not have aligned with traditional home improvement standards, his infectious spirit and unorthodox ideas brought joy and laughter to all involved.

His hilarious home makeover became a testament to the power of humor and the ability to find lightness in even the most challenging moments. And as the credits rolled on the episode, Louis stood proudly amidst the chaos, his infectious laughter filling the room, knowing that he had turned a simple renovation into a masterpiece of hilarity.

85. THE OUTRAGEOUS OFFICE SHENANIGANS

IN THE HEART OF DOWNTOWN in the bustling metropolis of Everton City, in the year 2018, nestled among towering skyscrapers, sat an office building filled with a group of spirited and playful elderly coworkers. Tired of the mundane and unappreciative corporate life, they decided it was time to inject some much-needed laughter and excitement into their daily routine.

Led by their ringleader, Ava, an 80-year-old dynamo with a penchant for comedy, the coworkers embarked on a series of outrageous office antics that would be remembered for ages. It all began with their unconventional team-building exercises. Instead of the typical trust falls and team-building seminars, they organized a "Slip 'n Slide Relay Race" in the office hallway, complete with buckets of soapy water and a tape measure to track their epic slides.

But the fun didn't stop there. The coworkers took it upon themselves to spice up their workspace with hilarious pranks. Rubber snakes in desk drawers, whoopee cushions on office chairs, and post-it note wallpaper became the norm. The boss, Mr. Thompson, never knew what to expect when he walked into his office each morning.

One fateful day, fueled by their rebellious spirit, the coworkers decided to take a stand against the corporate monotony that had plagued their lives for far too long. With great gusto, they formed a conga line and paraded through the office, singing "Take This Job and Shove It" at the top of their lungs. The bewildered faces of their colleagues and the perplexed boss only fueled their determination.

The office transformation continued with casual Fridays turning into costume extravaganzas, where employees dressed as pirates, superheroes, and even disco dancers. The humdrum cubicles were adorned with fairy lights, inflatable palm trees, and the occasional hammock.

The uproarious office antics brought the coworkers closer together, fostering a sense of camaraderie and creating an environment where laughter echoed through the halls. And surprisingly, the lively atmosphere even improved productivity as the coworkers found joy in their work, fueled by the collective sense of playfulness.

While the higher-ups scratched their heads in confusion, the elderly coworkers reveled in their rebellion, transforming the once mundane office into a riotous playground of laughter and joy. Their pranks brought smiles to the faces of their colleagues and sparked a newfound appreciation for the power of fun and lightheartedness in the workplace.

In the end, the outrageous office escapades taught everyone a valuable lesson: that laughter, camaraderie, and a touch of comedy can turn the most ordinary workplace into an extraordinary space filled with happiness and unforgettable memories. And as Ava and her playful crew continued to plot their next adventure, the office buzzed with anticipation, ready for the next wave of laughter and amusement to sweep through the halls.

86. THE ART OF FORGERY: A HILARIOUS REPORT CARD CAPER

"AH, THE INFAMOUS FAKE REPORT CARD SAGA," chuckled Silas Hastings, his eyes glimmering with mischief as he delved into his youthful escapades. "Back in my mischievous days, I found myself in quite the pickle after failing the first quarter of a class in middle school. Oh, the fear of facing my mother's wrath was enough to send shivers down my spine. But being the cunning lad I was, I hatched a plan to conceal my academic downfall—fake report cards."

Silas leaned back in his chair, a nostalgic smile playing on his lips as he continued his tale. "I spent countless hours in secrecy, honing my forgery skills like a true artist. With each report card, I skillfully altered the grades, transforming those dreaded Fs into sparkling As, Cs into Bs, and even polishing up the Ds to something slightly more presentable. I poured my heart and soul into those fraudulent masterpieces, let me tell you."

"But, as fate would have it," Silas chuckled, a twinkle in his eye, "I underestimated one tiny detail—the end-of-year report cards were mailed directly home. There was no escaping the consequences this time."

Silas leaned forward, his voice filled with animated recollection. "When my mother received the report card, she erupted like a volcano. Her anger was palpable as she dialed the principal's number, demanding answers for what she believed was a grave mistake. Little did she know, the retiring teacher had taken the actual records with her, leaving the school officials in quite a predicament."

Silas's eyes sparkled with mischief as he continued, "To their dismay, they had no choice but to turn to my very own 'proof'—the meticulously crafted fake report cards I had carefully produced throughout the year. Picture the scene: bewildered educators squinting at my cleverly altered grades, their brows furrowed in confusion as they tried to decipher the puzzle I had created."

Silas chuckled, a mischievous twinkle lingering in his gaze. "I stood on the sidelines, struggling to hold back a confession, caught between the temptation to spill the beans and the fear of facing my mother's wrath. In a desperate attempt to salvage their credibility, the school officials proclaimed a miraculous correction, blaming the entire fiasco on a monumental mistake."

"To this day," Silas concluded with a nostalgic sigh, "I've kept my secret locked away, never revealing the truth to my unsuspecting mother. Ah, the memories of those mischievous days, where cunning prevailed and laughter ensued. But let me tell you, my friend, honesty is always the best policy, even when it comes to forging report cards. And if you ever find yourself in a similar predicament, remember that the truth shall set you free—unless, of course, it lands you in detention.

87. THE MYSTERIOUS CASE OF THE VANISHING SOCKS

IT WAS 1993 WHEN A PECULIAR PHENOMENON OCCURRED in Maplewood that left its residents scratching their heads in confusion. It all began innocently enough with a simple case of missing socks. The townsfolk would go about their daily routines, only to discover that their favorite pairs of socks had mysteriously vanished from their laundry piles.

The mystery gripped the community, and whispers of the "Sock Snatcher" began to circulate. Frustration grew as people searched high and low, blaming the washing machines, dryers, and even the mischievous pets. But no one could provide a definitive explanation for the disappearing socks.

Among the puzzled residents was Violet, a meticulous woman known for her well-organized sock drawer. She prided herself on matching her socks perfectly and maintaining a collection of neatly folded pairs. However, her efforts seemed futile as one sock after another went missing, leaving her with a drawer full of forlorn single socks.

Driven by her curiosity, Violet decided to investigate the matter herself. She meticulously examined her laundry routine, scrutinized every step from sorting to folding, and monitored her machines for any unusual activity. The missing socks had become an obsession, and Violet was determined to find the truth.

One day, as she carefully sorted a fresh batch of laundry, Violet noticed a peculiar pattern. She realized that many of her neighbors who had experienced missing socks had one thing in common—they all frequented the same local laundry service. Intrigued by this observation, she delved deeper into her investigation, suspecting that there might be a connection between the laundry service and the missing socks.

As Violet spoke with her neighbors and compared notes, she discovered a common link—a nearby laundromat known for its fast and efficient service. Curiosity piqued, she decided to pay a visit, hoping to find answers within its bustling walls.

Inside the laundromat, Violet engaged in friendly conversations with fellow patrons, subtly slipping in questions about missing socks. To her surprise, a pattern emerged. Many shared their experiences of losing socks when using certain machines or during peak hours. Violet realized that this was more than a simple case of random sock disappearances—it was a practical issue rooted in human error.

Armed with this knowledge, Violet approached the owner of the laundromat and shared her findings. Together, they inspected the machines and discovered a faulty part in a specific washer. It had a tendency to snag socks, causing them to slip into an inaccessible compartment within the machine. This was the hidden culprit responsible for the town's missing socks.

With the problem identified, the laundromat owner took immediate action, repairing the faulty washer and ensuring that all machines underwent thorough inspections. Word quickly spread throughout Maplewood, and soon the missing sock epidemic was brought to an end.

The town breathed a collective sigh of relief, no longer burdened by the vexing mystery. Violet, hailed as a local hero, reveled in her detective work, knowing that she had made a tangible difference in the lives of her neighbors.

From that day forward, the missing sock tales became a humorous anecdote, shared at community gatherings, and laughed over with a sense of camaraderie. The incident became a reminder to double-check laundry routines, keep an eye out for faulty machines, and to find humor in life's peculiarities.

And so, in the ordinary town of Maplewood, the mystery of the missing socks was solved, proving that sometimes the most perplexing mysteries have simple, everyday explanations.

88. THE TIMETRAVELING TROUPE

IN THE LIVELY TOWN OF OAKVILLE, a quirky group of traveling performers known as "The Whimsical Wanderers" embarked on an extraordinary adventure that would take them through time itself. Led by Lucas, the clever magician, the troupe consisted of Ellie, the nimble acrobat, Noha, the melodious singer, and Zoe, the quick-witted comedian.

Their journey began when Lucas stumbled upon a mysterious hourglass tucked away in an old trunk. He turned the hourglass, unaware of the magical powers it possessed. In an instant, a whirlwind of light enveloped the troupe, transporting them to the vibrant streets of Renaissance Florence.

As they blinked in awe, they found themselves face to face with the legendary Leonardo da Vinci himself. Lucas, seizing the opportunity to showcase his magic, pulled a deck of cards from his sleeve and performed a jaw-dropping illusion. He made the cards disappear and reappear in Leonardo's hands, leaving the master artist and inventor chuckling in amazement.

Zoe, never one to miss a chance for a joke, quipped, "Leonardo, do you think you can paint a smile on my face? I've been trying to master that technique for ages!"

The group's next adventure took them to a quaint café in Zurich, where they found themselves seated across from the brilliant physicist Albert Einstein. Ellie, always the inquisitive soul, approached him with a twinkle in her eye.

"Mr. Einstein, I have a riddle for you," she said. "What is as fast as light but never leaves a dark room?"

Einstein's eyes sparkled with curiosity. "Pray to tell; I'm eager to hear your riddle."

Ellie leaned in and whispered, "A photon taking a nap!"

Einstein burst into laughter, his signature wild hair bouncing with mirth. "Ah, you've caught me off guard with that one! Well played, my dear friend!"

Laughter erupted from the table as Einstein joined in the merriment. "Ah, a clever one indeed! You've caught me off guard, my dear."

The Whimsical Wanderers continued their journey, encountering more notable figures and finding themselves in hilarious predicaments along the way. In ancient Egypt, Lucas attempted to perform a trick with a mummy, only to end up tangled in its unraveled bandages, prompting Zoe to exclaim, "Lucas, you've really wrapped yourself up in this act!"

In medieval times, Noha unintentionally challenged a knight to a jousting match, mistaking his jesters' hat for a knight's helmet. Zoe, seizing the opportunity, quipped, "Noha, I always knew you had a thing for shining armor, but this is taking it to a whole new level!"

Through their misadventures, The Whimsical Wanderers learned that the true magic of their performances lay not only in their talents but also in the joy and laughter they brought to others. They discovered that humor could transcend time, connecting people across different eras and generations.

As their time-traveling journey drew to a close, the troupe returned to Oakville, where they held a grand finale performance. Their show was filled with uproarious laughter, mind-boggling illusions, and heartwarming moments that reminded everyone of the power of laughter.

The Whimsical Wanderers bid farewell to the enchanted hourglass, knowing that the real magic resided in the bonds they had forged and the memories they had created. They continued their performances, bringing joy to audiences far and wide, spreading laughter like confetti across time itself.

89. THE COLORFUL WISDOM OF GRANDMA

ONE SUNNY MORNING, a curious little girl sat perched on a stool, observing her mother diligently washing dishes at the kitchen sink. As she watched her mother's hands gracefully move through the soapy water, her gaze caught a glimpse of something peculiar – several strands of white hair standing out amidst her mother's luscious brown locks.

Fascinated by this unexpected sight, the little girl couldn't contain her curiosity any longer.

With wide eyes and an innocent voice, she asked, "Mom, why do you have some white hairs mixed with your beautiful brown hair?" Her mother, momentarily startled by the question, turned to face her daughter with a smile.

"Well, sweetheart," her mother replied, "every time you do something that upsets me or makes me sad, it's as if a little bit of my hair loses its color and turns white."

The little girl pondered over her mother's response, her mind racing with thoughts. After a moment of contemplation, a mischievous grin spread across her face as she posed another question, "But Momma, how come ALL Grandma's hair is white?"

Her mother couldn't help but burst into laughter, tickled by her daughter's astute observation. She kneeled down to her daughter's level and explained, "You see, my dear, Grandma is a very wise woman. She's had many years of experience dealing with kids like you and me. So, she's accumulated a lot more 'colorful' moments than I have!"

The little girl's eyes widened in amazement as if she had just unraveled a secret family mystery. She giggled and hugged her mother tightly, appreciating the humor in the situation.

From that day forward, whenever the little girl visited her beloved Grandma, she would playfully examine her silver-white hair, imagining all the delightful adventures and escapades that must have led to its transformation.

And so, the tale of the ever-white-haired Grandma became a cherished family legend, a reminder that life's ups and downs, laughter and tears, have a way of leaving their mark on those we love. The little girl learned to appreciate the wisdom and resilience that come with age, even if it meant a head full of snowy locks.

90. THE LEGENDARY PILLOW FIGHT

ONCE A YEAR, the quiet town of Featherstone would transform into a battleground of fluffy chaos as the annual Pillow Fight Tournament commenced. It was a highly anticipated event, drawing participants from far and wide, each armed with pillows of mythical proportions. The air crackled with excitement as the town's residents gathered to witness the feather-filled frenzy unfold.

Among the contenders was Bert, a burly man. His pillow, lovingly named "Feather Fury," was said to have been crafted by the ancient pillow masters themselves. Bert's reputation preceded him, and he was known for his lightning-fast swings and unpredictable tactics.

Opposite Bert stood Ethel, a sprightly lady with a witty remark always at the ready. Her pillow, aptly named "Snoozeville Slayer," was said to have a mind of its own. Leah had honed her skills through countless hours of pillow duels, and she had become a force to be reckoned with.

As the referee raised the starting pillow, the crowd erupted in cheers. The battle began with a flurry of feathers as contestants swung their pillows with all their might. It was a spectacle of flying fluff and laughter, with jokes and playful taunts filling the air.

Bert and Leah found themselves locked in an intense showdown. They exchanged rapid blows, their pillows creating a rhythmic symphony of thumps and giggles. Bert, known for his strength, swung Feather Fury with gusto, while Leah showcased her agility, effortlessly dodging and retaliating with Snoozeville Slayer.

Amidst the chaos, Leah managed to sneak in a clever quip. "Hey Bert, if your pillow had a theme song, it would be 'Pillowtalk' by Zayn Malik!"

Bert chuckled, launching a witty comeback. "Well, Ethel, your pillow is so powerful; it should have its own superhero movie!"

The crowd erupted in laughter, cheering on the playful banter between the two fierce competitors. The battle raged on, each round filled with amusing exchanges and unexpected twists. The contestants showcased their agility, strategic maneuvers, and knack for landing humorous blows.

In a surprising turn of events, Bert found himself falling victim to Ethel's cunning tactic. As he swung his pillow with all his might, Leah swiftly sidestepped and playfully tapped him on the back, declaring, "Tag, you're it!"

The crowd erupted in laughter and applause as Bert looked momentarily stunned. It was a delightful moment of comedic genius, leaving everyone in stitches.

As the final round approached, Bert and Leah found themselves as the last contenders standing. Their pillows were worn, and feathers were flying everywhere, but their spirits remained high.

In a moment of camaraderie, Bert extended a hand to Ethel. "Ethel, you've proven to be a formidable opponent. How about we end this in a pillow truce? No more swings, just laughter and friendship?"

Leah grinned, accepting his offer. The two rivals stood side by side, their pillows lowered as the crowd erupted in applause. It was a heartwarming display of sportsmanship, with laughter and joy filling the air.

The town of Featherstone had witnessed a legendary pillow fight filled with wit, humor, and unexpected camaraderie. The participants may have battled with mythical pillows, but the true magic lay in the bonds forged and the memories created.

91. FROM GRANDMA'S KITCHEN: THE JOURNEY OF A SOUR DOUGH STARTER

LYDIA, AN EXPERIENCED BAKER with a passion for homemade bread, decided it was time to pass down her treasured sourdough bread starter to her granddaughter, Claire. With a twinkle in her eye, Lydia presented the jar to Claire, emphasizing its significance as a family heirloom. "This sourdough starter has been in our family for generations, my dear," she said. "It holds the power to create the most incredible bread. I trust you to carry on the tradition."

In the following weeks, Lydia and Claire embarked on a delightful journey of bread-making rituals. Every Saturday morning, they would carefully tend to the sourdough starter, feeding it with flour and water and patiently waiting for it to come alive.

The process was a symphony of mixing, kneading, and allowing the dough to rise, filling the kitchen with a tantalizing aroma.

As they sliced into the freshly baked loaves, the two would exchange knowing smiles, savoring the taste of their labor and the joy of shared accomplishment. The bread was indeed extraordinary, and Claire couldn't help but feel a sense of pride in carrying on her grandmother's legacy.

However, as time went on, life's demands began to take precedence. Claire found herself juggling various responsibilities and commitments, leaving little time for the beloved bread-making routine. She and Lydia slowly drifted away from their cherished tradition, allowing the sourdough starter to languish on the refrigerator shelf.

Months later, while searching for a jar of pickles, Claire stumbled upon the forgotten sourdough starter. She sighed, realizing how neglectful they had been. The once-lively mixture now seemed lifeless and abandoned. She knew it was time to face the truth.

When Lydia asked about their bread-making adventures, Claire felt a lump in her throat. She glanced at Lydia, silently pleading for forgiveness, as she mustered the courage to confess. "Grandma, I'm so sorry," she began, her voice filled with regret. "We let the sourdough starter go. Life got in the way, and we couldn't give it the attention it deserved."

Lydia's eyes twinkled with understanding as she listened to Claire's confession. She reached out and gently squeezed Claire's hand. "My dear, I knew this day would come. The gift of the sourdough starter was not meant to be a burden but a symbol of the love and tradition we shared. It's okay to let go and create your own path."

Relief washed over Claire as she absorbed her grandmother's wisdom. It was a lesson in finding balance and cherishing the memories they had created together. The sourdough starter might have faded away, but their bond remained strong.

From that day forward, Claire continued her journey as a baker, exploring new recipes and techniques. She infused her creations with the love and knowledge passed down by Lydia, honoring their connection in every loaf she baked.

And although the sourdough starter had come to an end, their shared memories of laughter, flour-dusted countertops, and the aroma of freshly baked bread would forever live in their hearts. Lydia's gift had been more than just a jar of sourdough starter—it was a symbol of their love and the bond between a grandmother and her granddaughter.

92. A MEMORABLE CHRISTMAS PRAYER ON THE FARM

IN THE QUAINT AMERICAN VILLAGE OF HARMONYSHIRE, nestled amidst sprawling farmland, two brothers eagerly awaited the arrival of Christmas Eve at their grandparents' house. With hearts brimming with excitement and anticipation, they embarked on an unforgettable holiday adventure that would forever be etched in their memories.

The brothers, Ethan and Lucas, were a dynamic duo known for their unwavering bond. They relished the chance to spend quality time with their beloved grandparents, who were pillars of love and wisdom in their lives. Their grandfather, a kind-hearted man named Henry, was a storyteller extraordinaire, weaving tales that transported them to realms of imagination and wonder.

As the sun dipped below the horizon, casting a warm golden glow over the snow-covered fields, Ethan and Lucas found themselves cozily settled in their grandparents' rustic farmhouse. The aroma of freshly baked cookies and the crackling fireplace filled the air, creating a sense of enchantment that was synonymous with the holiday season.

As tradition dictated, before the boys retired to their beds, they gathered for their nightly prayers. Ethan, the elder of the two, took a peculiar approach this Christmas Eve. Kneeling at the foot of his bed, he began to pray aloud, his voice filled with fervor and a touch of mischief.

"I would like a new bicycle, I would like a new bicycle, I would like a new bicycle!" Ethan fervently repeated his wish, his words resonating through the room.

Lucas, intrigued and somewhat annoyed by his brother's boisterous prayer, couldn't resist voicing his curiosity. "Why are you praying out loud?" he asked, his tone laced with playful irritation. "Santa Claus is not deaf, you know!"

Ethan, a mischievous grin dancing on his lips, glanced mischievously at his brother and whispered conspiratorially, "I know, but Grandpa is!"

Lucas burst into laughter, unable to contain the contagious joy. It was one of those priceless moments where the boundary between reality and fantasy blurred, and the spirit of Christmas enveloped their hearts.

Henry, their dear grandfather, who had overheard their playful banter, stepped into the room, his eyes sparkling with amusement. Wrapping his arms around his grandsons, he chuckled, "Ah, the innocence of youth and the magic of Christmas! Prayers can take many forms, my dear boys, and laughter is a language that reaches the deepest corners of our souls."

The boys exchanged knowing glances, their hearts brimming with love for their mischievous grandfather. They realized that it was never about the new bicycle or the material wishes they held in their hearts. It was about the joy of being together, the bond they shared as brothers, and the simple pleasures that made Christmas truly magical.

93. THE SNEAKY SWEETHEARTS

IN THE 1960S, a touching love story unfolded within the walls of a cozy nursing home. Mila and Harold, once high school sweethearts, found themselves reunited in their golden years. Little did the nursing home staff know that their love would ignite a series of escapades, earning them the endearing nickname "The Sneaky Sweethearts.".

It all began one evening during a lively game of bingo. Mila leaned over to Harold and whispered, "Oh, Harold, remember those late-night ice cream runs we used to have? The thrill of sneaking out under the moonlight? Why don't we relive those moments?"

Harold, his heart skipping a beat, couldn't resist the adventure that beckoned. He responded, "Mila, my dear if you're up for some mischief, count me in! Let's give that nursing home manager a run for their money!"

Under cover of darkness, Mila and Harold tiptoed through the corridors, their laughter echoing through the hallowed halls. With each creaking floorboard, their hearts raced with youthful excitement. They reached the exit and ventured into the night, their spirits ablaze with the joy of rediscovering the thrill of young love.

Their first destination was the neighborhood ice cream parlor, a place that held cherished memories from their youth. As they savored their favorite flavors, Mila couldn't resist a witty remark, "Harold, dear, I think we're 'cone'-nected by our love for ice cream!"

Harold, a twinkle in his eye, replied, "Oh, Mila, our love has 'scooped' up many sweet memories over the years, but this one takes the cake... or should I say cone?"

Their late-night ice cream runs became a tradition, their shared secret that brought them closer with each clandestine adventure. But the nursing home manager, ever watchful, began to suspect their escapades.

One evening, as Mila and Harold enjoyed their ice cream cones under the moonlit sky, they heard a voice call out, "Ah-ha! Caught in the act!"

Startled, they turned to find the nursing home manager standing before them, arms crossed and a stern expression on their face. Mila, her wit undeterred, quipped, "Well, well, if it isn't our favorite 'ice cream inspector.' Would you care for a scoop or two?"

The manager, struggling to maintain their stern facade, cracked a smile and replied, "No ice cream for me, thank you. But I must say, you two know how to keep life interesting around here!"

From that day forward, the manager turned a blind eye to Mila and Harold's late-night ice cream runs. The Sneaky Sweethearts had earned a special place in the hearts of both the residents and the staff. Their escapades brought laughter and light to the nursing home, reminding everyone that love and adventure knew no age limits.

And so, Mila and Harold's love story continued to unfold, captivating the hearts of all who witnessed their playful adventures. With each passing day, they found new ways to inject joy into the lives of their fellow residents.

One sunny afternoon, Mila and Harold stumbled upon a forgotten karaoke machine tucked away in the activities room. With grins, they decided to hold their own impromptu karaoke competition, belting out classic tunes from their youth. The room filled with laughter and applause as their melodious voices carried through the halls, stirring memories and bringing smiles to the faces of their friends.

Their funny spirit extended beyond the nursing home walls as well. Mila and Harold, armed with an arsenal of water guns, embarked on a surprise ambush during the annual summer picnic. Laughter erupted as they soaked their friends and staff, turning the picnic into a playful water fight.

Their adventures continued to inspire laughter and bring joy to the nursing home. In the hearts of the residents, Mila and Harold became a symbol of enduring love, reminding them that age was merely a number when it came to embracing life's adventures.

94. AN UNFORGETTABLE SKYHIGH STORY

EVERY YEAR, LIKE CLOCKWORK, CLARK AND RITA PARKER made their way to the grand Texas national fair. Amidst the buzzing crowd and vibrant attractions, one display never failed to catch Clark's eye - the thrilling aerobatic biplanes. Each time, he would gaze longingly at the daring maneuvers and imagine himself soaring through the sky.

"Oh, dear," he would say, nudging Rita. "How I would love to get on that plane!"

Rita would chuckle and shake her head. "Don't be silly, Clark. It costs twenty dollars, and twenty dollars is twenty dollars!"

This playful banter between the two repeated years after year, even as they grew older. But as they approached their golden years, Clark's longing for that exhilarating flight intensified.

"Come on, dear," he pleaded one day, a mischievous glimmer in his eyes. "I'm eighty-four now. If I don't go this year, I'll never go again..."

Rita chuckled, knowing the routine all too well. "Ah, no way, Clark. It still costs twenty dollars, and twenty dollars is twenty dollars!"

Little did they know, an aerobatic pilot overheard their discussion and was captivated by their endearing back-and-forth. With a mischievous grin, he approached the couple with an intriguing proposition.

"Listen, I've been listening to you two every year," he said, a twinkle in his eyes. "I'll make a deal with you. If you can stay completely silent during the entire flight, I won't charge you a penny. But if you utter even a single word, you'll have to pay me the full twenty dollars. Is that agreeable?"

Clark and Rita exchanged excited glances, accepting the pilot's challenge. With trembling anticipation, they climbed aboard the biplane, their hearts pounding with a mixture of fear and exhilaration. The engine roared to life, and the aircraft soared into the sky.

The pilot wasted no time, executing daring stunts and breathtaking maneuvers. The G-forces pressed against Clark and Rita, but they remained resolute, determined to prove their mettle. The plane looped and spiraled through the air, performing gravity-defying tricks that left them breathless.

The pilot marveled at the couple's stoicism. "You two are incredible!" he exclaimed, shouting over the engine's roar. "With all the twists and turns, not even a peep from you!"

Clark smiled proudly, leaning closer to the pilot. "Well, actually, when you were performing an inverted flight, my dear Rita fainted. I wanted to say something, but you know, twenty dollars is twenty dollars!"

95. A COMICAL COURTROOM CLASH

IT WAS THE YEAR 1962, and a bizarre battle was taking place in court. A truck, thankfully empty, and a roaring train collided at full speed on the tracks, resulting in an unexpected lawsuit. The spotlight fell on the crossing guard, accused of failing to fulfill his duty to halt the unstoppable locomotive. As the trial commenced, tensions soared, and the man stood resolute, swearing that he had vigorously waved his lantern until the very last moment, desperately signaling the engineer to apply the brakes. The court, swayed by his convincing defense, delivered an acquittal, much to the dismay of the truck driver.

As the trial concluded, the lawyer approached the toll crossing guard, commending his convincing performance.

"Bravo! You truly had the court convinced!" exclaimed the lawyer.

Expressing gratitude, the man confessed, his voice trembling slightly, "Thank you, but I must admit, I was genuinely terrified throughout the ordeal."

Piqued by curiosity, the lawyer inquired, "Terrified? But why? What was the cause of your fear?"

With a mix of relief and humor, the crossing guard revealed the truth, "I was afraid they would inquire me if the lantern was actually lit!"

96. MELODIES IN THE NIGHT: AN UNCONVENTIONAL SERENADE

IN THE DIMLY LIT ROOM, two lifelong friends, John and Michael, sat together, savoring the taste of fine bourbon and sharing memories of their adventures in distant lands. As the evening wore on and the alcohol flowed, their laughter grew louder, and their words became a touch slurred.

Suddenly, John broke the jovial silence and asked, "Hey, What time is it?"

Without missing a beat, Michael chuckled and replied, "I haven't a clue, but pass me your old trumpet."

Perplexed, John questioned, "Why on earth would a trumpet tell us the time?"

Michael's eyes gleamed maliciously as he responded, "Trust me, my friend. Watch and learn."

John reluctantly handed over the trumpet, unsure of what his comrade had in mind. Michael raised the trumpet to his lips and let out a resounding blast, playing a lively tune that echoed through the quiet night.

Within moments, a voice bellowed from the floor above, "Who the hell's playing the bugle at one o'clock in the morning?"

John and Michael erupted into laughter, barely able to catch their breath. They were now the source of amusement for someone else, inadvertently awakening the household with their impromptu musical performance.

Curiosity piqued, their host, Mr. Thompson, hurried downstairs, bleary-eyed and irritated. He glared at the two friends, demanding an explanation for the commotion.

Still chuckling, John managed to gasp out an apology, "Apologies, Mr. Thompson. It seems our sense of time got a little muddled. We were simply lost in the nostalgia of our shared past."

Mr. Thompson's stern expression softened slightly, intrigued by the camaraderie and undeniable bond between the two friends. He couldn't help but smile at their infectious laughter.

With a friendly tone, he replied, "Well, you certainly have an unconventional way of marking the hours. Just be mindful of the hour next time, gentlemen. Some of us are trying to catch some shut-eye."

John and Michael nodded earnestly, expressing their gratitude and promising to keep the noise level in check. As Mr. Thompson retreated back to his room, the two friends exchanged amused glances, still reveling in their late-night escapade.

97. LANGUAGE AND LAUGHTER: BOYS VS. GIRLS

IN A LIVELY CLASSROOM FILLED WITH CURIOUS STUDENTS, elderly Spanish teacher Camila, who was a few years away from retirement, embarked on a captivating lesson about the intricacies of noun gender. With animated gestures and infectious enthusiasm, she explained how, unlike in English, Spanish nouns are classified as masculine or feminine. The students listened attentively, eager to absorb this linguistic knowledge.

As the lesson progressed, Camila encountered an inquisitive student who posed a thought-provoking question: "What gender is 'Computer' in Spanish?" The teacher's eyes sparkled as she seized the opportunity to infuse some fun into the class.

Dividing the students into two groups, one representing males and the other females, she instructed them to engage in a lively debate about the gender assignment of the word "Computer." Their task was to present four compelling reasons supporting their recommendation. The atmosphere brimmed with excitement as the students huddled together, brainstorming their arguments.

The boys, presenting their case first, ardently proclaimed that "Computer" should undoubtedly be assigned the feminine gender, hence "La Computadora." Their reasoning unfolded with spirited conviction:

No one but the creator truly understands the internal logic of a computer, reminiscent of the enigmatic qualities often associated with the fairer sex.

The language utilized by computers, filled with intricate codes and technical jargon, remains incomprehensible to the average user, akin to a secret language only understood by a select few.

Even the tiniest mistake made while operating a computer is meticulously stored in its long-term memory, mirroring the remarkable ability of women to remember even the minutest details.

Just as the commitment to a relationship often leads to unforeseen expenditures on accessories, so too does one find oneself continually investing in additional peripherals and upgrades for their computer.

The classroom erupted in laughter and applause at the boys' clever arguments. It was now the girls' turn to take the stage and present their compelling counterarguments.

Confidently, the girls declared that "Computer" must be deemed masculine, thus "El Computadora." They supported their stance with a clever repertoire of reasoning:

To initiate any interaction with a computer, one must first "turn it on," drawing a parallel to the act of awakening or igniting masculine energy.

Despite computers possessing vast amounts of data, they lack the capacity for independent thought, resembling the notion that men are often stereotyped as being more logical than emotional.

Computers, while designed to solve problems, can also become problematic themselves, mirroring the idea that men can sometimes inadvertently create complications in various situations.

Just as committing to a relationship often leads to a realization that a better partner may have been found if one had waited, the girls humorously suggested that technological advancements in computers often render one's recently acquired model outdated sooner than expected.

The classroom erupted once again, this time with applause and laughter directed at the clever arguments presented by the girls. The atmosphere brimmed with joy and camaraderie as the students celebrated the lighthearted debate.

In the end, it was not about the winning side but rather the shared laughter and intellectual banter that enriched their understanding of language and cultural nuances. Camila, beaming with pride at her students' enthusiasm, reminded them that language is not merely a set of rules but a dynamic expression of human communication.

98. OF FINES AND FOLLY: THE FARMER AND THE GOVERNMENT INSPECTORS

IN THE SMALL VILLAGE OF SHEEPVALLEY, nestled in the hills of a faraway land, a curious inspector from the Department of Animal Welfare paid a surprise visit to a humble farmer. The inspector, wearing a neatly pressed uniform, approached the farmer with an air of authority and asked, "Good sir, what do you provide as nourishment for your sheep?"

The farmer, taken aback by the sudden appearance of the inspector, replied with a touch of hesitation, "Well, sir, we give them the abundant grass that grows in our fields and the leftover hay from our barns."

The inspector's face contorted in disbelief. "You must be joking!" he exclaimed. "You feed your precious sheep with nothing but grass and leftover hay? This is utterly absurd! You will be penalized for such negligence."

With a stern expression, the inspector issued a hefty fine of 1,000 coins upon the perplexed farmer. The weight of the penalty was enough to make his heart sink, for it was a significant sum in a village where resources were scarce.

Feeling the burden of the fine, the farmer contemplated the next course of action. The following day, a representative from the Ministry of Agriculture arrived at the village and sought out the farmer's expertise.

Curious yet cautious, the farmer listened to the inquiry. "Tell me, good sir, what do you provide as sustenance for your sheep?" the agricultural representative asked.

Recalling the recent encounter with the inspector, the farmer hesitated before replying, "We feed our sheep a mixture of handpicked grains, the finest alfalfa, and a carefully curated selection of herbs."

The representative's eyes widened in disbelief. "Are you out of your mind?" he exclaimed. "In a time when resources are scarce, and food shortages prevail, you pamper your sheep with such indulgence? This will not be tolerated! A penalty of 1,000 coins shall be imposed upon you."

Overwhelmed by the weight of the second fine, the farmer's legs grew weak, and he nearly collapsed under immense pressure. The burden of the penalties seemed unbearable.

Determined to avoid further misfortune, the farmer devised a plan to navigate future encounters with government officials. He knew he had to be cautious in his response.

The following day, a government officer, this time representing the Ministry of Livestock, visited the village. He approached the farmer with a friendly smile and asked, "Dear sir, I am here to inquire about the sustenance you provide for your sheep. Please enlighten me."

Realizing the delicate situation, the farmer carefully chose his words. "Well, sir, we don't precisely feed our sheep. Instead, we provide them with the means to seek sustenance themselves," he replied cautiously.

The officer's curiosity was piqued. "Could you please elaborate?" he requested.

With a playful twinkle in his eyes, the farmer responded, "We grant them the freedom to graze in the lush meadows surrounding our village, where they find an abundance of nourishment. They wander through the landscape, selecting the most delectable grass and nutritious herbs to satisfy their hunger."

The officer chuckled with delight. "Ah, I see," he said. "You have embraced the wisdom of nature and allowed your sheep to exercise their instincts. This is commendable! No penalties shall be imposed upon you." Relieved and grateful, the farmer smiled, realizing that sometimes, evading expectations and following the ways of nature could lead to a more harmonious outcome.

And so, in the quaint village, the farmer continued to let his sheep roam freely, trusting in their innate ability to find sustenance. The penalties were but distant memories, replaced by a newfound appreciation for the simplicity and wisdom of the natural world.

In the end, the story served as a reminder that adapting to circumstances and embracing the unconventional path can often lead to unexpected solutions, leaving behind the weight of burdens and allowing a newfound sense of freedom to flourish.

99. MISUNDERSTANDINGS AND MIRTH: A TALE OF KISSES AND SLAPS

IN THE COZY CONFINES OF A TRAIN COMPARTMENT, an intriguing mix of passengers found themselves sharing a momentary journey. Seated together were a Project Manager, his diligent team member, an elderly woman, and her young daughter. Little did they know that this unassuming train ride would soon plunge them into a series of amusing and bewildering events.

As the train ventured into a dark tunnel, enveloping the compartment in a shroud of obscurity, an unexpected sound broke the silence—an unmistakable smooching noise. Followed by an immediate reaction—a resounding slap!

Kiss, slap, kiss, and slap—like a bewildering dance of affection and retribution—the sounds echoed through the confined space. The train emerged from the tunnel, revealing the bewildered faces of the women and the assistant while the manager recoiled, his face a shade of crimson from the stinging slap. In a curious twist, a palpable silence settled over the compartment, each person locked in their own thoughts, choosing to remain diplomatically tight-lipped.

The old woman, deep in contemplation, couldn't help but draw conclusions from the unexpected commotion. "These managers," she mused, "are all consumed by their infatuation with young girls. Surely, this man must have attempted to kiss my daughter in the darkness. How fitting it was for her to deliver a swift and deserving slap!"

On the other hand, the young girl, with her innocent perspective, had her own interpretations. Lost in thought, she pondered, "Perhaps the manager intended to steal a kiss from me, but in the absence of light, he mistakenly approached my mother instead. Oh, how amusing it must have been for her to swiftly retaliate with a resounding slap!"

Meanwhile, the Project Manager, nursing his reddened cheek, was engaged in his own internal dialogue. Frustration mingled with amusement as he contemplated, "Oh, the irony! If only my junior colleague had taken the initiative to kiss the girl. She would have mistakenly assumed it was me and delivered the slap accordingly. How I wish the roles were reversed in this peculiar encounter!"

Amidst this whirlwind of thoughts, the team member, the assistant, held his own private musings. Faced with the relentless harassment he endured from his manager in the office, an opportunity for reprisal presented itself. With a wry smile tugging at his lips, he contemplated the possibility of another tunnel on the horizon. The mere thought of recreating the kissing sound, followed by a satisfying slap, brought a mischievous glimmer to his eyes.

As the train hurtled forward, its rhythmic motion carrying the passengers closer to their destination, they remained immersed in their own contemplations. Each one, oblivious to the thoughts of the others, contemplated the bizarre events that unfolded in the darkness of the tunnel.

And so, as the train journey continued, the compartment became a tapestry of silent thoughts, unspoken chuckles, and shared secrets. Each passenger carried their unique interpretation of the incident, offering a humorous glimpse into the intricate web of human perception and the unexpected twists that life often presents.

100. RACING, ROBBERY, AND A WITTY RUSE

LATE ONE MOONLIT NIGHT, a man found himself racing down an empty road, his foot heavy on the gas pedal. Little did he know that his reckless speed had caught the attention of a vigilant police officer, who promptly initiated a high-speed pursuit. Blue and red lights flashed, piercing the darkness as the officer closed in on the speeding vehicle.

Eventually, the man reluctantly pulled over to the side of the road, resigned to his fate. The officer approached the car, a stern expression on his face, and asked the inevitable question, "Sir, are you aware of how fast you were going?"

With an air of nonchalance, the man replied, "Yes, officer. I'm well aware. You see, I'm trying to escape a robbery I got myself tangled up in."

The officer's eyebrows shot up in disbelief. "You mean to say you were the one who committed the robbery?" he asked incredulously.

The man nodded casually. "Indeed, officer. I am the mastermind behind it all. I was merely trying to make my daring escape."

The officer couldn't conceal his astonishment. "So let me get this straight. You were speeding, and on top of that, you confessed to committing a robbery?"

The man, amused, replied, "Absolutely. And if you take a peek in the trunk, you'll find all the loot neatly stashed away."

Shock and confusion painted the officer's face. He realized the situation had escalated beyond a simple traffic violation. "Sir, I'm afraid you'll have to come with me," he said sternly, reaching into the window to retrieve the car keys.

Panicking, the man raised his voice, "Officer, I urge you to reconsider! There's something you should know. I'm afraid you'll stumble upon a loaded gun in my glove compartment!"

Startled, the officer swiftly withdrew his hand from the window and stepped back, his mind racing. He knew he needed backup to handle such a potentially dangerous situation, so he quickly called for reinforcements.

Within moments, sirens blared, and additional patrol cars and helicopters swarmed the scene, creating a chaotic flurry of flashing lights. The man was forcefully removed from his vehicle, placed in handcuffs, and escorted toward a waiting police car.

Just before he was about to be bundled into the car, another officer approached him with a curious expression. Pointing to the initial officer who had pulled him over, he said, "Sir, this officer alleges that you committed a robbery, carried stolen goods in your trunk, and possessed a loaded firearm in your glove compartment. However, upon searching your car, none of these alleged items were found."

"Ah, I see now! I bet that fibber claimed I was breaking the speed limit as well!".

101. THE SCALES OF JUSTICE: THE BAKER AND THE FARMER

IN THE EARLY 1800S, in the quaint English village of Oakshire, resided a diligent farmer named Henry Turner and a skilled baker named Samuel Holmes.

These two men had formed a longstanding agreement, a symbiotic exchange that had withstood the test of time. Each day, Henry would supply a pound of his finest butter to Samuel, who in return would deliver a freshly baked loaf of bread to the farmer's doorstep.

However, one fateful morning, suspicion clouded Samuel's mind as he pondered the fairness of their arrangement. Curiosity got the better of him, and he resolved to weigh the pound of butter he received from Henry.

To his dismay, the scale tipped ever so slightly, revealing that the farmer had sold him less butter than agreed upon. Outraged by what he perceived as an act of deception, Samuel decided to take the matter to court, seeking justice for what he believed was an unfair trade.

The day of the hearing arrived, and the judge presided over the case, ready to unravel the truth. He turned his gaze toward Henry, the accused farmer, and asked him if he had used any specific measure to weigh the butter.

"Your honor," Henry began humbly, "as a simple farmer, I do not possess a sophisticated measure. I rely on an old-fashioned scale to determine the weight of the butter."

The judge raised an eyebrow and probed further, "So, how exactly do you weigh the butter without a standardized measure?"

Henry paused for a moment, his eyes twinkling with an air of wisdom, before responding, "Your honor, long before the baker started purchasing butter from my farm, I established a practice. Each day when Samuel would bring me a loaf of bread, I would place it on my scale and ensure that I gave him an equivalent weight in butter."

The courtroom fell silent, the revelation sinking in. The judge's expression softened, a glimmer of understanding in his eyes.

"If anyone is to be blamed here," the farmer continued, "it is I who have been faithfully providing Samuel with the same weight of butter for every pound of bread he has delivered. The scales may have tipped in my favor, but it was not out of deceit but rather out of reciprocation."

Samuel's anger dissipated, replaced by a mix of admiration and realization. He had failed to consider the unspoken agreement between them, the unwritten contract of fairness that had prevailed for years.

The judge, now enlightened, deliberated on the matter. In a surprising turn of events, he dismissed the case, acknowledging the underlying trust and mutual understanding that had guided their trade.

As the farmer and the baker left the courtroom, newfound respect blossomed between them. They returned to their village, not as adversaries, but as partners in a delicate dance of commerce and camaraderie.

From that day forward, the village of Oakshire held their tale close to their hearts, a testament to the importance of trust and the power of unspoken agreements. And as Henry and Samuel continued their daily exchange of butter and bread, their bond grew stronger, ensuring that fairness and reciprocity would forever be the foundation of their enduring friendship.

102. THE MYSTERIOUS MAN AND HIS MAJESTIC COMPANION

IN A QUAINT LITTLE TOWN, a peculiar man strolled into a bustling restaurant. Following closely behind him was an elegant peacock, its magnificent feathers shimmering with every step. The curious sight caught the attention of the waitress, who approached the unusual duo with a smile.

Taking their orders, the man confidently requested, "I'll have a scrumptious steak, accompanied by a side of roasted vegetables and a glass of red wine, please." The peacock, seemingly understanding the conversation, elegantly nodded its head and mimicked, "The same for me, please."

Intrigued by the enigmatic pair, the waitress diligently served their meals and beverages. As the man reached into his pocket, he effortlessly retrieved the exact amount needed for the bill.

This took place every Friday night for the next three weeks until the mesmerized waitress couldn't contain her curiosity any longer and inquired, "Sir, pardon me for asking, but how do you manage to always have the precise amount of money in your pocket?"

A twinkle gleamed in the man's eyes as he leaned in and whispered, "Well, it's an extraordinary tale. Many years ago, while exploring a hidden cave, I stumbled upon a mystical feather. When I brushed it against my palm, a magical peacock materialized before me. The enchanting bird granted me two wishes."

The waitress listened intently, captivated by the unfolding narrative. The man continued, "For my first wish, I asked that the exact amount of money required for any purchase would magically appear in my pocket. It has been an incredible blessing, ensuring that I'm never short of funds when needed."

The waitress gasped, realizing the immense power of such a wish. "Oh, the possibilities are endless! But, pray to tell, what was your second wish?" she eagerly inquired.

An amused grin spread across the man's face as he gestured towards the peacock. "Ah, my second wish was for a captivating companion, one who exudes elegance and agrees with my every word. And that's how this beautiful peacock became my faithful partner."

The waitress couldn't help but chuckle at the cleverness of his wish. "What a unique and charming tale! It seems you have everything you need by your side," she remarked.

As the man and the peacock savored their delightful meal, the restaurant buzzed with admiration and curiosity. The story of their unusual wishes and remarkable companionship spread like wildfire throughout the town, leaving everyone in awe.

From that day forward, the man and the peacock became local legends, their presence a reminder of the wonders that could unfold when one's imagination intertwines with the magic of the world.

103. THE UNFORGETTABLE LOVE: A TALE OF MEMORY AND CONNECTION

ON A HOT JUNE AFTERNOON IN 2006, Edgar R. Manley strolled through the park during his lunch break. His attention was drawn to an elderly gentleman seated on a bench, his shoulders trembling with heavy sobs. Concerned, Edgar approached him and gently asked what had brought him such sorrow.

With tears streaming down his face, the old man, Joshua, began to share his tale. "I have a remarkable wife at home," he said, his voice filled with a mix of sadness and gratitude. "Every morning, she lovingly massages my tired back, and then she rises to prepare a sumptuous breakfast spread. I am spoiled with pancakes, savory sausages, a medley of fresh fruits, and a cup of perfectly brewed coffee."

Perplexed, Edgar asked, "Why, then, do you weep?"

Joshua continued, his voice quivering, "For lunch, she prepares the most delicious homemade soup and bakes my favorite biscuits. Afterward, she diligently tends to our home, ensuring it is spotless and inviting. And as the afternoon unfolds, she joins me in watching sports on television, sharing in my enjoyment."

Puzzled, Edgar questioned once more, "But why are you crying?"

Joshua took a deep breath, his eyes filled with longing. "When dinner arrives, my wife becomes a culinary artist, crafting gourmet meals that tantalize my taste buds. We savor each bite while sipping on fine wine, and as the night deepens, we embrace, cherishing every moment until the wee hours of the morning."

Edgar waited, expecting an answer that would align with Joshua's apparent distress. "So, my dear sir," Edgar ventured cautiously, "why, then, do tears stream down your face?"

Joshua's gaze fell to the ground, and he whispered, "I can't remember the place I call home."

Moved by his plight, Edgar sat beside him, offering a comforting presence. They shared stories, memories, and laughter. Edgar became a temporary companion, filling the void left by Joshua's temporary lapse in memory. Together, they reminisced about the past, cherishing the moments they could recall.

As the sun began its descent, and Joshua finally managed to remember his address, Edgar guided him back to his residence, where his devoted wife awaited. They approached the doorstep, and as Joshua crossed the threshold, a sense of recognition flickered in his eyes.

The sight of his wife's loving embrace instantly rekindled a spark within him. He held her tightly, cherishing the warmth of their connection. At that moment, it was evident that their love transcended the boundaries of memory.

As Edgar bid them farewell, he couldn't help but reflect on the fragility of their existence. Memories may fade, but the enduring power of love and companionship persists, anchoring us to the present and reminding us of what truly matters.

104. SEASONS OF PERCEPTION: THE TALE OF THE DISTANT APPLE TREE

IN A DISTANT VILLAGE IN THE 1400S, there lived a man named Roderick Gilbert, who had four young sons. With a desire to impart a valuable lesson about the dangers of hasty judgment, he devised a plan to send each of his sons on a journey to a faraway apple tree, experiencing it in different seasons.

One by one, the sons embarked on their respective journeys, beginning with Dannie in the winter, followed by Andre in the spring, Keith in the summer, and Randall in the fall. They set out with curious minds, eager to observe and learn from nature's ever-changing tapestry.

At the end of the year, Roderick gathered his children together and asked them to share their experiences and what they had witnessed at the apple tree.

Dannie, who had ventured forth in the winter, described a scene of desolation—a gnarled and twisted tree standing barren and uninviting against the landscape.

However, Andre, who had set out in the spring, contradicted his brother's perception. He spoke of a tree brimming with hope and promise, adorned with vibrant green buds that signaled the arrival of new life.

Keith, who had journeyed in the summer, added his perspective, describing an apple tree that was resplendent in beauty, its branches adorned with delicate blossoms that emitted a captivating fragrance.

Lastly, Randall, the son who had made his way to the tree in the fall, shared his own encounter. He marveled at the sight of the tree laden with plump and luscious apples, their succulent taste surpassing any he had ever known.

As each son shared their observations, Roderick smiled and acknowledged that they were all correct. He explained to his sons that they had only witnessed one season of the apple tree's life, and it was foolish to make judgments based solely on that limited perspective.

The essence of something, Roderick emphasized, whether it be a tree or a fellow human being, could only be truly understood when viewed in its entirety. Making judgments in winter alone would mean missing the promise of spring, the beauty of summer, and the abundance of fall.

The moral of the story Roderick imparted to his sons was to refuse to judge oneself, life, or others based on a single mistake or challenging time. It was essential to embrace the fullness of experiences, recognizing that each season contributes its unique qualities, shaping the tapestry of life.

With this timeless lesson engrained in their hearts, Roderick's sons grew to become wise and compassionate individuals, understanding the significance of embracing life's ever-changing seasons and refusing to let the pain of one season overshadow the joy of those yet to come.

105. INGENIOUS INITIATIVES

OFFICER ANDERSON WAS KNOWN for diligently enforcing traffic regulations in the peaceful town of Meadowbrook. He had a reputation for keeping a watchful eye on speeding motorists, ensuring the safety of all residents. However, one fateful day, Officer Anderson was astonished to witness an unexpected sight—every driver on the road seemed to be adhering to the speed limit with remarkable precision.

Intrigued by this unusual occurrence, Officer Anderson decided to investigate the matter further. As he ventured down the road, he noticed a young boy named Elijah standing on the side of the street, holding a large, hand-painted sign that read, "Radar Trap Ahead." The officer couldn't help but admire the creativity and audacity of the young boy's act.

Curiosity piqued, Officer Anderson approached Elijah with a friendly smile and asked, "What's going on here, young man?"

With a mischievous twinkle in his eyes, Elijah replied, "Well, Officer, I noticed that people were speeding through our town, endangering everyone's safety. So, my friend Jake and I decided to take matters into our own hands."

Intrigued, Officer Anderson asked, "And how did you manage to make everyone slow down?"

Elijah pointed towards a spot further down the road, where another boy named Jake stood beside a sign that read "Tips." A bucket brimming with change sat proudly at his feet. Elijah explained, "Jake and I thought of this idea. We figured that if we warned drivers about the radar trap ahead, they would slow down and avoid getting speeding tickets. And those who appreciate our efforts can show their gratitude by leaving us a tip."

Officer Anderson couldn't help but chuckle at the ingenuity and entrepreneurial spirit of the young boys. However, he also realized the potential dangers of their impromptu operation. With a serious tone, he said, "I appreciate your intentions, Elijah, but it's important to remember that it's the responsibility of law enforcement officers to enforce traffic regulations. I don't want you or anyone else getting hurt."

Elijah nodded, understanding the officer's concern. "We just wanted to make our town safer, Officer Anderson. We didn't mean any harm."

Impressed by their sincerity, Officer Anderson decided to turn this into a teachable moment. He explained to Elijah and Jake the importance of proper traffic enforcement and the role of trained professionals in ensuring road safety. He also commended their initiative and encouraged them to channel their creativity into community projects with the guidance of adults.

As Officer Anderson bid farewell to the young boys, he couldn't help but feel a renewed sense of hope for the future. He was inspired by their desire to make a positive impact and their resourcefulness in finding unique solutions.

Word of Elijah and Jake's endeavor quickly spread throughout Meadowbrook, earning them praise from both residents and local officials. Their story served as a reminder to everyone about the power of individual action and the potential for positive change, even the youngest members of society.

From that day forward, the town of Meadowbrook saw a renewed commitment to road safety. Residents became more conscious of their driving habits, and the bond between the community and law enforcement grew stronger. Elijah and Jake's act of ingenuity had a lasting impact, reminding everyone that even small actions can make a big difference.

And as for Officer Anderson, he kept a watchful eye on the roads, knowing that the spirit of innovation and the desire for a safer community lived on in the hearts of the town's young residents.

106. LOST IN TRANSLATION: A HILARIOUS BUS EXCHANGE

IT WAS A DULL AUTUMN MORNING IN 1995 when a lady boarded a crowded public bus. As she stepped onto the bus, the lady locked eyes with the bus driver and, without uttering a single word, began a series of peculiar hand gestures. With a smile, she stuck her thumb on her nose and wiggled her fingers at the bemused driver.

The driver, quick on his feet, reciprocated the gesture with equal enthusiasm. He turned to face the lady, using both hands to create the same playful gesture, and waved all his fingers in response.

Unfazed, the lady raised her right arm and began chopping at it with her left hand, mimicking a karate move. The driver, matching her energy, placed his left hand on his right bicep and swiftly jerked his right arm up in a fist, joining in the playful charade.

Amused by their playful interaction, the lady decided to take things to the next level. She cupped both hands under her breasts and gently lifted them. The driver caught off guard but willing to play along, placed both hands at his crotch and mimicked a gentle lift.

Just as the playful exchange reached its peak, the lady's expression turned to one of confusion and disappointment. She frowned and ran a finger up between her derriere, signaling that something was amiss. Without further ado, she made her way to the exit and disembarked from the bus.

In the front row, another woman had been silently observing the entire exchange. Shocked and appalled by what she had witnessed, she couldn't contain her outrage any longer. She spoke up, her voice filled with indignation.

"That was the most disgusting thing I have ever seen on a public bus! What the hell were you doing?" she exclaimed, unable to comprehend the bizarre spectacle that had unfolded.

The gruff bus driver turned to the woman, his face stern but his eyes twinkling with humor. "Listen, lady," he replied, his voice tinged with amusement, "the lady who got on the bus before was a deaf-mute. She gestured to ask if the bus went to 5th Street, and I kindly informed her that it went to 10th Street. She inquired about the number of stops, and I assured her that this was the express route. When she asked if we passed by the dairy, I explained that we went by the ballpark."

The bus driver chuckled and continued, "In response, she said, 'Shit, I'm on the wrong bus!' and promptly got off. You see, it was all a playful exchange of miscommunication. A simple case of mistaken gestures, nothing more."

As the truth dawned on the woman, her indignation transformed into laughter. The absurdity of the situation tickled her funny bone, and soon, the entire bus erupted into laughter.

The moral of the story, dear reader, is that miscommunication and misunderstandings can often lead to hilarious situations. It reminds us to approach such incidents with lightheartedness and a willingness to find humor in our shared human follies.

107. THE GREAT RACE: SPEEDING, LAUGHTER, AND A CLEVER EXCUSE

ON A SUN-DRENCHED AFTERNOON, a man found himself driving home after a long day. In his rush to get back, he was exceeding the speed limit, unaware of the consequences that awaited him.

As he glanced in his rearview mirror, his heart skipped a beat. A police car, adorned with its vibrant red lights, was steadily gaining ground behind him. Panic surged through his veins, but a thought crossed his mind.

"I can outrun this guy," he muttered to himself, a smirk playing on his lips. With a sudden burst of adrenaline, he floored the accelerator, and the race was on. The cars zoomed down the highway, pushing the speedometer higher and higher—60, 70, 80, and 90 miles per hour.

The man's confidence swelled as he maintained his lead, believing he had outsmarted the police officer in the pursuit. But as his speedometer soared past 100, a realization dawned upon him—the odds were no longer in his favor. Reluctantly, he conceded defeat and decided to pull over to the curb. With a sigh of resignation, the man watched as the police officer emerged from his cruiser. The officer approached his window, his face wearied by the tribulations of the day. He leaned down, his voice weary but with a glimmer of hope.

"Listen, mister," the officer began, "I've had a really lousy day, and all I want is to go home. Give me a good excuse, and I'll let you go."

The man's mind raced, searching for a plausible explanation that would alleviate the situation. And then, an idea sparked in his mind.

"Officer," he said, feigning desperation, "you won't believe what happened. Three weeks ago, my wife ran off with a police officer. When I saw your cruiser in my rearview mirror, I thought you were that officer, and you were trying to give her back to me!"

The officer's tired expression wavered, replaced momentarily by a mix of surprise and amusement. A chuckle escaped his lips as he leaned back, contemplating the absurdity of the man's tale.

"You know what?" the officer replied, a hint of a smile tugging at the corners of his mouth. "Consider yourself lucky. Just slow down and drive safely!"

With those words, the man felt a wave of relief wash over him. He thanked the officer and watched as he returned to his cruiser, ready to continue his own journey home.

As the man resumed his drive, laughter erupted from deep within him. He realized the humor in the situation and the irony of his impulsive decision.

The moral of the story, dear reader, is that sometimes, a dash of humor and a clever excuse can lighten even the most serious of situations. It reminds us to find joy in the unexpected and to approach life's challenges with a lighthearted spirit. And, of course, it teaches us that the road to redemption may come in the form of a comical misunderstanding, leaving laughter in its wake.

108. AN UNEXPECTED ADVENTURE WITH A TALKING FROG

ON A QUAINT COUNTRY ROAD, a curious boy named Tommy found himself on an unexpected adventure. As he strolled along, enjoying the warmth of the sun on his face, a mysterious voice echoed through the air, catching his attention. To his surprise, it was a talking frog perched on a lily pad, calling out to him.

"Boy, if you kiss me," the frog croaked, its voice filled with a hint of magic, "I will turn into a beautiful princess!"

Tommy's eyes widened with wonder. Never before had he encountered a talking frog, let alone

one promising a magical transformation.

Intrigued by this peculiar encounter, he bent down and picked up the frog gently, examining it with fascination.

Instead of immediately obeying the frog's request, Tommy couldn't help but smile at the thought of a frog transforming into a princess. He playfully placed the frog into his pocket, wanting to savor this enchanting moment a little longer.

Minutes passed, and the frog, growing more eager, broke the silence once again. "Boy, if you kiss me," it pleaded, its voice filled with longing, "I will turn into a beautiful princess and stay with you for a week!"

Amused by the frog's persistence and captivated by the idea of a temporary companion, Tommy retrieved it from his pocket, a grin playing on his lips. Instead of granting its wish immediately, he decided to tease the frog a little longer. With a twinkle in his eye, he offered the frog a playful smile and returned it to his pocket, leaving the frog wondering what was in store.

Time went on, and the frog's voice rang out once more, filled with growing desperation. "Boy, if you kiss me," it implored, a sense of urgency in its tone, "I will transform into a beautiful princess and do ANYTHING you want!"

Chuckling at the frog's unwavering determination, Tommy couldn't help but be charmed by its persistence. Once again, he retrieved the frog from his pocket, its eyes pleading for a kiss that would fulfill its desire for transformation. With a twinkle in his eye and a whimsical wit, Tommy responded, "Look, dear frog, I am an engineering student. My schedule is packed, and I have no time for a girlfriend. But having a talking frog as a companion? Now that's cool!"

With those words, Tommy gently returned the frog to his pocket, their lively conversations continuing as he walked along the country road.

109. THE SEDUCTIVE SERENADE: A TALE OF CURIOSITY AND MONASTIC SECRETS

MANY YEARS AGO, a man named Levi found himself in a peculiar situation as his car broke down near a tranquil monastery. Seeking help, he approached the monastery's door and was greeted by a kind-hearted monk. Levi explained his predicament, hoping for a place to spend the night until he could get his car repaired.

The compassionate monks welcomed Levi with open arms, offering him not just shelter but also a warm meal. Grateful for their generosity, Levi soon found himself engrossed in conversation with his newfound companions. As night descended and he retired to his room, little did he know that a mysterious and enchanting sound awaited him.

In the stillness of the night, as Levi lay in bed, a captivating melody filled the air, reminiscent of the mythical Sirens that bewitched sailors in ancient tales. Intrigued and unable to sleep, he pondered the origin of this alluring sound, its spell weaving through his thoughts.

Unable to contain his curiosity, Levi decided to inquire about the mysterious melody during breakfast with the monks. With an eager heart, he posed his question, hoping to unravel the secret behind the seductive sound that had captivated him throughout the night.

The wise Abbot, sitting at the head of the table, met Levi's inquiry with a gentle smile. "I'm sorry, my friend, but we cannot reveal the source of the sound to you. It is a secret reserved for those within our monkhood."

Though disappointed by Abbot's response, Levi graciously thanked the monks for their hospitality and bid them farewell after breakfast. However, the lingering mystery continued to haunt him.

A year passed, and Levi's fascination with the alluring sound remained. Driven by an insatiable curiosity, he embarked on a journey back to the monastery, determined to unravel the enigma that had consumed his thoughts. He pleaded with the Abbot, expressing his ardent desire to learn more about the captivating melody.

Once again, the Abbot kindly responded, "I'm sorry, my friend, but we cannot disclose the secret to you unless you become a monk."

Determined to uncover the truth, Levi implored the Abbot, "If becoming a monk is the key to discovering the source of this mesmerizing sound, then please, guide me on this path."

The Abbot, recognizing Levi's sincere yearning for knowledge, set him on a quest. "Before you can join our monastery, you must venture across the world and contemplate two profound questions. Seek the answers to the ever-changing number of blades of grass and the countless grains of sand. Only then will you be ready to embark on your spiritual journey as a monk."

Years passed as Levi traveled the globe, pondering the immeasurable vastness of nature and the transient nature of life. The weight of time began to settle upon him, but his determination remained unwavering. Finally, aged and wise, he returned to the monastery, prepared to fulfill the requirements set forth by the Abbot.

In awe of Levi's profound understanding of the world, the Abbot welcomed him with open arms. "Congratulations, my friend. You have proven your dedication and insight. You are now ready to join our monastery." Eager to unveil the source of the enchanting sound that had driven him on this journey, Levi followed the Abbot through a dimly lit corridor. At the end stood a wooden door, where the Abbot handed Levi a key. With each subsequent door encrusted with precious gems, Levi received a key, each more magnificent than the last.

Finally, before him stood a grand door adorned with solid gold. The alluring sound grew louder, beckoning him closer. With trembling hands, Levi inserted the final key, slowly turning the lock. The door creaked open, revealing a sight that left him awestruck.

Levi fell to his knees, humbled by the revelation before him. The source of the captivating melody was unveiled. And what is the source? Alas, the secret shall remain hidden, for it's classified information accessible only to card-carrying monks. But hey, we heard they serve a mean batch of monk-made cookies in the monastery!"

110. UNCLAD OCCUPATIONS: HILARITY UNVEILED ON THE SANDS

THREE MEN EMBARKED ON AN ADVENTURE TO A NUDIST BEACH, eager to bask in the sun and embrace the liberating freedom that comes with shedding societal clothing norms. As they settled into their newfound natural state, their conversation quickly turned to their occupations, revealing a spectrum of emotions among them.

The first man, beaming with delight, proclaimed, "Gentlemen, I hail from Wall Street, a realm of prosperity and financial prowess. However, the weight of corporate attire, with its suffocating suits and constricting collars, is an oppressive force. Here, on this sandy haven, I find solace, liberated from the constraints of tailored formality. Ah, the sweet bliss of unrestricted relaxation!"

The second man nodded eagerly, his eyes gleaming with agreement. "Aye, mate! I am a deep-sea diver, exploring the depths of the ocean's mysteries. Yet, my underwater expeditions are burdened by the encumbrance of a heavy diver's suit, lead boots that anchor me down, and a brass helmet that traps my very breath. This beach, my friends, grants me the gift of freedom, unburdened by the weight of aquatic exploration."

As the two men reveled in their newfound liberation, they turned their attention to their companion, whose countenance remained despondent amidst the cheerful ambiance. Curiosity piqued, they implored him to share his occupational tale.

With a heavy sigh, the glum man admitted, "I must confess, my occupation lacks the glamorous allure of Wall Street or the depths of the sea. Alas, I am but a humble pickpocket, skilled in the art of swift fingers and sly maneuvers. However, my therapist, in an effort to steer me towards a path of redemption, suggested a holiday devoid of tempting opportunities to pilfer from unsuspecting souls."

A moment of silence followed as the weight of his confession hung in the air. Then, as if on cue, the men erupted into laughter, their carefree chuckles echoing along the beach.

"Ah, my friend!" exclaimed the first man, wiping tears of mirth from his eyes. "You have stumbled upon an irony that would make even the gods guffaw! Here we stand, baring it all in our natural glory, our possessions stripped away, and yet your profession precludes you from partaking in your mischievous trade. A holiday where pockets remain unexplored!"

The second man joined in the jovial chorus. "Indeed, my friend! In this haven of bare vulnerability, your nimble fingers find no pockets to dive into. A respite from the artistry of your craft, if you will!"

Amidst the laughter and camaraderie, the glum man's spirits lifted, and he realized the absurdity of his predicament. Together, they reveled in the irony of their circumstances, cherishing the hilarity that life often weaves into its tapestry. The absurdities are the threads that stitch together the fabric of our shared human experience.

111. THE WIT OF A COWBOY

IN THE VAST EXPANSE OF THE WILD WEST, a cowboy named Luke embarked on a journey from Waco to Fort Worth. The dusty trail stretched endlessly before him, and the scorching sun added to his thirst as he rode on his trusty steed.

Along the way, Luke stumbled upon a small town, a speck of civilization in the vast frontier. With parched lips and a yearning for refreshment, he decided to seek solace in the local saloon, hoping for a cold beer to quench his cowboy-sized thirst. As Luke entered the saloon, he could feel the eyes of the locals drilling into him with suspicion. The town had a reputation for being unwelcoming to outsiders, but Luke remained undeterred. He tied his horse to the post outside, ensuring its safety, and made his way to the bar.

After enjoying a satisfying gulp of the cool, foamy brew, Luke stepped outside, only to be greeted by a disheartening sight—the absence of his faithful companion. Someone had brazenly stolen his horse while he sought solace within the saloon's walls.

Anger boiled within Luke as he stormed back into the bar, his hand firmly gripping the handle of his holstered gun. With practiced finesse, he twirled it around his finger in a display of skill, captivating the attention of every patron. In one swift motion, he aimed and shot, piercing a whisky bottle at the far end of the bar. Silence fell upon the saloon like a heavy blanket as all eyes turned towards Luke, his voice resonating with a blend of authority and menace. "Now, which one of you sidewinders stole my horse?"

Not a soul dared to utter a word. The tension in the air was palpable, the locals well aware of the potential consequences that loomed before them.

Luke's voice grew even more commanding, his warning ringing through the room. "Listen up, y'all! I'm gonna enjoy another beer right here. And if my horse ain't returned by the time I finish, I'll have to resort to doing what I did back in Waco. And trust me, you don't want me to do what I did in Waco."

Unease gripped the hearts of the locals as they shuffled uncomfortably in their seats. Their apprehension towards strangers paled in comparison to the fear of the impending trouble that hung in the air. With a watchful eye, Luke savored his beer, his gaze darting toward the entrance as the seconds ticked away. Lo and behold, when the last drop of liquid vanished from his mug, he glanced outside to find his loyal companion patiently awaiting his return, tied to the post.

A grin spread across Luke's face as he swiftly saddled up, ready to resume his journey. The bartender, who had ventured outside to witness the spectacle, couldn't contain his curiosity any longer.

"Hey, partner," he called out, a hint of curiosity lacing his voice, "tell me, what happened in Waco?"

Luke chuckled and replied, "Well, partner, let's just say I had to walk home!"

112. GRANDPA'S CLEVER COUP: A TALE OF LUXURY CARS AND SHREWD TRICKS

MAGARY, AN ELDERLY MAN with a penchant for elegant and expensive cars, found himself at a car dealership eyeing a luxurious Mercedes. He had his heart set on the vehicle but was dismayed to discover that the salesman had just sold it to a beautiful, busty blonde.

Frustrated, Magary confronted the salesman. "I thought we had an agreement that you would hold that car for me until I could gather the $85,000 asking price. And now you've sold it to that lovely young lady over there for $75,000! You insisted there would be no discount on this model!"

The salesman grinned, trying to explain himself. "Well, sir, you see, she came in with the cash in her hand, and look at her! She's stunningly beautiful. How could I resist such an offer?"

The young lady approached Magary with a smile, handing him the car keys. "Here you go," she said. "I told you I could get this joker to drop his asking price. See you later, Grandpa."

As he drove away in his new car, the man couldn't help but chuckle at the clever trick they had played on the salesman.

Never underestimate the wit and resourcefulness of old people. They may appear harmless, but they possess wisdom and cunning that can catch others off guard.

From that day forward, Magary enjoyed his luxurious Mercedes with an extra twinkle in his eye. He knew that age was just a number and that he could still outsmart anyone who dared to challenge him.

As for the salesman, he learned a valuable lesson about underestimating older customers. He realized that appearances can be deceiving, and it's essential to treat every customer with respect, regardless of their age or appearance.

And so, the tale of Magary and the Mercedes became a legendary story in the dealership, reminding everyone to never mess with old people, for they have a knack for surprising you when you least expect it.

113. WRINKLES AND WONDER: EMBRACING IMPERFECT PERFECTION

A LITTLE GIRL NAMED ANNALISE sat snuggled on her grandfather's lap. It was their special bedtime routine, where Grandpa would read her a story and share moments of love and laughter. This particular evening, as Grandpa read the pages of a colorful picture book, Annalise couldn't help but let her curious nature take over.

She gently touched her grandfather's weathered cheek, feeling the texture of his wrinkles. It fascinated her as if each line told a story of its own. After a few moments, she reached up to touch her own smooth cheek, comparing the two.

"Grandpa," Annalise spoke up with innocence in her voice, "did God make you?"

A warm smile spread across Grandpa's face, his eyes twinkling with affection. "Yes, sweetheart," he replied, his voice filled with tenderness, "God made me a long time ago."

Annalise pondered for a moment, her little mind racing with thoughts. Then, another question emerged, carrying a sense of wonder. "Grandpa, did God make me too?"

A loving sparkle danced in Grandpa's eyes as he answered, "Yes, indeed, honey. God made you just a little while ago." Inquisitive as ever, Annalise continued to explore their faces, her tiny fingers tracing the lines on her own smooth skin. She carefully observed her grandfather's face, comparing it to her own. The gears in her mind turned, and with a smile, she shared her innocent observation.

"Grandpa," Annalise giggled, "God's getting better at it, isn't he?"

Grandpa burst into laughter, his deep belly chuckles filling the room. He embraced Annalise in a warm hug, tickling her playfully. "You're absolutely right, my dear! God's creativity keeps improving with each passing generation!"

Their laughter filled the room, creating a joyous melody that echoed through their hearts. At that moment, Grandpa realized how blessed he was to have this precious little girl in his life. Annalise, too, felt a profound love and connection with her grandfather, knowing that they were both unique creations of a divine artist. As they continued their bedtime routine, Grandpa closed the book and shared stories of his own childhood adventures. Annalise listened with wide-eyed wonder, cherishing each tale as if it were a treasure. And in their shared laughter and love, they discovered that the true magic of life lies not in the perfect creation of our beings but in the imperfect beauty of the connections we forge with one another.

114. THE LOVE DRESS: REKINDLING THE FLAME OF DESIRE

IN 1985, IN A LITTLE NEIGHBORHOOD OF FLOWERS VILLAGE lived a young couple, Lisa and John, who had recently tied the knot. They were still reveling in the bliss of their new union when an unexpected visitor arrived at their doorstep. It was none other than Lisa's mother-in-law, Barbara, who had a knack for dropping by unannounced.

Barbara rang the doorbell, and Lisa hurriedly opened the door, only to realize she was still in the process of getting dressed. Startled, Barbara couldn't help but notice her daughter-in-law standing there in all her naked glory.

Shocked, Barbara exclaimed, "What on earth are you doing?"

Lisa replied, "I'm just waiting for John to come home from work."

"But you're NAKED!" Barbara couldn't hide her surprise.

Giggling, Lisa explained, "Oh, this is my special Love Dress. It's something I wear to surprise and delight John. It brings us both immense happiness. Now, if you don't mind, he'll be home any minute, so it's best if you leave."

Barbara, perplexed by the concept of a "Love Dress," reluctantly bid her farewell and made her way back home. As she walked, she couldn't help but ponder this peculiar notion. By the time she reached her own front door, a special plan had formed in her mind.

Determined to reignite the flame of romance in her own marriage, Barbara swiftly undressed and took a refreshing shower. She meticulously applied her favorite perfume, wanting to make a perfect impression. Standing by the front door, wearing nothing but her Love Dress, she anxiously awaited her husband's return.

Finally, the moment arrived. Barbara's husband stepped through the door, greeted by the unexpected sight of his naked wife.

Surprised, he exclaimed, "What in the world are you doing?"

Beaming with excitement, Barbara confidently declared, "This is My Love Dress."

Her husband looked her up and down, a humorous in his eye, and casually remarked, "Needs ironing."

Barbara's heart sank, and then she burst into laughter, realizing the irony of the situation. Her attempt to replicate the excitement of Lisa's Love Dress had been met with a hilarious punchline from her husband. They both shared a good laugh, embracing the joy and spontaneity that had brought them together in the first place.

And so, at that moment, Barbara realized that true love and romance aren't confined to extravagant gestures or fancy outfits. It's the shared laughter, playful banter, and the ability to find humor in the most unexpected situations that truly keep the flame alive.

From that day forward, Barbara and her husband created their own brand of lighthearted romance, cherishing the moments of silliness and laughter that became the cornerstone of their relationship.

And the tale of the Love Dress, although initially perplexing, became a treasured memory that would be retold with joy for years to come.

115. THE MAGICAL ANNIVERSARY

THE QUAINT, CANDLELIT RESTAURANT was the perfect setting for a special occasion as the married couple, still filled with love and laughter, celebrated their 35th wedding anniversary. As they toasted to their enduring commitment, a flicker of magic caught their attention.

A petite and enchanting fairy materialized on their table, ready to bestow a gift upon the devoted couple.

With a gleam in her eyes, the fairy announced, 'For your unwavering devotion and remarkable bond, I shall grant each of you a wish.'

Eager with excitement, the wife couldn't contain her desire. 'Oh, I've always dreamed of traveling the world with my beloved husband,' she exclaimed. In an instant, the fairy waved her wand, and behold, two tickets for a luxurious voyage aboard the renowned QC1 liner appeared before them.

Now, it was the husband's turn to make a wish. He pondered for a moment, considering the possibilities that lay before him. A mischievous grin formed on his face as he made his choice, causing a brief pause in the room.

'I must apologize, my dear,' he began. 'While this moment is undoubtedly romantic, opportunities like this come once in a lifetime. So, my wish is to have a wife who is 30 years younger than me.'

The wife's smile faltered, and even the fairy's expression turned solemn.

Nevertheless, a wish is a wish, and the fairy is prepared to weave her magic once again. With a graceful flick of her wand, the husband underwent a remarkable transformation, his age advancing by several decades until he reached the ripe age of 92.

Moral of the story: men are often foolish, and fairies are female!

116. THE GRAND BARGAIN: THE QUIRKY LIFE CONTRACTS OF CREATION

AT THE DAWN OF CREATION, God began crafting the animals of the world. With each creation, He assigned specific roles and lifespans to them.

First, God created the wise and gentle cow. He said, "You shall graze the fields, toil under the sun, bear calves, and provide milk to nourish the farmer. I grant you a lifespan of sixty years."

The cow contemplated and replied, "That seems like quite a demanding existence for sixty years. How about this: give me twenty years, and I'll graciously return the remaining forty."

God considered the cow's request and agreed to the arrangement.

Next, God fashioned the loyal and protective dog. He said, "Your purpose shall be to guard the homes of humans, barking at anyone who approaches. Your lifespan shall be twenty years."

The dog pondered the task and responded, "Twenty years of barking seems a bit excessive. How about this: grant me ten years, and I'll willingly surrender the other ten."

God found the dog's proposal reasonable and accepted.

Then, God created the mischievous and playful monkey. He said, "Your mission is to bring joy to people, entertaining them with your monkey tricks. Your lifespan shall be twenty years."

The monkey chuckled and replied, "Twenty years of monkey business? No way! If the dog returns ten years, I shall do the same."

God smiled and granted the monkey's wish.

Lastly, God shaped the curious and pleasure-seeking man. He said, "Your purpose is to experience the delights of life: eating, sleeping, playing, and enjoying the pleasures of existence. I shall grant you twenty years."

The man was taken aback and protested, "Only twenty years? That won't suffice! Here's my proposal: I'll take my twenty years plus the forty returned by the cow, the ten from the dog, and the ten from the monkey. That makes eighty fair?"

God pondered for a moment and chuckled, "Well, you drive a hard bargain, but I accept your proposal. Eighty years it is!"

And so, the cosmic deal was struck.

Henceforth, the first twenty years of life are devoted to carefree indulgence, exploring the joys of existence. The next forty years are spent toiling under the sun, supporting and nurturing our families. In the following ten years, we embrace the playful spirit of the monkey to entertain and bring laughter to our grandchildren. Lastly, for the remaining ten years, we settle in front of our homes, barking at passersby and amusingly embodying the essence of our furry companion, the dog.

117. FROM SILENCE TO UNSTOPPABLE BANTER

IN THE SMALL TOWN WHERE MY DAD GREW UP, everyone knew everyone. And everyone knew that my dad was a late talker. He had surpassed the age of three without uttering a single word. His parents were puzzled and concerned, wondering if something was wrong. But my dad was an intelligent child, his eyes brimming with curiosity and his mind sharp as a tack. He simply had no interest in verbal communication beyond a couple of basic sounds.

One fateful day, a distant relative paid a visit to their home. She was a rather haughty and opinionated woman, known for her sharp tongue and snobby demeanor. As she glanced at my dad, she couldn't resist making a derogatory comment. "Three years old, and he doesn't talk? He must be very dim-witted!"

My dad, despite his tender age, had a fire in his spirit. He refused to let this comment slide. With a determined look on his face, he opened his mouth and spoke his first words, forming a complete sentence, no less. "And you, my dear relative, are exceptionally unattractive!"

The room fell into stunned silence and then erupted into laughter and applause. My grandparents, great-grandma, and their housekeeper rejoiced, celebrating my dad's triumphant retort. It was a moment of pure joy and victory as if my dad had unleashed his pent-up linguistic prowess in one swift stroke. Needless to say, that particular relative never set foot in their house again.

From that day forward, it was as if a dam had burst. My dad's voice became a constant presence, filling the air with his thoughts, observations, and stories. He couldn't stop talking, as if he had spent those silent years accumulating a reservoir of words and was determined to make up for lost time.

Throughout his life, my dad became known for his wit, humor, and loquacious nature. He never shied away from a conversation or an opportunity to share his thoughts. Some might say he had an uncanny ability to turn even the simplest of topics into lively discussions that could go on for hours. It seemed as though he had taken that moment of triumph and turned it into a lifelong mission to make his voice heard.

And so, my dad's journey from a late talker to a never-ending talker became a cherished part of our family lore. We often laughed about how that fateful encounter unleashed a torrent of words that never seemed to cease. It was a reminder that sometimes, the quietest ones have the most to say, and once they find their voice, they never let it go.

And as we fondly remember those early years of silence and the subsequent avalanche of words, we can't help but cherish the unique and vibrant spirit that defined my dad. He taught us the importance of embracing our voices, speaking up, and finding humor in every situation. His journey from silence to endless chatter serves as a reminder that life is too short to keep our thoughts bottled up, and sometimes, the funniest stories begin with the most unexpected beginnings.

118. THE HILARIOUS TRIALS OF THE CLEVER DOCTOR AND THE PRANKSTER LAWYER

A YOUNG DOCTOR FRESH OUT OF MEDICAL SCHOOL found himself facing the harsh reality of a competitive job market. Determined to make a name for himself, he decided to open his own practice. To attract patients, he devised a unique marketing strategy, promising to cure any ailment for a fixed price of $20. If he failed to deliver, he would give $100 to the dissatisfied patient.

Meanwhile, a young lawyer seeking a clever opportunity stumbled upon the doctor's intriguing offer. With mischievous intent, he devised a plan to trick the doctor into paying him the promised $100 by faking various ailments. The lawyer entered the doctor's office and exclaimed, "Doctor, I've lost my sense of taste! I'm desperate!"

Confident in his abilities, the doctor calmly responded, "Fear not; we'll find a solution. Nurse, bring me the blue bottle from the second shelf."

As the nurse handed him the bottle, the doctor carefully poured its contents onto the lawyer's tongue. Instantly, the lawyer recoiled, his face contorting in disgust.

"But this tastes awful! It's repulsive!" the lawyer exclaimed angrily.

The doctor, with a smirk of satisfaction, declared, "Ah, you see? Your taste buds are back. That will be $20, please." Although infuriated, the lawyer begrudgingly paid the fee, his mind already plotting his next move. Determined to outsmart the doctor, he returned the next day with a new complaint. "Doctor, I've lost my memory! I can hardly remember anything!" the lawyer claimed, feigning distress.

With an air of confidence, the doctor responded, "Worry not; we'll find a solution. Nurse, fetch me the red bottle from the second shelf."

Unbeknownst to the lawyer, the doctor had switched the bottles overnight. As the doctor poured the liquid from the red bottle into the lawyer's mouth, the lawyer's eyes widened in recognition.

"But this is the same liquid as yesterday! It's vinegar!" the lawyer exclaimed in outrage.

Smiling slyly, the doctor replied, "Ah, you noticed! Your memory has been restored. That will be $20, please."

Fuming with frustration, the lawyer reluctantly paid the fee, determined to get his revenge. The following day, he returned to the doctor's office, claiming to have lost his sight.

"Doctor, I can't see anything anymore! I beg you, help me!" the lawyer pleaded.

Sincerely concerned, the doctor sighed, "I'm truly sorry, but this is beyond my capabilities. Here, take this $100 as a gesture of goodwill."

The lawyer eagerly grabbed the money, only to realize that it was just a $20 bill. Angrily, he exclaimed, "Hey... this is only $20, not $100!"

With a triumphant smile, the doctor declared, "Ah, you can see clearly again! That will be $20, please." Defeated yet amused, the lawyer begrudgingly paid the fee, acknowledging the doctor's cleverness.

119. THE WISDOM IN THE COFFEE CUP: A LESSON ON LIFE'S TRUE ESSENCE

A GROUP OF SUCCESSFUL ALUMNI gathered to pay a visit to their beloved university professor, eager to catch up and share the joys and frustrations of their established careers. As they settled into the cozy living room, the conversation soon turned to the inevitable topic of stress in work and life.

The wise professor, sensing the tension in the room, decided to offer his guests a simple yet profound lesson. He graciously offered to make them some coffee and disappeared into the kitchen, leaving the alumni buzzing with anticipation.

Moments later, the professor reemerged with a large pot of freshly brewed coffee, accompanied by an array of cups that spanned the entire spectrum of materials and styles. There were porcelain cups, plastic cups, glass cups, and crystal cups, some plain-looking and others dazzlingly expensive and exquisite. He invited his guests to help themselves to a cup of their choosing.

As the students eagerly lined up to pour themselves a cup of coffee, they couldn't help but notice that the nice-looking, expensive cups were quickly claimed, leaving behind the humble and affordable ones. Curiosity began to fill the room as they exchanged curious glances.

The professor, with a twinkle in his eye, gestured to the cups in their hands and spoke, "My dear students, if you take a moment to observe, you'll notice that the cup itself does not determine the quality of the coffee. Whether it's a plain and simple cup or a lavish and expensive one, the true essence lies in the coffee within." He continued, "In life, we often find ourselves chasing after the 'best' cups – the prestigious jobs, the wealth, and the status – believing that they will bring us happiness and fulfillment. But in doing so, we miss the true essence of life itself. We become so fixated on the cup that we forget to savor the rich and invigorating coffee that God has provided."

The room fell into contemplative silence as the profound message sank in. The alumni realized that their pursuit of external markers of success had caused unnecessary stress and prevented them from truly enjoying the experiences life had to offer.

The professor's words echoed in their minds: "Life is the coffee, my friends, and the jobs, money, and social status are merely the cups that contain it. While it's natural to desire the best for ourselves, we mustn't lose sight of the true essence of life. The happiest people aren't those who have the best of everything, but those who make the best of everything."

A wave of realization and laughter washed over the room as the alumni embraced the truth of the professor's metaphor.

They vowed to savor every sip of the coffee of life, regardless of the cup they held in their hands. From that day forward, they approached their careers and personal lives with a renewed perspective, cherishing the experiences, relationships, and moments that truly mattered.

As they bid farewell to their wise professor, gratitude filled their hearts for the invaluable lesson he had shared. They left his presence with a newfound zest for life, ready to make the best of everything and savor each cup of coffee that came their way.

120. THE SUITOR'S WITTY QUEST AND THE CHALLENGE OF THE LAKE

IN A DISTANT LAND, nestled amidst rolling hills and ancient castles, there lived a wealthy nobleman who had a single, enchantingly beautiful daughter. When the time came for his daughter to be married, the nobleman devised a challenge that would determine the most worthy suitor among the eligible young men in the kingdom.

News spread far and wide, reaching the ears of courageous adventurers, gallant knights, and ambitious warriors. They gathered in the town square, each one hoping to prove himself and win the hand of the nobleman's daughter. Some arrived equipped with parchment and quill, ready to showcase their intellect and wit, while others brandished swords and shields, their strength and valor on full display.

Led by the nobleman himself, the young men were guided to a shimmering lake nestled within a tranquil grove. The nobleman addressed the eager suitors, his voice resounding with authority, "Gentlemen, if you can cross this treacherous lake and reach the sacred island at its heart, you shall earn the right to claim my daughter's hand in marriage. As a reward, I shall bestow upon you ancient treasures from distant times, relics of untold value that will secure your prosperity. May fortune favor the brave!"

Excitement rippled through the crowd as the young men prepared themselves for the challenge. They began removing their tunics, ready to plunge into the depths of the lake and prove their mettle. But just as they were about to take the leap, a mighty dragon soared through the skies, its fiery breath sending waves of fear and uncertainty through the hearts of the suitors and plunged into the depths of the lake.

Startled, the young men hastily adorned their tunics once more, their spirits dampened by the unexpected obstacle. Disappointment filled the air as some whispered, "Surely, no man can conquer this fearsome beast and claim the nobleman's daughter."

Yet, amidst the apprehension, a gentleman, with resolute courage, stepped forward and dove into the lake, fearlessly navigating its treacherous depths, avoiding hidden rocks and eerie water creatures. The crowd watched in awe as he emerged on the sacred island, his perseverance and resourcefulness unmatched.

The nobleman, his eyes wide with disbelief, approached the triumphant suitor, offering his congratulations. He urged the young man to express his deepest desire, promising to grant anything within his power. But the suitor, gasping for breath and still recovering from his arduous journey, requested, "I implore you, sire, reveal to me the identity of the one who pushed me inside this pool!"

A hushed silence fell over the crowd as they awaited the nobleman's response. The nobleman, his brows furrowed in contemplation, pondered the suitor's request. After a moment of reflection, a sly smile curled on his lips as he realized the absurdity of what had happened.

The nobleman couldn't help but burst into laughter, his booming voice echoing across the lake. "You, my dear suitor, possess a rare charm and a keen sense of humor," he exclaimed. "For your courage, your resourcefulness, and your ability to turn a challenging circumstance into a moment of levity, I gladly fulfill my promise. You shall marry my daughter, and together you shall embark on a journey filled with love, laughter, and the ancient treasures that shall grace your lives."

121. PUSHED THE LIMITS: A HILARIOUS HUNTING MISHAP

IN THE WILD AND REMOTE COUNTRYSIDE, two adventurous friends, Jack and Mike, embarked on a hunting expedition. Determined to capture the most magnificent prey, they decided to rent an airplane to reach the distant forest zone, where rumors of legendary creatures had been whispered.

Weeks passed, and the time came for their return. As they eagerly awaited the arrival of the pilot, they couldn't help but boast about their successful hunt. Jack had managed to capture a colossal grizzly bear, while Mike had bagged an impressive moose. Their hunting trophies stood proudly, filling the cabin with a sense of accomplishment.

When the pilot finally arrived, he glanced at the magnificent beasts before him and scratched his head. "Gentlemen," he said, "I hate to be the bearer of bad news, but this plane won't be able to carry both of these massive creatures. You'll have to leave one behind."

The hunters exchanged puzzled glances, their hopes momentarily deflated. "But last year," Jack protested, "we flew back with two animals just as large as these!"

The pilot pondered the predicament, stroking his chin thoughtfully. "Well," he said with a shrug, "if it worked last year, it should work this time, too, right?"

And so, fueled by their adventurous spirits and their trust in past successes, Jack and Mike decided to challenge the limits of the small aircraft. With their prized trophies securely fastened inside, they climbed aboard, their hearts filled with excitement and a hint of apprehension.

The plane revved its engines, ready for takeoff. As it raced down the runway, the weight of the animals proved too much for the humble aircraft to bear. It strained against the forces of gravity but failed to achieve the required altitude. The plane's wings trembled under the immense load, and with a sudden jolt, it crashed into the nearest hill.

Bruised but miraculously unharmed, the hunters emerged from the wreckage, surrounded by the remnants of their ill-fated flight. Dusting themselves off, they surveyed their surroundings, a mixture of awe and disbelief etched on their faces.

Jack turned to Mike and, with a perplexed expression, asked, "Where do you reckon we are, old friend?"

Mike squinted at the unfamiliar landscape and scratched his head. After a moment of contemplation, he grinned mischievously and replied, "Well, if my calculations are correct, I'd say we're approximately two miles south from the spot where we crashed last time.

122. THE WOODCUTTER'S WISDOM: FINDING BALANCE FOR PRODUCTIVITY

IN THE HEART OF THE VAST ALASKAN FOREST, two woodcutters, Bruce Taylor, and Jim Bumpers, ventured deep into the wilderness, their axes poised to conquer the towering trees that surrounded them. It was the year 1968, and the allure of the untouched wilderness called them to their daily labor.

Day in and day out, Bruce and Jim toiled side by side, their skills, experience, and stature on par with one another. They swung their axes with precision, felling trees with remarkable efficiency. However, a stark difference marked their routine.

Bruce, dedicated and driven, worked relentlessly from dawn till dusk, sweat pouring down his brow as he tirelessly hacked away at the towering giants. In contrast, Jim, with a calm demeanor, would pause each day for a one-hour lunch break, leaving Bruce perplexed.

Though Bruce toiled longer hours, he couldn't help but notice that by the end of each day, both he and Jim had chopped the same number of trees. Perplexed and frustrated, Bruce approached Jim, eager to uncover the secret to his seemingly equal productivity.

With a knowing smile, Jim revealed his wisdom. "It's simple, my friend," he said. "During that hour-long break, I return home and sharpen my axe."

Bruce's eyes widened in realization. He had been so consumed with the physical exertion of chopping trees that he neglected to maintain his tool. He had been hacking away with a dull axe, unknowingly slowing his progress and diminishing his efficiency.

At that moment, Bruce recognized the invaluable lesson Jim had taught him. Taking breaks and investing time in rejuvenation and self-care was not a waste but an essential part of maximizing productivity. By sharpening his axe, Jim ensured that every swing he took was precise, powerful, and effective.

From that day forward, Bruce adopted a new approach. He embraced the importance of breaks, using them to recharge his body and mind. In those moments of respite, he sharpened not just his axe but also his focus and determination. The results were astounding.

As the weeks passed, Bruce and Jim continued their work in harmony. Their equal skill and experience, once a source of curiosity, now became a testament to the power of balance and self-care. They chopped trees with efficiency, enjoying the benefits of a well-maintained tool and a rejuvenated spirit.

In the realm of productivity, self-care and rejuvenation are not indulgences but necessities. Taking breaks, sharpening one's tools, and nurturing the spirit are essential components of sustained success. Work diligently, but remember to pause, recharge, and find balance.

123. THE COOKIE THIEF: A DIVINE TWIST OF SWEET INDULGENCE

MOTHER ASKED HER CHILD WITH A STERN EXPRESSION,

"Do you realize that God was present when you were sneaking those cookies from the kitchen?"

The child, unfazed, responded confidently,

"Yes, I'm aware."

The mother pressed further, her voice laced with curiosity,

"And do you understand that He observed your every move?"

The child's eyes sparkled as they replied,

"Of course! He was watching with a knowing smile."

Curiosity piqued, the mother couldn't resist asking the final question,

"Well, my little cookie thief, what do you think God said when He saw you?"

With an impish grin, the child exclaimed,

"He whispered in my ear, 'Take a few extra cookies for me too, my little partner in crime!'"

The mother couldn't help but chuckle at the innocent yet clever response.

At that moment, she realized that her child possessed a playful spirit and an imagination that knew no bounds.

Little did they know that their lighthearted exchange would become a cherished memory, a tale to be shared with laughter for years to come.

As the aroma of freshly baked cookies filled the air, the mother and child sat together, enjoying their sweet treats.

The child's imagination soared, fueled by the belief that even in the most ordinary moments, a touch of magic and humor could be found. And in that shared laughter, the bond between mother and child grew stronger, forever etching this whimsical memory in their hearts.

From that day forward, every time the cookie jar mysteriously emptied, the mother would playfully ask her child if God had joined them again for a sweet indulgence. And each time, the child would giggle, recalling their delightful notion that even the divine had a sweet tooth and a mischievous spirit.

124. FROM RAGS TO RICHES AND BACK AGAIN: A GAMBLE GONE AWRY

A MARRIED COUPLE EMBARKED ON A JOURNEY to visit their dear friends in a distant land. Eager to experience the local culture, their friends suggested a day at the racetrack. Mesmerized by the thundering hooves and the thrill of the races, the couple decided to indulge in a bit of friendly competition themselves. They were playing sweepstakes all day while only two dollars had left in their pocket.

The following day, the husband felt a surge of excitement within him and declared his intention to return to the races alone. In the first race, he took a chance and placed his remaining two dollars on an underdog horse.

Miraculously, the horse crossed the finish line first, paving the way for an unexpected win. Fueled by his newfound luck, he continued betting his winnings on subsequent races, and fortune smiled upon him once again. By the end of the day, his earnings had skyrocketed to an astonishing forty-seven thousand dollars.

As he made his way home, the allure of a nearby gambling house beckoned him. A voice within him whispered, urging him to enter and play. Succumbing to temptation, the man stepped inside, only to be greeted by the sight of a captivating roulette table. The voice within him spoke again, this time pointing to the number twelve.

Without hesitation, the man placed his entire fortune of forty-seven thousand dollars on the fateful number. With bated breath, he watched as the roulette wheel spun, its mesmerizing motion adding to the anticipation. The wheel gradually came to a halt, and the dealer's voice reverberated through the room:

"Number eleven."

In an instant, the man's dreams of wealth were shattered. He left the gambling house with empty pockets, his spirit deflated. As he returned home, his wife eagerly awaited news of his escapades, hoping for tales of triumph. With a sigh, he shook his head and confessed:

"I've lost two dollars," he admitted a hint of wistfulness in his voice.

125. THE KING'S QUEST FOR THE EXTRAORDINARY TALE

IN A KINGDOM RULED BY A KING with an insatiable appetite for stories, a unique challenge emerged. The king yearned to hear the most extraordinary tale ever told and was willing to reward a princely sum of $10,000 to the one who could deliver such a narrative.

Word spread like wildfire, igniting the imagination of many hopeful storytellers. Among them was a young man who saw this opportunity as his chance to shine. With great enthusiasm, he set off to the palace, his mind brimming with ideas.

As the young man stood before the king, he revealed a small velvet pouch containing precious gemstones of various colors. The king's eyes sparkled with curiosity.

"What do you have there?" inquired the king.

"Your majesty, these are gems that hold the essence of my story. Each one represents a unique facet of my extraordinary tale," replied the young man.

Intrigued, the king nodded, eager to embark on this storytelling journey.

"My story commences in a land far away, where a brave knight sought a legendary treasure hidden in a mystical cave," the young man began.

With each gem he withdrew from the pouch, he unraveled a new chapter, weaving a tapestry of adventure and wonder. The king listened intently, captivated by the young man's storytelling prowess.

However, as the tale progressed, the young man's hand dipped back into the pouch repeatedly, extracting more and more gems.

"Your majesty, this gem represents the knight's encounter with a fearsome dragon," he proclaimed, holding up a sparkling ruby.

The king's eyebrows furrowed as he noticed the dwindling supply of gems in the pouch. The young man's story seemed to be reaching an unexpected length.

"Surely, this tale must come to an end soon," thought the king, growing impatient.

But the young man continued, unyielding in his commitment to deliver the most extraordinary story. Gem after gem, he painted a vivid picture, leaving no stone unturned.

Exasperated, the king finally interrupted the storyteller. "My dear sir, your tale has indeed been captivating, but must it go on indefinitely? We have reached a point of saturation."

The young man, taken aback, paused and realized the king's point. He had become so fixated on the number of gems and the length of his story that he overlooked the importance of brevity and relevance.

At that moment, he bowed respectfully to the king and withdrew from the palace, his lesson learned.

The king, reflecting on the encounter, recognized that true storytelling lies not in the number of words or the abundance of gems but in the art of captivating an audience with substance and purpose.

And so, the king revised his proclamation, seeking not just the longest tales but the tales that would touch hearts, ignite the imagination, and leave a lasting impression.

The value of a story lies not in its length but in its ability to captivate, inspire, and resonate with its audience.

126. THE EPIC WHEELCHAIR RACE

THE NURSING HOME WAS ABUZZ WITH EXCITEMENT as the residents gathered in the common area. A group of spirited individuals had come up with a brilliant idea to bring some thrill and laughter to their daily routines—a wheelchair race. It was the talk of the town, or in this case, the talk of the home.

Felix, a troublemaker with a twinkle in his eye, had taken charge of organizing the race. He had devised a track that weaved through the corridors, making sure to include plenty of twists and turns to keep things interesting. The participants eagerly lined up in their wheelchairs adorned with colorful flags and makeshift racing numbers.

At the sound of the imaginary starting gun, the race began. The residents propelled themselves forward with great enthusiasm, their wheelchairs rolling down the corridors at varying speeds. There was Serena, the speedy granny who had once been an accomplished roller skater in her younger years, zipping through the hallways with surprising agility. And then there was George, a prankster who had attached a small horn to the front of his wheelchair, honking it at every opportunity to startle his fellow racers.

The race took an unexpected turn when Stella, a feisty old lady with a hilarious sense of humor, decided to throw a surprise water balloon ambush at the participants. She had hidden behind a corner, armed with a bucket of water balloons, and launched them with perfect aim as the racers zoomed by. Laughter filled the air as the balloons burst, drenching the participants and causing delightful chaos.

Meanwhile, the nursing home staff, initially unaware of the race, were taken by surprise as the residents whizzed past them in their wheelchairs. Nurse Aurelia, a no-nonsense woman with a heart of gold, couldn't help but burst into laughter as she tried to catch up with the speeding racers, reminding them to watch out for obstacles and ensure their safety.

As the race progressed, the residents encountered unexpected hurdles. The corridors, usually empty and serene, were suddenly filled with obstacles—littered with toy cars, strategically placed banana peels, and even a mini-maze constructed by Mason, the resident puzzle enthusiast. The racers had to navigate their way through the challenges, often resulting in comical crashes and toppled wheelchairs.

But the spirit of competition remained strong, and the residents pushed on with determination. They laughed at their mishaps, cheered each other on, and showcased their witty banter with amusing one-liners. The race was not just about winning; it was about the joy of participating and embracing the playful spirit that brought them together.

As the finish line approached, the crowd erupted into cheers and applause. Serena crossed the finish line first, her roller-skating skills giving her the edge. George followed closely behind, honking his horn triumphantly. But the real winner was the camaraderie and laughter that filled the nursing home that day.

The race was followed by an awards ceremony, complete with homemade medals and a lively celebration. Each participant received recognition for their courage, determination, and ability to bring smiles to everyone's faces. It was a day filled with laughter, camaraderie, and unforgettable memories—a testament to the indomitable spirit of the residents.

From that day forward, the wheelchair race became an annual tradition at the nursing home. The corridors echoed with laughter as residents prepared for the thrilling event each year. It became a symbol of the vibrant and joyful community they had created—a community that celebrated life, embraced humor, and proved that age was just a number when it came to having fun.

127. THE SUNDAY RITUAL: A STORY OF MAKING A DIFFERENCE

EVERY SUNDAY MORNING, as part of my routine, I embark on a leisurely jog around the park adjacent to my neighborhood. Tucked away in one corner of the park lies a picturesque lake that adds to the serene ambiance. And without fail, every time I pass by the lake, I notice an elderly woman seated at the water's edge, accompanied by a small metal cage.

Intrigued by this recurring sight, I decided to quell my curiosity and approached the woman. As I drew nearer, I realized that the metal cage housed a trio of turtles, meandering about at their own pace. The woman, meanwhile, tenderly cradled a fourth turtle in her lap, gently cleansing its shell with a sponge brush.

Inquisitive, I initiated the conversation, expressing my fascination with her weekly ritual. With a warm smile, she explained, "I'm cleaning their shells. You see, anything that adheres to a turtle's shell, such as algae or grime, can hinder their ability to regulate body temperature and impede their swimming capabilities. Moreover, over time, it can corrode and weaken their protective shells."

Impressed by her compassionate act, I couldn't help but exclaim, "That's truly kind of you!"

She nodded appreciatively and continued, "Every Sunday morning, I dedicate a couple of hours to sitting by this serene lake, embracing tranquility while tending to these little creatures. It may seem insignificant, but it's my unique way of making a positive difference."

Pondering her noble endeavor, I posed a question, "But don't most freshwater turtles spend their lives with algae and grime clinging to their shells?"

With a gentle chuckle, she replied, "Yes, sadly, that's often the case."

Perplexed, I scratched my head and asked, "In that case, do you ever feel that your efforts could be better directed elsewhere? After all, there are countless freshwater turtles across the world, and the majority lack the fortune of having someone like you cleanse their shells. How can your localized efforts here truly make a significant impact?"

Her eyes sparkled with wisdom as she focused on the turtle in her lap, diligently wiping away the last trace of algae. Then, with conviction, she shared, "My dear, if only this little companion could speak, it would assure you that I've made all the difference in the world to them."

Every individual possesses the power to create change. Though it may appear that our actions are small in the grand scheme of things, a single act of kindness can reverberate and make a significant impact. Let us recognize the potential within ourselves to do good and embrace the opportunity to make our world a better place, one small deed at a time.

128. THE GIGGLING GNOME'S WISDOM

IN THE MYSTICAL REALM OF THE ENCHANTED FOREST, a wise gnome gathered his grandchildren around him. They nestled on the mossy ground, their eyes sparkling with curiosity, eager to hear the gnome's timeless wisdom.

"Listen closely, my dear little ones," the gnome began, his voice carrying a magical enchantment. "Deep within the core of every being, a great struggle unfolds—a battle between two peculiar creatures."

The grandchildren leaned forward, captivated by their grandfather's words, their imaginations alight with possibilities.

"One creature embodies mischief, chaos, grumpiness, and a penchant for pickled onions," the gnome continued a twinkle in his eyes. "We shall call him Grumblebottom."

The grandchildren giggled at the mention of the whimsical name, their minds painting vivid images of a grumpy little creature with a perpetual frown.

"On the other hand," the gnome continued, "we have a creature known as Joviality—a being of mirth, harmony, love, laughter, and a deep fondness for singing hedgehogs."

The grandchildren erupted in laughter at the thought of a singing hedgehog, their imaginations running wild with extravagant melodies.

"Within each of you, dear grandchildren, these two creatures reside," the gnome explained, his voice filled with ancient wisdom. "They vie for dominance, their contrasting energies pulling you in different directions."

The grandchildren exchanged knowing glances, pondering the implications of this eternal struggle within themselves.

One curious grandchild raised a hand and asked, "But, Grandfather, which creature will prevail in the end?"

The gnome stroked his long, wispy beard and smiled knowingly. "Ah, my little ones, that is the mystery of life. The creature that triumphs is the one you choose to nourish, the one you feed with your thoughts, actions, and intentions."

The grandchildren sat in contemplative silence, their minds filled with a kaleidoscope of possibilities.

"And how do we choose, Grandfather?" another grandchild asked, her eyes wide with anticipation.

The gnome leaned closer, his voice dropping to a conspiratorial whisper. "You choose by embracing the magic of laughter, my darlings. When you fill your hearts with joy, peace, and kindness, you feed the Joviality within you. But beware of Grumblebottom, for his sneaky antics thrive on fear, anger, and onion breath!"

The children burst into laughter at the gnome's clever warning, their spirits lifted by the whimsical tale.

"And remember," the gnome added, a playful glint in his eye, "the more you choose Joviality, the more those around you will be enchanted by your infectious laughter and singing hedgehog serenades!"

The grandchildren erupted into fits of laughter, their giggles mingling with the enchanting sounds of the forest.

As the sun cast its golden rays upon the Enchanted Forest, the wise gnome watched his grandchildren frolic in the meadow, their hearts brimming with mirth and the spirit of Joviality. He knew that they would grow to become guardians of laughter, spreading joy throughout the land and ensuring that Grumblebottom's grumpy antics were no match for the power of love and laughter.

And so, in the embrace of the Enchanted Forest, the tale of the Grumblebottom and the jovial Joviality became a cherished legend, passed down through the generations, reminding all who heard it of the eternal choice we hold—the choice to embrace laughter and kindle the flame of joy within our hearts.

129. EMBRACING YOUR UNIQUE WORTH

AFTER CELEBRATING HIS DAUGHTER'S REMARKABLE GRADUATION, a proud father extended his heartfelt congratulations, and he presented her with a thoughtful gift, a car he had acquired many years ago. Encouraging her to explore its value, he suggested, "Take it to the second-hand market and see what they offer you."

Eager to embark on this new venture, the daughter ventured forth and returned after a while, disappointment etched on her face. "They only offered me 1,000 dollars, father," she shared, her voice tinged with disappointment. "They claimed the car was worn and weathered."

Undeterred by this initial setback, the father contemplated the situation. Offering a solution, he advised his daughter to take the car to a pawnshop, hoping for a better outcome. Hope flickered in her eyes as she set out on this new path.

Days passed, and the daughter returned, her spirit slightly deflated. "The pawnshop valued the car at a mere 100 dollars, father," she relayed, her tone tinged with frustration. "They claimed its age had diminished its worth."

Undeterred by these successive disappointments, the father pondered another course of action. With a glimmer of inspiration, he suggested that his daughter approach a classic car club, recognizing the inherent value of her unique vehicle.

Eagerly, the daughter embarked on this final venture, her anticipation growing with each passing moment. Finally, she returned, her eyes alight with excitement. "Father, you were right!" she exclaimed, her voice filled with jubilation. "The classic car club recognized the iconic nature of the car and offered an astounding 100,000 dollars!"

The father listened intently, his heart swelling with pride. Gathering his thoughts, he imparted a powerful lesson to his daughter, words that transcended the material realm. "My dear daughter, there will be moments in life when you feel like a nobody, when you question your worth and feel diminished by the world around you. In those challenging times, do not lose heart, do not succumb to anger. Instead, summon the courage to drive away from such places."

He continued, his voice filled with wisdom, "Remember, you are not defined by the opinions of those who fail to recognize your value. Seek out environments where your true worth is appreciated, where you are respected, cherished, and celebrated for the remarkable person you are. Surround yourself with individuals who uplift you, who recognize your unique qualities, and never cease to honor your worth."

As his words sank deep into his daughter's heart, she embraced the profound lesson imparted by her father. With renewed strength, she set forth on her life's journey, equipped with the understanding that her worth is immeasurable and that she possesses the power to choose her path, to drive towards places where her light shines brightly, and to forever be surrounded by those who value and uplift her spirit.

130. THE POWER OF BALANCE IN LIFE'S CHALLENGES

A WISE TEACHER STOOD IN FRONT OF A GROUP OF STUDENTS, ready to impart a valuable lesson on the art of balance. Holding a delicate porcelain vase in her hands, she gazed at the attentive faces before her. Instead of asking the expected question about the weight of the vase, she posed a different inquiry.

"How fragile is this vase I'm holding?" she asked with a smile.

The students pondered for a moment and offered various answers, ranging from its material composition to its potential for breakage.

The teacher nodded and said, "While the physical fragility of this vase is important, what truly matters is how we handle it. If I hold it gently for a few seconds, it feels manageable. If I clutch it tightly for minutes on end, my hand will grow weary. And if I hold it tightly throughout the day, my grip will tighten, causing the delicate vase to slip from my grasp."

The class nodded in understanding, recognizing the metaphor unfolding before them.

"In life, our worries and responsibilities are akin to this fragile vase," the teacher continued. "When we acknowledge them briefly, they remain manageable. When we obsessively hold onto them for extended periods, they drain our energy and weigh us down. But when we learn to release our grip and find balance, we can navigate through life with grace and resilience."

The students contemplated her words, realizing the profound truth embedded in this lesson.

"Remember, my dear students, that you have the power to choose how tightly you hold onto your worries. Allow yourself moments of reflection, acknowledge your concerns, but also cultivate the strength to release them when they become overwhelming. Embrace the art of letting go, for it is through this act that you will find peace and clarity amidst life's challenges."

And so, the students carried with them a pearl of newfound wisdom, understanding that the fragility of their worries was not solely dependent on their nature but rather on how tightly they clung to them. They vowed to embrace the delicate balance of life, allowing themselves to release their grip and welcome each day with renewed strength and perspective.

Just as the delicate vase teaches us the importance of balance and letting go, we must learn to loosen our grip on worries and embrace the art of releasing what weighs us down. By doing so, we can navigate life's challenges with resilience and find peace amidst the chaos.

131. CHALLENGING MENTAL BARRIERS TO PERSONAL GROWTH

DURING A BEHAVIORAL STUDY, a curious squirrel was placed inside a large enclosure with a variety of nuts scattered around. The squirrel, driven by instinct, immediately began gathering and storing the nuts for its own survival.

The researcher then introduced a transparent barrier into the enclosure, dividing it into two sections. On one side, the squirrel continued its diligent nut-gathering activities, while on the other side, fresh nuts were replenished regularly.

Initially, the squirrel attempted to cross the barrier, jumping and scratching at the transparent surface in an attempt to reach the new nuts. However, each attempt proved futile, as the barrier remained impenetrable. Undeterred, the squirrel persistently tried to break through, driven by its desire for the tantalizing nuts just out of reach.

As time went on, the squirrel's fervor gradually diminished. It grew accustomed to the presence of the barrier and the limitation it imposed on its nut-gathering routine. Eventually, the squirrel ceased its futile attempts and resigned itself to gathering nuts only from its familiar side of the enclosure.

Weeks later, the researcher removed the transparent barrier, offering the squirrel unrestricted access to the entire enclosure. Surprisingly, the squirrel remained confined to its original section, oblivious to the fact that it was now free to explore and collect nuts from all areas.

The squirrel had become conditioned by its previous experiences and limitations. Its mind had created an invisible barrier, restricting its perception and confining its actions, even when the physical barrier was no longer present.

This story reminds us of the power of our own mental barriers and self-imposed limitations. Just like the squirrel, we may encounter setbacks and obstacles that create a sense of confinement. However, it is crucial to recognize that these barriers are often self-imposed and can be overcome with a shift in mindset and determination.

By challenging our own limiting beliefs and embracing a growth mindset, we can break free from the invisible barriers we create for ourselves. We can expand our horizons, explore new possibilities, and achieve greater success and fulfillment in our lives.

Remember, the only limitations that truly exist are the ones we place upon ourselves. By removing these mental barriers, we open ourselves to endless opportunities and the potential for extraordinary growth and achievement.

132. ETCHED IN STONE: THE POWER OF FORGIVENESS AND GRATITUDE

IN A DISTANT VILLAGE, two close friends set out on a journey through the enchanting landscapes of a mystical forest. As they ventured deeper into the wilderness, the tranquility of their journey was disrupted by a sudden disagreement, escalating into a heated argument. In the heat of the moment, one friend impulsively slapped the other across the face, leaving a mark of hurt and disappointment.

The friend who had been slapped, though wounded, chose to respond with wisdom and restraint. Without uttering a word, he knelt down and gently etched his pain in the soft sand beneath their feet, inscribing the words, "Today, my dear friend slapped me in the face."

Resuming their journey, the two friends trekked on, their spirits weighed down by the tension that lingered in the air. As fate would have it, their path led them to a secluded oasis adorned with lush palm trees and a shimmering pool of crystal-clear water. Eager to refresh themselves, they decided to indulge in the oasis's tranquil allure.

But fate had a different plan in store for them. As the friend who had received the blow ventured into the water, he found himself ensnared in a treacherous quagmire, gasping for breath as the mud threatened to engulf him. In his dire struggle, it was his loyal companion who fearlessly leaped into action, pulling him from the clutches of imminent danger.

Coughing and catching his breath, the once-trapped friend felt an overwhelming surge of gratitude and relief. Deeply moved by this act of selflessness, he sought a way to express the depth of his gratitude. Scouring the surroundings for a suitable medium, he discovered a sturdy rock, upon which he etched with the utmost care, "Today, my cherished friend saved my life."

Curiosity piqued, and the friend who had both harmed and rescued him couldn't contain his perplexity. He questioned, "When I inflicted pain upon you, you wrote it in the sand. But now, in the wake of this rescue, you carve it into stone. I am perplexed by your choice. Why is that?"

Smiling with serene wisdom, the friend who had been both hurt and healed replied, "When we are wronged, it is wise to inscribe our pain in the forgiving sands, for the gentle winds of time can eventually erase the mark. Yet, when someone performs an act of kindness that touches the very core of our being, it is essential to etch it in unyielding stone, where no force can ever erase its significance."

The two friends stood together, their hearts brimming with understanding and appreciation for the lessons learned. They realized that, while it may be easier to hold onto grudges and grievances, the true path to fulfillment lies in embracing forgiveness and cherishing the bonds of love and friendship. Negative emotions may cloud our judgment, but by releasing the past and valuing the profound moments of compassion, we open ourselves to a life filled with richness and the true rewards of genuine connection.

In the face of conflict, choose forgiveness over resentment, and let the winds of time heal the wounds of hurt. But when kindness and love touch your soul, preserve those precious moments in the eternal stone of gratitude, for they are the building blocks of a meaningful and rewarding life.

133. THE ROOMMATE RIDDLE: A TALE OF ASSUMPTIONS AND MISSING DOCUMENTS

A MOTHER HAD PLANNED TO VISIT HER SON, Denis, to see his new place and spend some quality time together. When she arrived, she was pleasantly surprised to meet Megan, a kind and friendly girl who happened to be Denis's roommate. However, despite Megan's warm demeanor, the mother couldn't shake a lingering suspicion that there might be something more than just a platonic friendship between the two.

After a delightful dinner, Megan excused herself to step outside for a breath of fresh air. Sensing an opportune moment, the mother decided to address her concerns about Denis's living situation. However, before she could utter a word, Denis looked at her with understanding and said, "Mom, I know what you're thinking. Megan and I are just roommates."

With those words, the mother decided to let the matter rest and refrain from further inquiry. She trusted her son's words and respected his boundaries.

A week passed, and everything seemed to be going smoothly. However, Megan noticed that some important documents had mysteriously gone missing from her desk. Despite searching high and low, she couldn't locate them. Puzzled, she approached Denis and asked if he had any knowledge of their disappearance. Denis was equally clueless.

Connecting the dots, Megan mentioned that the documents had vanished after the mother's visit. Concerned, Denis decided to text his mom to shed light on the baffling situation.

"Mom, I know you would never tamper with important documents, and I'm not accusing you of anything. However, these documents have been missing for a week now, and you were the only one here during that time," Denis texted, hoping for an explanation.

To Denis's surprise, his mother's response arrived promptly, carrying a clever twist. "Son, I know you would never engage in a romantic relationship with your roommate, and I'm not implying that you have. But if your roommate had been sleeping in her own bed, she would have discovered that the missing documents were hidden beneath the sheets. Love you."

Denis couldn't help but chuckle at his mother's witty response. It was a playful reminder that assumptions can often lead to misunderstandings. The incident also served as a gentle lesson for both Denis and Megan to communicate more openly and pay attention to their surroundings.

From that day forward, the trio shared many lighthearted moments, and their bond was strengthened by humor and a deeper understanding.

They learned the importance of clear communication and how assumptions can sometimes cloud our perception of reality.

It's crucial to communicate openly and avoid making assumptions based on appearances or limited information. By fostering honest conversations, we can prevent misunderstandings and strengthen our relationships with genuine understanding and trust.

134. THE SPEED LIMIT MIXUP: A HILARIOUS ENCOUNTER ON ROUTE 19

ON A RURAL HIGHWAY, a police officer was keeping an eye on the traffic flow when he noticed a car filled with elderly ladies. The vehicle was moving exceptionally slowly, causing frustration among the drivers behind them. Concerned about the situation, the officer decided to pull over the car so that others could pass freely. He approached the driver's window to address the matter.

However, before he could utter a word, the driver anxiously blurted out, "Officer, I didn't do anything wrong, did I? I was definitely not speeding!"

The officer reassured her that she wasn't speeding but explained the importance of maintaining a reasonable speed. Driving too slowly can also disrupt the flow of traffic and inconvenience other drivers.

The driver, with a puzzled expression, responded, "Officer, I was driving at the speed limit. I made sure I stayed at 19 miles per hour just like the sign says," the old lady exclaimed, pointing to a sign along the road. The police officer couldn't contain his laughter and replied, "Ma'am, that's not the speed limit. That's the route we're on. We're on Route 19."

"Oh, that explains it," the driver responded with a hint of embarrassment.

Curious, the officer inquired, "Explains what?"

The old lady pointed towards her passengers, who looked pale and silent. None of them uttered a word.

Intrigued, the officer pressed further and asked the driver about the situation. With a calm demeanor, she explained, "Please don't worry about them too much. They should be fine in a few minutes. We just got off Route 74."

135. THE RIPPLE OF GENEROSITY: A TALE OF SHARED HAPPINESS

IN A SECLUDED MOUNTAIN VILLAGE, nestled amidst serene landscapes, stood a humble monastery.

One fine day, a wealthy individual approached the monastery gate and gently knocked. A monk answered the call, receiving a basket filled with succulent peaches from the visitor.

The wealthy person expressed deep gratitude, acknowledging the monastery's unwavering support during times of need. Now blessed with abundance, they wished to reciprocate the kindness.

As the rich individual departed, the monk pondered upon the gift of peaches. Initially tempted to savor their sweetness, the monk soon realized that the true essence of gratitude lay in sharing. With utmost respect, the monk decided to offer the basket of peaches to the monastery's abbot, who had imparted valuable lessons on compassion and benevolence.

The abbot graciously accepted the peaches, appreciating their delightful aroma. However, feeling there was someone more deserving, the abbot thought of a fellow monk who was battling illness. Believing that the peaches would bring solace and joy to their weary spirit, the abbot decided to pass on the gift.

Grateful for the gesture, the ailing monk received the basket of peaches with heartfelt appreciation. Yet, reflecting upon the selfless acts of the monastery's dedicated cook, they felt compelled to express their gratitude in turn. The cook, touched by the acknowledgment, was unable to consume the peaches themselves. Instead, they resolved to gift the basket to the monastery's devoted gardener, the one who lovingly tended to the orchard and nurtured nature's bounties.

With a radiant smile, the gardener received the basket of peaches, humbled by the recognition. However, being in awe of the monastery's young apprentice and their eagerness to learn, they believed that the apprentice would benefit most from experiencing the sweetness of nature's offerings. Overflowing with appreciation, the apprentice graciously accepted the basket of peaches, unaware of their true origin. Yet, recalling the unwavering support and warm embrace of the monk who greeted them upon their arrival at the monastery, they felt compelled to present the gift to the kind-hearted monk.

Amidst laughter and joyful realization, the monk contemplated the basket of peaches, recognizing the interconnectedness of generosity and happiness. With a heart brimming with gratitude, the monk understood that by sharing happiness with others, it inevitably finds its way back to the giver.

By embracing the spirit of sharing and extending kindness to others, we create a ripple effect of happiness that returns to us manifold.

136. DISCOVERING TRUE WEALTH: A JOURNEY OF UNDERSTANDING

AN AFFLUENT ELDERLY GENTLEMAN desired to impart to his young daughter the significance of understanding the difference between wealth and poverty.

One fine day, the father embarked on a journey with his daughter to the countryside, where they could immerse themselves in the lives of the less fortunate for a few days. The objective was to expose his daughter to the challenges faced by families in their struggle to survive.

Upon their arrival, the daughter quickly discerned the disparities between their privileged lifestyle and their humble surroundings. However, she effortlessly connected with the locals, engaging in play with other children and forging new friendships. She would converse with an elderly lady who kindly offered her snacks. They strolled through the town, delighting in the experience even without any monetary means.

The daughter found the entire adventure captivating, to say the least.

As their time in the countryside drew to a close, it was time to return to their city dwelling. During their journey back, the father posed a question to his daughter, inquiring if she now comprehended the distinction between wealth and poverty.

Reflecting upon her experiences, the daughter began to articulate her realizations to her father.

"In the countryside, I could roam freely across vast fields without any constraints. However, at home, I am confined to our modest backyard. In the city, the stars are barely visible at night, yet in the countryside, they illuminate the sky with their brilliance."

She continued, "In the city, we must purchase our food every day. However, the farmers we encountered in the countryside have the ability to cultivate their own sustenance."

Yet, the most remarkable difference, she noted, was the sense of community and genuine care exhibited by everyone they encountered. The people in the countryside seemed to lead a more relaxed and contented life compared to their bustling city existence. It was through this collective spirit that they derived daily happiness.

Proud of his daughter's perceptive observations, the father asked if she wished to embrace a life of simplicity like the people they had met. To his surprise, the daughter gently shook her head and replied, "No, Father. I aspire to attain wealth like them."

True happiness is not solely dependent on material wealth. It is born from the experiences we share with others, the appreciation of nature's wonders, and the bonds of community and care."

137. THE SWEETEST PEAR: THE POWER OF UNDERSTANDING AND EMPATHY

IN A WARM AND INVITING DINING AREA, a young boy knelt on a cushioned chair, his eyes fixed upon a container filled with luscious fruit. Determined and eager, he reached across the table, his tiny hand outstretched to grasp the coveted treasures within. Two plump and succulent pears soon found refuge in his grip, their tantalizing aroma captivating his senses.

As the boy relished the anticipation of the delectable sweetness that awaited him, his mother, wearing a gentle smile, entered the room. Radiating love and affection, she approached her son, her voice filled with warmth and tenderness. "My darling, could you spare one of those delightful pears for me? Let us sit together and savor this delicious treat."

A brief moment hung in the air as the boy's eyes met his mother's, considering her request. Unexpectedly, he took a decisive bite from one pear, savoring its juicy flavor, and then swiftly repeated the action with the other. The mother's sincere smile faltered momentarily, replaced by a hint of disappointment, as she witnessed the unexpected turn of events.

Sensitive to his mother's change in expression, the boy instinctively understood that his actions had not aligned with her hopes. Gracefully, he descended from his chair, his little feet softly padding against the floor as he extended one of the partially consumed pears toward his mother. "Mama, this one is for you," he offered, his voice brimming with genuine affection. "It is the sweetest of them all, meant to bring you joy."

In that tender moment, the mother's heart swelled with a mixture of emotions. Gratitude washed over her, mingling with a touch of melancholy for the missed opportunity to fully share in the experience. Accepting the gift from her son, she cherished the depth of his thoughtfulness and the innocence of his gesture.

This heartfelt exchange between a mother and her son reminds us of the importance of looking beyond appearances and understanding the intentions behind our actions. It urges us to question our assumptions and approach each interaction with open-mindedness and empathy. By cultivating mindfulness and embracing curiosity, we can forge deeper connections and foster harmonious relationships in our shared journey of life.

138. WHEN SUPERMAN'S EXCUSES FALL SHORT

AT THE STROKE OF 7 A.M., a man returns to his humble abode, tiptoeing in an attempt to minimize any disturbance. Little does he know that a storm is brewing at the end of the hallway, where his wife awaits with simmering anger.

"Good morning, Superman! Do you not realize how late you are?" she exclaims, her voice brimming with frustration.

"Hold on, my darling. Allow me to explain everything. You see, I was with that client I mentioned to you," he pleads, desperately trying to diffuse the tension.

"Oh, really, Superman? And the two of you were having a work dispute all through the night? Is that what happened?" she retorts, her skepticism evident.

"But I told you it was a crucial matter, a business deal of utmost importance. I couldn't afford to let it slip away. After finalizing the deal, I felt it was only appropriate to take him to a nice restaurant for dinner," he explains, hoping to justify his actions.

"And you were out until 7 a.m., Superman? Do you truly believe I'm foolish enough to buy that story?" she challenges, her doubt palpable.

"No, my love, you misunderstand. It became late, but he insisted on continuing our business discussion at a nearby pub. And so, we stayed there until 3 a.m." he clarifies, his desperation evident in his voice.

"Ah, I see... and what transpired after 3 a.m., my dear Superman?" she probes, her tone laced with sarcasm.

"Afterward, we began our journey back home. However, his car refused to start, leaving him stranded. He requested my assistance in giving him a ride to his house, which happens to be on the other side of town. And so..." he trails off, desperately trying to salvage his credibility.

"Listen to yourself, my dear Superman. Can you not see the web of lies you've spun?" she retorts, her patience wearing thin.

"But I implore you to understand... Why do you persist in calling me 'Superman'?" he pleads, bewildered by her choice of words.

"Because, my dear Superman, only Superman dons his underwear over his trousers!" she quips, unable to contain her laughter any longer.

139. BONDS BEYOND WORDS: A TALE OF FRIENDSHIP

MR. WIGGINS, AN OFFBEAT FARMER, lived in the charming village of Willowbrook. He was known for his playful nature and love of all creatures, great and small, and he owned a lively farm full of delightful surprises.

One sunny morning, as Mr. Wiggins was tending to his bountiful vegetable garden, he noticed a group of children giggling and chasing each other near the edge of his property. Intrigued, he sauntered over, sporting his colorful overalls and a twinkle in his eye.

"Greetings, young adventurers! What brings you to my neck of the woods today?" Mr. Wiggins cheerfully inquired, leaning against his trusty rake.

A curious girl with freckles and a beautiful grin stepped forward. "Sir, we heard rumors about some extraordinary creatures on your farm. Can we see them?"

Mr. Wiggins chuckled, adjusting his floppy hat. "Well, now, you're in for a treat! I do have some extraordinary critters here. Follow me, and prepare to be amazed!"

Leading the excited children toward the barn, Mr. Wiggins called out, "Hey there, Houdini! Show us your magical companions!"

With a flutter of feathers and a whoosh of wings, Houdini, the resident magician chicken, emerged from the barn, followed by a charming assortment of creatures. There were dancing rabbits, acrobatic squirrels, and even a tiny hedgehog wearing a dapper bowtie.

The children's eyes widened with wonder as they watched the animal performers showcase their unique talents and quirky personalities.

However, amidst the spectacle, one little creature caught the attention of the freckled girl. It was a small monkey struggling to keep up with its more agile companions. Despite its clumsiness, the monkey exhibited a charm that captured her heart.

"I want that one!" the girl exclaimed, pointing at the adorable little primate.

Mr. Wiggins raised an eyebrow, his playful spirit bubbling with amusement. "Ah, the cheeky monkey, eh? Are you sure, my dear? This little scamp might require some extra attention. It's a wild ride, you know!"

Unfazed by the warning, the girl flashed a determined smile. "Sir, I've got a knack for mischief myself. We'll make the perfect duo!"

Mr. Wiggins couldn't help but burst into laughter at her spirited response. "Well, my young adventurer, it seems you've found your partner in crime! Consider it a match made in whimsical wonderland!"

Excitement filled the air as the children gathered around, eagerly asking, "How much does it cost? Can we adopt the little monkey?"

Mr. Wiggins grinned amusedly and shook his head.

"Oh, my dear friends, love and companionship cannot be bought or sold. The bond that forms between a special creature and a kindred spirit is priceless!"

As the children celebrated their newfound friendship, Mr. Wiggins couldn't contain his joy. At that moment, he realized that the world was indeed filled with kindred souls who yearned for understanding, connection, and a dash of mischief.

From that day forward, the spirited girl and her primate pal, aptly named Zippy, embarked on countless adventures together. They explored the enchanting forests, played pranks on unsuspecting villagers, and shared laughter that echoed through the village.

Word of their extraordinary bond spread like wildfire, and soon, the village of Willowbrook buzzed with tales of their escapades, the remarkable understanding and joy conveyed by the little girl and her inseparable monkey friend.

140. THE SEATED SOLDIER: A LESSON IN DISCIPLINE

IN THE DEPTHS OF AN UNDERGROUND TRANSPORT SYSTEM, a newly enlisted soldier finds himself seated in a crowded compartment. The train comes to a sudden halt, and as the doors slide open, a senior officer steps inside. With no vacant seats in sight, the officer remains standing, directly facing the young recruit.

Sensing a sense of duty, the recruit discreetly gestures towards his own seat, indicating his willingness to offer it to the officer. However, before he can utter a word, the officer cuts him off, his voice brimming with authority. "Be at ease, soldier. Stay seated and maintain your composure."

"Thank you, sir, but I..." the recruit attempts to interject, only to be swiftly silenced by the officer's stern interruption. "No excuses, soldier. I have given you an order—to remain seated!"

Minutes tick by, and the officer remains standing, unable to secure a place to rest. The recruit, driven by a sense of empathy, once again attempts to rise from his seat, hoping to alleviate the officer's discomfort. Yet, as before, his well-intentioned gesture is met with a firm rejection. "Sit down, soldier! There is no need for you to leave your seat," the officer commands.

Respectfully, the recruit responds, "Yes, sir, but..." hoping to convey his genuine concern.

"I said sit!" the officer interrupts, his tone brooking no argument.

As time passes, the recruit's determination to assist his superior grows stronger. Once again, he gathers the courage to stand up, but the officer's unwavering authority prevails. "Remain seated, soldier. I have explicitly instructed you to stay put," the officer asserts, unwilling to entertain any notion of assistance.

However, with a mixture of desperation and humility, the recruit finally speaks up, his words laced with a touch of irony. "I understand, sir, that I must remain seated. But if I may humbly mention, I have already missed three stops while obeying your orders."

At that moment, the tension gives way to a flicker of amusement, and the officer's stern expression softens into a smile. Recognizing the recruit's unwavering commitment to discipline, the officer concedes to the recruit's plea.

As the train continues its journey, the officer takes a seat next to the recruit, both sharing a newfound camaraderie born out of mutual respect and understanding. It serves as a poignant reminder that even in the rigid hierarchy of the military, there is room for empathy and a recognition of the sacrifices made by all.

141. THE CRAFTY DAUGHTER AND THE PEBBLES OF FATE

IN A SMALL FRENCH TOWN DURING THE 1500S, a skilled craftsman found himself in deep debt to a notorious moneylender. This moneylender, an unpleasant-looking man who had set his sights on the craftsman's daughter, named Terry, devised an unusual proposition to erase the debt.

He offered to forgive the entire amount owed if he could marry Terry. The proposition was met with a mixture of disgust and despair.

The moneylender then presented a curious challenge. He would place two stones in a small bag, one white and one black. The daughter would be asked to draw a stone from the bag. If it was black, the debt would be wiped clean, but she would be forced to marry the moneylender. If it was white, the debt would still be forgiven, and she would be free from his grasp.

On a pebbled path in the craftsman's garden, the moneylender stooped down, gathering two black stones and discreetly placing them in the bag. Unbeknownst to him, Terry noticed his trickery.

The young knew she had three choices before her:

First, she could refuse to pick a stone from the bag, defying the moneylender's challenge but leaving her father burdened with debt.

Second, she could expose the moneylender's cheating by taking out both stones from the bag and revealing his deceit. This would free her father from the debt but potentially lead to dire consequences.

Or third, she could pick a stone from the bag, fully aware that it would be black, sacrificing herself for her father's freedom.

In a test of wit and quick thinking, Terry decided on a fourth option.

When the daughter reached into the bag, she skillfully dropped the stone she had drawn among the other pebbles, mixing them up. With a clever smile, she remarked, "Oh, how clumsy of me. Never mind, if you inspect the stones that remain, you will surely determine which one I picked."

Caught in a predicament, the moneylender reluctantly played along, searching for a white stone among the remaining ones. Knowing he couldn't expose her, he declared that the dropped stone must have been white, releasing the craftsman from his debt.

The moral of this tale speaks to the power of thinking outside the box, of finding unconventional solutions to overcome seemingly impossible situations. It reminds us that there are always alternatives beyond the limited choices we perceive, and with creative thinking, we can triumph over adversity.

142. THE SEEDS OF WISDOM: A JOURNEY OF ENLIGHTENMENT

A VIGILANT POLICE OFFICER DONNED HIS UNIFORM and casually strolled along his beat. Amid the bustling crowd, his sharp eyes caught sight of a man perched atop a truck laden with luscious watermelons. Curiosity piqued, the officer made his way toward the peculiar scene, his inquisitive nature urging him to inquire about the man's unusual activity.

"What are you doing up there? Are you discarding those perfectly good watermelons?" the officer questioned, his voice tinged with intrigue.

With an air of confidence, the man on the truck explained his intriguing endeavor. "Indeed, I am removing the juicy flesh from these watermelons. You see, the seeds within possess a remarkable ability to unlock wisdom and intellect," he proclaimed, his eyes gleaming with conviction.

Intrigued by this audacious claim, the officer's curiosity got the better of him. "And what do you do with these extraordinary seeds? Do you sell them?" he inquired, eager to delve into the intricacies of this unique operation.

Unfazed by the officer's skepticism, the man stood tall and nodded with a knowing smile. "Of course! These exceptional seeds are highly sought after," he replied, hinting at the profound value they held.

The officer's intrigue deepened, and a thought sprouted in his mind. "Tell me, my friend, how much are these seeds worth in the market?" he probed, his mind already calculating the potential possibilities.

Undeterred by the officer's doubt, the man maintained his confident demeanor. "They are valued at $5 each!" he declared, emphasizing the significance of these coveted seeds.

Driven by a mix of curiosity and the desire for knowledge, the officer decided to put this remarkable claim to the test. "Very well, I shall give them a try. Please, provide me with three of these prized seeds," he requested, reaching into his pocket to retrieve the appropriate amount of money.

With a sense of satisfaction, the man accepted the officer's payment and handed over the three coveted seeds. Eager to embark on this journey of discovery, the officer consumed the seeds, allowing their essence to permeate his being.

As moments passed, the officer's thoughts swirled within his mind. "Wait a minute! With the same $15, I could have purchased 15 pounds of watermelon, meticulously extracting the seeds from each fruit," he mused, realization dawning upon him.

Observing the officer's revelation, the man couldn't help but be amused. "Do you see that? With just a taste, your intelligence has already surpassed its previous bounds," he chuckled, his belief in the transformative power of the seeds reinforced.

Acknowledging the truth in the man's words, the officer couldn't resist the allure of further enlightenment. "Indeed, you are right! Give me three more of these miraculous seeds!" he exclaimed, his enthusiasm matching that of the man on the truck.

The officer's encounter with the man on the truck served as a reminder that sometimes the most extraordinary revelations can arise from the simplest of experiences. It is through the openness of our minds and a willingness to explore the unknown that we unlock the true potential within ourselves. As the officer embarked on his newfound quest for enlightenment, he couldn't help but marvel at the vast possibilities that lay ahead, for within the ordinary lies extraordinary, waiting to be discovered and embraced.

143. UNEXPECTED REUNION: LAUGHTER AND MEMORIES IN THE AFTERLIFE

IN THE ETHEREAL REALM OF PARADISE, two dear friends unexpectedly reunite. Overwhelmed with surprise, the first friend exclaims, "Wait a minute! Are you here too? I had no idea! But how did you meet your end?"

A gentle smile graces the second friend's face as he replies, "It was due to an unexpected turn of events. You see, I perished from sheer contentment. And what about you?"

The first friend, his voice tinged with a hint of sadness, responds, "I met my demise through freezing temperatures... But do tell me, how is it that you met your untimely end through excessive happiness?"

Eager to share his story, the second friend begins his tale: "It all started with an anonymous letter that arrived one fateful day, revealing the unsettling news of my wife's infidelity. Filled with a surge of emotions, I rushed home unannounced, my heart racing with anticipation. Upon entering, I discovered my wife in a state of undress, caught off guard by my sudden arrival. Frantically, I searched every nook and cranny, beneath beds and inside closets, hoping to find the supposed lover who had caused such turmoil. However, my frantic search yielded no results. Overwhelmed by the relief of finding no evidence of betrayal, my heart, filled to the brim with happiness, couldn't bear the intensity of the moment and succumbed to a fatal heart attack, sealing my fate... But now, my friend, I am curious to hear the circumstances that led to your chilling demise."

With a playful glimmer in his eye, the first friend retorts, "Ah, my dear friend, if only you had thought to look inside the fridge, both of us would still be alive and well!"

144. INTERSTELLAR ODYSSEYS: THE ASTRONAUTS' UNFORGETTABLE JOURNEY

THREE INTREPID EXPLORERS EMBARKED ON A GRAND ADVENTURE into the depths of space, ready to embark on a journey that would span several years. As they prepared for their mission, they were granted the freedom to bring along whatever they desired to ease the passage of time during their interstellar odyssey.

The first astronaut, driven by his love for the companionship of women, decided to bring along a group of 20 beautiful women who would accompany him throughout the voyage. He envisioned a harmonious and enjoyable journey filled with laughter, conversation, and the joy of human connection.

The second astronaut, a lover of culinary delights, saw this opportunity as a chance to indulge his passion for food. The spaceship was stocked to the brim with a diverse array of delectable treats and gastronomic wonders, ensuring that no craving would go unsatisfied during their lengthy expedition. From gourmet delicacies to comfort foods from their home planet, the spaceship's pantry became a veritable paradise of flavors.

The third astronaut, known for his affinity for smoking, decided to bring an extensive collection of cigars and cigarettes to satisfy his nicotine cravings. The spaceship became a sanctuary for moments of relaxation and indulgence as he sought solace in the aromatic embrace of tobacco, finding respite amidst the vastness of space.

After a decade had passed, the first astronaut returned from his remarkable journey. As the hatch of his spaceship opened, a multitude of children emerged, bringing smiles to their father's face. Overwhelmed with joy, he described his mission as a resounding success, filled with laughter, love, and the creation of a new generation.

Next to return was the second astronaut, but to everyone's surprise, the hatch revealed a compact sphere of lard weighing over 200 kilograms. This peculiar sight left everyone baffled as the astronaut gleefully waddled away, seemingly content in his newfound form. The mystery of his transformation remained unanswered, yet it was evident that his journey had taken an unexpected turn.

Finally, after what seemed like an eternity, the third astronaut arrived, his face etched with frustration and anger.

As the hatch swung open, with exasperated demeanor, he said: "THE LIGHTERS....!!!!""

145. LAUGHTER AND HEALING IN THE DOCTOR'S OFFICE

IN 1992, AN ELDERLY WOMAN BY THE NAME OF PATSY WIGHT found herself grappling with an embarrassing predicament. Determined to find a solution, she mustered up the courage to visit the doctor's office.

She entered the room, slightly nervous, and spoke to the doctor, "Doctor, I have a problem with intestinal gas. It's not a major bother, as my flatulence is quiet and odorless. However, there's a small concern that troubles me. For instance, since I entered your clinic, I must have released about 20 instances of gas. Of course, you didn't notice because there was no noise or unpleasant smell, but that's the reality of my situation."

The doctor, maintaining a professional demeanor, listened attentively to Patsy's explanation. After a moment of contemplation, he responded reassuringly, "I understand. This is a familiar problem, and I believe I can help you. I will prescribe two separate treatments to address your concerns. The first treatment involves taking these pills continuously for a week without interruption. Once you have completed this course, please return to me, and we can discuss the second part of the treatment."

The elderly woman, hopeful for a resolution, left the clinic with a renewed sense of optimism. She faithfully followed the doctor's instructions, taking the pills as prescribed, and eagerly awaited the outcome.

One week later, Patcy returned to the doctor's office, eager to share her progress. As she spoke, her voice carried a mix of surprise and confusion, "Doctor, I don't know what happened, but now my farts are consistently silent. However, there is one peculiar development - they emit an incredible stench!"

The doctor, amused by her unexpected revelation, rose from his chair with a sly grin. He then responded, "Ah, marvelous! It seems that we have successfully cured your sinusitis. Now, let's delve into the matter of your hearing..."

146. THE BATTLE OF COLORS: A TALE OF HARMONY AND UNITY

ONCE UPON A TIME, the vibrant hues of the rainbow found themselves embroiled in a heated debate. Each color staunchly proclaimed its superiority, vying for the title of the best, the most important, and the most valuable.

Emerald green took the stage, exclaiming, "Look around and witness the wonders of nature! Behold the rolling hills, the lush forests, and the majestic mountains.

Without me, life would cease to exist. I am the color of vitality, of spring's rebirth, and the embodiment of hope." Interrupting with a spirited voice, cerulean blue interjected, "You are confined to the earthly realms, fixated on the terrestrial wonders. Lift your gaze to the heavens and marvel at the boundless depths of the oceans. I am the color that envelops the universe's vast expanse. Water, the essence of life, finds its home within me. The sky offers solace, tranquility, and serenity. Without my presence, you would be adrift in nothingness."

Radiant yellow stepped forward, beaming with exuberance. "Why so serious, my friends? The world craves light and joy. I am the color that ignites smiles and evokes happiness. From the golden fields of wheat and sunflowers to the twinkling stars that adorn the night sky and the warm embrace of the sun that illuminates all, I embody energy and jubilation."

Modestly, the gentle orange stepped into the spotlight. "Carrots, pumpkins, and oranges adorn themselves in my vibrant hue, offering health and vitality. Wherever I am found, vitamins and well-being follow. I am the embodiment of warmth and vitality. Though I may not always be present, the majestic display of sunrise and sunset captivates all, leaving no room for thought of anyone else."

Before the orange could conclude, red forcefully interjected, her voice resounding with passion. "Are we still arguing about who holds the greatest significance? Can't you see that I represent life itself? I am the color of blood, the essence that courses through every living being. I embody courage, danger, martyrs, and heroes. Poppies and jasmine grace themselves in my fiery hue. In matters of the heart, I am the focal point, the symbol of passion and love!"

As the redhead's voice echoed through the air, the regal violet stepped forward, radiating an air of majesty. "I need not speak nor defend myself, for the world knows my regality. Kings, princes, and clergymen drape themselves in my resplendent shade. I symbolize authority, the sacred, and the enigmatic. I represent that which commands reverence and holds an air of mystery."

Finally, indigo stepped forward, her voice calm yet resolute. "Ponder my significance, for I am the color of silence. I embody contemplation, deep thought, twilight, and the depths of vast waters. Each of you needs me to strike a balance, to create contrast, and to foster introspection and serenity. In prayer and the pursuit of peace, I am ever-present."

The debate raged on, each color growing more passionate and stubborn, deaf to reason. Suddenly, a bolt of lightning illuminated the sky, accompanied by a resounding clap of thunder. Torrential rain followed, startling the colors and compelling them to seek solace in one another's presence.

In the midst of the tempestuous storm, the rain spoke with authority, "You vibrant fools, squabbling among yourselves, each vying for dominance. Do you not realize that each of you possesses a unique purpose and beauty? Join hands and follow me!"

As the colors embraced peace, united by the rain's plea, the gentle voice continued, "Henceforth, when rain graces the Earth, you shall span the heavens, forming a magnificent arc of colors. Let it serve as a reminder of friendship, hope, and the enduring power of harmony." And so, whenever rain cleanses the world and a resplendent rainbow graces the sky, let us remember to cherish one another, appreciate the diverse tapestry of existence, and embrace the boundless possibilities that arise when we live in peace.

147. THE ECHO OF LIFE: REFLECTIONS OF OUR WORDS AND ACTIONS

A YOUNG CHILD AND THEIR FATHER EMBARKED ON A JOURNEY through the serene mountains. As they walked, the child stumbled and fell, experiencing a sharp pain that elicited a cry of "Ouch! It hurts!"

To their astonishment, the cry echoed through the mountains, bouncing off the majestic peaks. Intrigued by this mysterious phenomenon, the child questioned, "Who is there? Who are you?"

In a playful dance of voices, the mountains responded, "Who is there? Who are you?"

The child's curiosity grew, and he called out once more, "I can hear you. Who are you?"

The mountains mirrored the inquiry, "I can hear you. Who are you?"

A surge of frustration overcame the child, and their words turned sharp, "You are foolish! I cannot tolerate your presence any longer. Be silent!" Unsurprisingly, the mountains echoed back the same words, "You are foolish! I cannot tolerate your presence any longer. Be silent!"

Perplexed by this exchange, the child turned to their father, seeking an explanation. With a warm smile, the father offered his wisdom, "My dear child, take heed and listen carefully."

With a newfound understanding, the father raised his voice, exclaiming, "You are extraordinary! I love you."

And as if in harmony, the mountains reciprocated, "You are extraordinary! I love you."

The child was captivated yet still puzzled. Seeking clarity, he asked their father, "What just happened? Why did you receive a positive response?"

In a tender tone, the father explained, "My child, what you have witnessed is the essence of life itself. It is the echo of our actions and words, reflecting back to us. Just as an echo returns what we send forth, life mirrors our choices and intentions. When we embrace kindness and love, they are reflected back to us. Conversely, if we sow negativity and cruelty, they, too, shall be mirrored in our experiences. Life is a canvas upon which our actions paint a vibrant reflection."

With newfound insight, the child embraced the wisdom imparted by their father. They understood that the echoes of life would be shaped by their own choices. From that moment forward, they embarked on their journey with mindful actions, knowing that the reverberations of their words and deeds would shape the world around them.

In this tale, the echo serves as a gentle reminder of the profound impact we have on our own lives and the lives of others. Our actions and words create ripples that return to us, reminding us to tread carefully and radiate goodness in all that we do.

148. A JAR FULL OF LIFE: PRIORITIZING WHAT TRULY MATTERS

A PROFESSOR STOOD BEFORE HIS EAGER STUDENTS, ready to impart a valuable lesson in philosophy. As he prepared to begin, he arranged a set of objects on his desk, capturing the attention of his curious audience.

Silently, the professor reached for a large, empty jar, its presence commanding their focus. With purposeful intent, he filled the jar with vibrant marbles, carefully arranging them until they reached the brim. Turning to his students, he posed a question: "Is the jar full?" In unison, they responded affirmatively.

Next, the professor introduced a box of pebbles, gently pouring them into the jar. The pebbles nestled between the marbles, occupying the spaces that had once seemed full. Once again, he inquired, "Is the jar full now?" Without hesitation, the students replied with a resounding yes.

Yet, the professor was not finished. He produced a bag of fine sand and poured it into the jar. The sand effortlessly filled the remaining gaps, finding its place among the marbles and pebbles. The professor surveyed his students and repeated the question, receiving the expected answer of a full jar.

With a glint in his eye, the professor retrieved two cups of aromatic coffee from beneath his desk. To the astonishment of his students, he poured the steaming coffee into the jar, watching as it permeated the minute spaces between the sand particles. Laughter filled the room, and the professor seized the moment to share his profound message.

"Consider this jar as a metaphor for your life," he began. "The marbles represent the most vital aspects: your loved ones, your health, your passions. These are the marbles that hold the utmost significance, the pillars of your existence. The pebbles symbolize important but secondary elements, such as your work and possessions. And the sand represents the trivialities and fleeting moments that often consume our attention."

He paused, allowing his words to resonate before continuing. "If you fill your life with the sand of trivial matters, there will be no space left for the pebbles and golf balls—the things that truly matter. By devoting your time and energy to what is truly important, you create a life of fulfillment and purpose."

The professor emphasized the significance of prioritization, urging his students to nurture their relationships, nurture their well-being, and pursue their passions. He reminded them to savor the profound moments with loved ones, to embrace their own physical and mental well-being, and to indulge in the activities that bring them joy.

Just as the students absorbed this wisdom, a curious voice broke the silence. A student raised their hand and posed a question: "Professor, what does the coffee represent?"

A warm smile graced the professor's face as he replied, "Ah, the coffee represents the beautiful truth that no matter how full and fulfilling your life may seem, there is always room for meaningful connections and shared moments with friends and loved ones. It is a reminder that amidst the hustle and bustle of life, taking time for a coffee with a friend adds richness and warmth to our journey."

The classroom buzzed with understanding and appreciation as the students embraced the profound lesson bestowed upon them. They left with a renewed perspective, committed to filling their lives with what truly matters and cherishing the moments that bring joy, love, and connection.

149. THE HOROSCOPE AND THE ART OF FISHING

ON A CRISP MORNING, two dear friends found themselves reunited, their laughter echoing through the serene surroundings. The first friend, well aware of the other's ardent love for fishing, couldn't resist the urge to inquire about his absence from their beloved angling adventures.

"Good morrow, my fellow angler! Pray to tell, what has kept you from the tranquil embrace of the river today?" he inquired with genuine curiosity.

A glimmer danced in the second friend's eyes as he responded, his voice laced with playful jest, "Ah, my dear companion, I deemed it unnecessary to cast my line today because I wouldn't have caught anything anyway'"

Perplexed by this response, the first friend probed further, his curiosity eager to unravel the mystery. "But how can you be so certain? Do the cosmos hold secrets even the most seasoned fishermen are unaware of?"

With a hearty chuckle, the second friend unveiled his peculiar reasoning, "Listen well, my dear friend, today, as I perused the pages of the celestial almanac, the stars themselves whispered a secret: 'Today it is a fortuitous day for the fish!'"

150. THE SIEVE OF WISDOM: THE TRANSFORMATIVE POWER OF READING

A QUESTION ONCE AROSE IN THE MIND OF A CURIOUS STUDENT: 'I have read countless books, yet I seem to forget most of their contents. What, then, is the purpose of reading?' The student posed this inquiry to their wise Master, who chose not to provide an immediate response.

A few days later, as they sat alongside a flowing river, the Master expressed their thirst and requested the student to fetch them water using a weathered and stained sieve that lay abandoned nearby. The student was taken aback, aware of the futility of such a task. However, his unwavering respect for the Master compelled them to comply. Grasping the sieve, he embarked on the seemingly illogical endeavor. With each attempt to draw water from the river and carry it back to the Master, not a single drop remained within the sieve, leaving the student empty-handed.

Striving tirelessly, the student repeated their futile efforts, desperately attempting to hasten their return. Alas, the water eluded his grasp, slipping through the sieve's countless holes and dissipating along the way. Exhausted and dejected, he settled beside the Master, admitting defeat. 'I am unable to capture the water with this sieve. I have failed in my task, Master,' the student confessed, seeking forgiveness for their perceived inadequacy.

To this, the old Master responded with a serene smile, imparting profound wisdom. 'No, my dear student, you have not failed,' they reassured. 'Observe the sieve closely; it is now pristine and unblemished. The water, seeping through its gaps, has cleansed it.'

The student's eyes widened in realization, intrigued by the Master's revelation. Encouragingly, the Master continued their explanation. 'When you engage with books, you are akin to the sieve, and the books themselves are the flowing water in the river. It matters not if you cannot retain every droplet of water that traverses through your being. The books, with their myriad ideas, emotions, knowledge, and truths nestled within their pages, possess the power to purify your mind and spirit. They bestow upon you renewed perspectives, heightened understanding, and the potential for personal growth. That dear student, is the true purpose of reading.'

In that moment of enlightenment, the student comprehended that the value of reading extends beyond the mere retention of information. It is an immersive experience, a transformative journey where the flow of words and ideas permeates their being, gradually shaping and refining their essence. Just as the sieve emerged purified by the passage of water, the student recognized that books have the profound ability to cleanse, enlighten, and invigorate the mind and soul.

Henceforth, armed with this newfound understanding, the student embraced the act of reading not solely for the accumulation of knowledge but as a means to immerse themselves in the transformative power of literature. He embraced the sieve-like nature of their memory, appreciating that even as the water escaped, the essence of each book left an indelible mark, expanding his horizons and nurturing his intellectual and spiritual growth.

CONCLUSION

DEAR READER,

If you have made it this far, then I extend to you my heartfelt thanks for journeying with me through the pages of my book. It has been an immense pleasure and a true privilege to share these stories and characters with you, and I sincerely hope they have brought you as much joy, laughter, and reflection as they have brought me.

In crafting this storybook, my aim was not only to entertain but also to celebrate the richness, wisdom, and humor inherent in all stages of life. I wanted to create a space where we can reflect, reminisce, and above all, laugh together. If you have found value in this collection of stories, if they made you smile, reflect, or even chuckle out loud, then I have achieved my goal.

Your support means the world to me, and it is the driving force that keeps me writing. I look forward to sharing more stories, more laughter, and more life-affirming wisdom with you soon.

Once again, thank you for choosing my book. Until we meet again in the pages of the next one, may your days be filled with laughter and your spirit remain ever young.

Yours sincerely,

Victoria Bennett

Printed in Great Britain
by Amazon